ZAZU DREAMS

Between the Scarab

and the Dung Beetle

As told to
Cara Judea Alhadeff

Paintings by
Micaela Amateau Amato

© 2017 Cara Judea Alhadeff
Printed in the United States of America

All rights reserved. This publication is protected by Copyright, and permission should be obtained from the publisher prior to any prohibited reproduction, storage in a retrieval system, or transmission in any form or by any means, electronic, mechanical, photocopying, recording, or likewise.

Published by Eifrig Publishing,
PO Box 66, Lemont, PA 16851, USA
Knobelsdorffstr. 44, 14059 Berlin, Germany.

For information regarding permission, write to:
Rights and Permissions Department,
Eifrig Publishing,
PO Box 66, Lemont, PA 16851, USA.
permissions@eifrigpublishing.com, +1-888-340-6543

Library of Congress Cataloging-in-Publication Data

Cara Judea Alhadeff
Zazu Dreams: Between the Scarab and the Dung Beetle /
by Cara Judea Alhadeff, art by Micaela Amateau Amato
  p. cm.

Paperback: ISBN 978-1-63233-120-5
Hard cover: ISBN 978-1-63233-118-2
Ebook: ISBN 978-1-63233-119-9

[1. Juvenile Non-Fiction: Science and Nature 2. Ecosystems 3. Transdisciplinary Jewish History 4. Critical philosophy]

I. Amateau Amato, Micaela., ill. II. Title

21 20 19 18 2017
5 4 3 2 1

Printed in the USA on acid-free paper with recycled content. ∞

Praise for *Zazu Dreams*

"*Zazu Dreams* bursts forth from its cover, showering the reader with art, song, language, spirituality, joy, and history. In the spirit of *Le Petit Prince*, the door to adult reflection is opened by a child guide. With the query, "Who needs imaginary monsters or giants or evil empires when corporations like Nestle and PepsiCo, Merck and Monsanto destroy everything in their path?" *Zazu Dreams* challenges us with the notion that knowledge of evil, even for the very young, is the clearest path to good. From climate change to Big Oil, war to slavery, Zazu faces the worst of humanity, while simultaneously basking in the beauty that constantly amazes and surrounds, teaching that we must live in harmony with and as caretakers of this earth and all upon it, if we wish the same in return. Three generations take us on a journey to be enjoyed by all ages. A grandmother's artwork joins a mother's storytelling to create an adventure for her son into what it means to be human that is unrestricted by space, time or prejudice, only his—and through him our own—limitless imagination."
ANTONIA JUHASZ, author of *The Tyranny of Oil*.

"*Zazu Dreams* is a fascinating story that launches a new genre of book called edutainment. Amazing Research!" ARUN GANDHI, Founder/President, M. K. Gandhi Institute for Nonviolence / Grandson of Mahatma Gandhi

"*Zazu Dreams* thoughtfully and colorfully addresses the crucial need for young people to develop empathy for humanity and all life."
DR. JAMES E. HANSEN, Director of the Program on Climate Science, Awareness and Solutions, Earth Institute, Columbia University

"Cara Judea Alhadeff is remarkably unafraid to face up to the controlling influences of the chemical industry on the US government, causing great harm to our nation's children who are suffering from exposure to chemicals in their food, water, and vaccines. Alhadeff sees the world from a perspective that few others can achieve—addressing issues of toxic chemical exposure and the way the forces in power manipulate the population to fall in line towards unreasonable and in many cases unethical goals. Her original thinking will have significant impact on society."
DR. STEPHANIE SENEFF, Senior Research Scientist, MIT Computer Science and Artificial Intelligence Laboratory

"In *Zazu Dreams: Between the Scarab and the Dung Beetle*, Dr. Cara Judea Alhadeff elegantly tackles complex subject matter. A book for all ages, *Zazu Dreams* touches upon the complicated nature of human existence, from one end to another, with intelligence and beauty."
JOSEPH JENKINS, author of *The Humanure Handbook*

"We're in the midst of damaged life, and continuing with the same old modes of thought and imagination will almost certainly allow the damage to continue. *Zazu Dreams* generates a new imaginary that looks beyond sustainability to genuine transformation. Rather than survival as we are, *Zazu Dreams* raises the possibility of a creative and marvelous new world."
DR. CLAIRE COLEBROOK, author of *Death of the PostHuman*

"*Zazu Dreams* reclaims the power of language as both a poetic intervention into politics and storytelling and as a powerful force for reclaiming the radical imagination. *Zazu Dreams* moves across disciplinary borders, collapses genres, unsettles how we think about the planet and the need to keep it going, and inspires and energizes a sense of individual and social agency and collective hope as it unfolds. This is a brilliant book whose relevance cuts across generations, merges the space between adult and child, and gives the poetic as a force for struggle and hope a new and urgent political register."
DR. HENRY GIROUX, author of *Disposable Futures: Violence in the Age of the Spectacle*

"Every thought, word and action we put forth, no matter how tiny or huge, whether in the streets or in offices, underground or above, either hurts or helps the wave of prosperity to ensure a bright future for humanity, and for all life on this planet & beyond. *Zazu Dreams* is a beautiful example of keeping our work and our play focused on our most crucial mission, securing our survival and our freedom. Let every breath we take help that wave."
GREGORY "SHKG / HUMPTY-HUMP" JACOBS, Digital Underground

*Zazu Dream*s is "... absolutely fascinating with superb drawings and an innovative juxtaposition between a very serious subject and its narrative unraveling as a childlike adventure. ... [A] totally original concept for a sociologically relevant topic. ... The book is an extraordinary fusion of fanciful allegory, childhood perception, ecological prophecy and sociological parable . . . all woven together in a profound tapestry of consummate scholarship. Richly enlivened by the imaginative illustrations of Micaela Amato, Zazu's youthful curiosity propels him through a global succession of apocalyptic encounters and joyfully elevating adventures. In the most poetic way, his 'dreams' embody a microcosm of global conflicts, premonitions, celebrations, and spiritual aspirations. The unique accomplishment of this book is its capacity to simultaneously bridge the human condition through the innocent perceptions of a child and the world-weary apprehensions of an adult. *Zazu Dreams* is definitely an enlightening story for all ages."
JAMES WINES, Green Architect Founder of SITE architect

"In this original and intriguing book, history meets the age of the anthropocene in a big bang. Whimsical and instructive, fable-like and scholarly, this is a children's book that spares the young neither the bad news nor hope for the work ahead. It is a phantasmagoric read for adults and a visual feast for all generations!"
DR. DALIA KANDIYOTI, author of *Migrant Sites: America, Place, and Diaspora Literatures*

"*Zazu Dreams* is a truly magical tale for people of all ages and all faiths (or none)—a magnificent way to introduce children to the reality of the environmental crisis while simultaneously teaching some of the deep spiritual messages that are the common heritage of humanity. Your life and your children's lives will be greatly enriched by reading (and studying) this amazing story and its accompanying commentary!"
RABBI MICHAEL LERNER, author of *Jewish Renewal: A Path to Healing and Transformation*

Table of Contents

A Guide to *Zazu Dreams*	6
Chapter One: Beyond the Anthropocene	9
Chapter Two: Pirates of the Caribbean	17
Chapter Three: The Oldest Jews on the Planet	23
Chapter Four: "spooky action at a distance"	31
Chapter Five: "It takes a village…"	41
Chapter Six: *Mashallah*!	49
Chapter Seven: Quantum Entanglements	55
Chapter Eight: Between the Scarab and the Dung Beetle	61
Chapter Nine: Worms and Germs	71
A Möbius Chronology of Selected Geologic and Human Events Preceding Our Petro-Chemical Era	79
The 21st Century Arcades Project	85
Additional Resources	139
About the Author and Artist	140
Afterword	141

*We dedicate our story to forgotten Sephardim
who died during the Holocaust.
To mi hijo, Zazu, growing so big everyday.
For your relentless "Why?" questions.
You teach me my own breath.*

A Guide to *Zazu Dreams*
in case you are perplexed (a nod to Maimonides)

"The door to adult reflection is opened by a child guide" (Antonia Juhasz) as three generations imagine a world together—grandmother Micaela Amato Amateau illustrates the stories of her grandson Zazu, as told to his mother, Cara Judea Alhadeff. Framing our story in the form of a children's narrative situates the adult reader at a 'safe' distance, allowing entry into otherwise challenging topics; and, as with strategic uses of humor, our subject can be received with greater openness and less fear. By entering one's consciousness through the mediated vehicle of storytelling, we hope to surprise our readers (children and adults)—evoking the possibility of reconsidering consequences of one's habitual daily choices.

Like Salman Rushdie's *Haroun and the Sea of Stories*, Art Spiegelman's *Maus: A Survivor's Tale*, George Orwell's *Animal Farm*, Gertrude Stein's *To Do: A Book of Alphabets and Birthdays*, William Golding's *Lord of the Flies*, and Richard Adam's *Watership Down*, *Zazu Dreams: Between the Scarab and the Dung Beetle, A Cautionary Fable for the Anthropocene Era* explores the transformative power of the imagination and the necessity of storytelling to generate and nourish a community of parent-child culture-shapers. Dr. Seth Lerer describes *Zazu Dreams* as a world in which child and adult read together to create a culture of affect.

George and the Secret Key to the Universe, Stephen Hawking's collaborative trilogy written with his daughter Lucy, offers a rare example of transgenerational storytelling. In our story, like the Hawkings', the primary text and illustrations are for children, while endnotes for young adults and adults offer rich scientific, historical, socio-political, and literary exploration.

Reminiscent of Sfar's *The Rabbi's Cat*, Lester's *Stagolee*, Alexander's *The Remarkable Journey of Prince Jen*, Homer's *The Odyssey*, St. Exupery's *Le Petit Prince*, Swift's *Gulliver's Travels*, Juster's *The Phantom Tollbooth*, Martel's *Life of Pi*, and Al-Garnati's *World of Wonders*, our story's characters explore unfamiliar geographical and metaphysical terrain while they learn about social and environmental costs of subjugating others. Just as *Zazu Dreams* offers an opportunity for transgenerational dialogue about the Anthropocene, our narration of the histories of Sephardim and Mizrahim is our point of departure for an extensive discussion of ethnic erasure in the context of human rights, globalization, and corporate-driven democracies. We believe that only by understanding how all forms of oppression are interconnected can we understand that all forms of emancipation are equally interconnected.

Zazu Dreams is divided into two parts: the narrative — "A Cautionary Fable for the Anthropocene Era," and extended endnotes— "The 21st Century Arcades Project." These *arcade*s expand and historicize the illustrated text. The intended audience includes parents who read the narrative to their young children, as well as young-adults, educators, activists, and others who additionally choose to explore the environmental and cultural perils outlined within the endnotes. In the interface between the narrative of *Zazu Dreams* and its "21st Century Arcades Project," myth mingles with science, literature, and polyvalent histories in order to re-examine manufactured consent and miseducation. In their book, *Nurture Shock: New Thinking About Children*, Po Bronson and Ashley Merryman investigate the importance of discussing race/ethnicity with children as young as two years old. Similarly, the correspondences between the two sections of *Zazu Dreams* are key to understanding our capacities as communal, co-implicated beings; we advocate that symbiotic relationships be introduced to young children. Within the national debate about how to *emotionally* protect our children, many 'holistic-minded' parents conflate 'news' about terrorism, police brutality, school-shootings, etc. with environmental devastation—claiming all as taboo-subjects. Contrary to such fears, we suggest parents and educators teach our very young children *why* ecologically-conscious values and behaviors are both nourishing and critical for us all. Our cross-generational 'cabinet of curiosities' stimulates empathy in the child by encouraging a sense of awe and a sense of community within and beyond our human ecologies.

Zazu, the weaver of stories, hopes we will all reconsider the words of Egyptian Jewish scholar Andrè Aciman who said: "To be a Jew is to be in exile." Zazu wants us to know that *to be a Jew*, an outsider, is to practice *tikkun olam*, repair what has been broken, and *bal tashchit*, do not destroy or waste. "The 21st Century Arcades Project," the second portion of *Zazu Dreams*, offers such a practice. The title and provocation of this portion is derived from Walter Benjamin's *The Arcades Project*. His original essay was titled "*Pariser Passagen: Eine dialektische Feerie*" ("Paris Arcades: A Dialectical Fairyland"). Benjamin's work

> extend[s] from the literary and philosophical to the political, economic, and technological, with all sorts of intermediate relations…[exploring] the 'refuse' and 'detritus' of history, the half-concealed, variegated traces of the daily life of 'the collective.'… Not conceptual analysis but something like dream interpretation was the model. …At issue was what [Benjamin] called the 'commodification of things.' He was interested in the unsettling effects of incipient high capitalism on the most intimate areas of life and work. …[A]n unflinching realism was cultivated alongside a rhapsodic idealism. … '[P]hantasmagorical'…figures on the threshold…in the wakening to crisis (crisis masked by habitual complacency), [were] the link to present-day concerns…historical time is broken up into kaleidoscop[es]" (ix-xii).

In a similar vein, Rachel Carson wrote about her plan to "achieve…a synthesis of widely scattered facts, that have not heretofore been considered in relation to each other. It is now possible to build up, step by step, a really damning case against the use of these chemicals as they are now inflicted on us" (340). While Carson focused on the environment and Benjamin on the marketplace, *Zazu Dreams* integrates both for social, spiritual, and self-emancipation.

Precisely because of the complex interplay between the marketplace and the environment, *Zazu Dreams* is, in fact, a book *specifically* for children. In Mark Achbar, Jennifer Abbott, and Joel Bakan's 2004 documentary film, *The Corporation*, Noam Chomsky describes how profit-driven institutions begin to instill consumer-values at infancy; Ray Anderson, CEO of Interface, the world's largest commercial carpet manufacturer, calls corporate motivation a form of 'intergenerational tyranny.' Since children are at the root of sustaining commercially-mediated relationships that maintain how big business functions, shouldn't educators, activists, academics, parents, and those who oppose the monoculturalization of our minds (Vandana Shiva) address children directly? Branding and advertising certainly do. Lucy Hughes, Vice President for Initiative Media and co-creator of "The Nag Factor," proudly declares that Initiative spends $12 billion of media time to encourage children to 'nag' their parents into buying products, home videos, fast food and attending movies, theme parks, and "places like Chuck E Cheese." Initiative Media is the "biggest buyer of advertising time and space in the U.S. and in the world." She continues: "You can manipulate consumers into wanting and therefore buying your products—it's a game…[today's children are] tomorrow's adult consumers, so start talking with them now, build that relationship with them when they're younger and you've got them as an adult" (cited in *The Corporation*).

Zazu Dreams counters this manipulation.

Jeremy Rifkin, founder of The Foundation on Economic Trends, insists: "There are many tools for bringing back community, but the importance is not the tools…there is litigation, legislation, there's direct action, there's education, boycotts, social investment, there are many, many ways to address issues of corporate power, but in the final analysis what is really important is the vision. You have to have a better story."

Zazu Dreams is that story.

Citations accompanying the paintings throughout the narrative are sourced in "The 21st Century Arcades Project." The narrative, images, and arcades co-exist within a convivial, symbiotic framework. Ladino (Spanish-Jewish) proverbs are integrated throughout both portions of the text.

Aciman, André. *Out of Egypt: A Memoir.* New York: Picador, 1994.

Benjamin, Walter. *The Arcades Project.* Cambridge: MIT Press, 1988.

Lear, Linda. *Rachel Carson: Witness for Nature,* New York: Henry Holt and Company, 1997.

The Corporation. 2004. Directed by Mark Achbar, Jennifer Abbott, and Joel Bakan, based on Bakan's book, *THE CORPORATION: The Pathological Pursuit of Profit and Power.*

Lo ke se aprendre en la kuna, sien anios dura. (What you learn in the cradle lasts a hundred years.)

Chapter One
Beyond the Anthropocene

What do I smell?
Glancing at Cocomiso's furry bum,
I don't see anything.
Nope, nothing on the soles of my shoes.
What do I hear? Whale voices? Singing stars?
Millions of miles away on what looks like
the blue Planet Earth, past its wispy white clouds,
I can make out fragments of our biosphere.
I see a vast expanse of gold—
are those the aspens changing color back home in Colorado?
Down South, I see what looks like a giant glacier—
how is that possible?
Way over to the West, I see thick plumes of grey smoke.
What in the world is burning?
And to the East, are those the sprawling tendrils
of the Great Barrier Reef?
Whoa! I feel like I'm spiraling
—kind of like I'm inside of a conch shell?
Or strands of DNA?
Blasting through the primordial light, through clouds
of gas and stardust, I feel really dizzy!
—the cosmic mosaic flashing faster and faster,
thumping louder and louder…

Zazu's eyes pop open. Startled, he looks around his bedroom and mumbles to himself:

Cousteau and Carson books piled on my paint boxes, Malcolm X and Star Wars posters, globe-night light, drum trap-set....yup, all here. What just happened? Ouch, my hand hurts.

Someone is knocking on his door. "Hey, Zazu!"

Hi, Ari! Come on in!

It's Shabbat morning. Yawning and stretching, Zazu climbs out of bed, remembering his dreams from the night before when he and his imaginary friend, a malamute husky named Cocomiso, had gone for a long ride across many lands and many seas on the back of their friend, the humpback whale.[1]

Ari, what a wild adventure I had again last night! Every night I travel back through time and visit my ancestors in their diaspora.[2] My family has told me so many stories about these relatives who I am finally meeting in my dreams. And I learn about a history that we never hear about in school.

"Yeah, Zazu, my whole life I have felt invisible as a Black Jew. Maybe history is like an ancient mosaic[3]—a composite of many tiny fragments of stories—and we have to go on adventures to find out more and more about who we really are on planet earth and in the universe. These stories form constellations like the stars and planets in our solar system. It sounds like you are trying to put the pieces of a giant puzzle back together."

Zazu's mom's family is Sephardi and Mizrahi—Arab Jews[4] *who come from Iberia, the Middle East, and North Africa, the Mediterranean, the Balkans, and the Caribbean islands.*[5] *Zazu's dad's family is African-American from Barbados and India. Today is August 2nd, the 9th of Av, the same date as the ancient destruction of the First and Second Temples of Jerusalem, and the final day King Ferdinand and Queen Isabella expelled the last Jews from Spain during the Spanish Inquisition.*[6] *"Sobre Sepharad, ha caido el cielo la desgracia" (Over Spain had fallen a heaven of disgrace). Zazu and Ari sit in the sunshine together eating a delicious breakfast. Zazu loves to eat Sephardic foods for Shabbat breakfast—foods like leek kefticas with eggs, tahini on toasted pan, and pomegranates.*[7] *For their breakfast, Zazu's Nana and Papoo drink thick, sweet Turkish coffee that looks like mud! After taking her first sip, Nana always exclaims: "La alma se fué a su lugar!" (The soul returns home!)*[8] *Zazu's family speaks Ladino (Judezmo),*[9] *a language that combines medieval Spanish with Hebrew (Djudeo-Espanyol) and Judeo-Arabic.*[10] *They say "Shebbath Shalom" and sing Sh'bahoth.*[11]

Ari is Ashkenazic,[12] *so for Shabbat breakfast his family likes to eat lox and bagels. They speak Yiddish, a language that comes from German, and they say "Gut Shabbes." Ari's mother is African-American and his father is white Russian-Jewish.*

"Zazu, Tell me about your adventures last night!"

I dreamt Cocomiso and I hopped on the back of our friend the humpback whale and swam across the Atlantic Ocean to The Rock of Gibraltar[13] in the Mediterranean Sea, between Spain and North Africa. Ari, it was here that our expedition began![14]

After a long windy ride across the ocean under a full moon and clear, starry sky, we arrived just as the sun was rising on the southwestern coast of Spain. It was cold and I was kind of queasy from the ride. From Gibraltar, far in the distance we could see the tip of the Atlas Mountains of Morocco. We were so hungry after our voyage, and quickly found huge, sweet, ripe, purple figs that hung from giant trees near shore.[15] They tasted scrumptious with the *boyos* (stuffed savory pastries), *guichado* (spinach pie), and calamata olives we had brought in our backpack from home. As we ate we could hear the wailing sounds of *zingano, yifto* (gypsy)[16] voices coming from nearby caves, singing mesmerizing and melancholic songs of life in Sefarad, from so long ago.

I heard them sing: "*Estamos en galut.*" (We are in exile!) I wondered why gypsies were singing in Ladino. Why were they singing about the Andalusian Jews? A shiver of ran through me as I listened to their voices.

Have you ever seen the Rock of Gibraltar,[17] Ari? It's a giant rock that pops straight up out of the sea at the edge of Spain! You can see a treacherous rocky cliff on one side and a long sloping meadow on the other. This geography reminds me of the Sephardic trickster, Joha,[18] who also has two very different sides, two personalities— he's suspicious and scheming, but enchanting and loveable. Mommia tells me *guzma* (exaggerated stories) of Joha's mischieviousness. And his wild behavior makes me laugh at myself sometimes too! She says that's a good lesson for everyone to learn!

As Cocomiso and I walked up the grassy hillside towards the top of Gibraltar, we saw hundreds of Barbary macaque monkeys[19] scampering back and forth—*ginga*, side to side—all over the hills. We tried to pass them quickly since the macaques made high-pitched, eery, screeching sounds, and glared suspiciously at us over their shoulders, lip-smacking and teeth-chattering[20] as they pried open seeds with their long spidery fingers. A lot of the macaques were also eating out of potato chip bags found on the ground. Why on earth did the tourists leave their trash everywhere?

Quickening her step, Cocomiso looked anxiously at the macaques and nudged me forward with her furry wet nose. Suddenly a macaque leapt out in front of us and spoke to Cocomiso: "We heard you were coming here. You need to know that our families keep disappearing onto your shores—the land of masks and gloves.[21] Your scientists continue to steal our baby macaques to use for laboratory experiments. Please stop your people from hurting us!"

Cocomiso grew angry about what the mother monkey had shared. As she nursed her tiny baby,[22] the macaque told us her story. We listened carefully, and as she finished, we told her we would do whatever we could to keep their babies safe from medical experiments.

A macaque mama led Cocomiso to a dirt mound inside a nearby cave. As the sun was setting they finally emerged—Cocomiso wagging her tail, her muzzle and front legs covered in dry earth.

The mama handed me a fist-sized nutshell that contained something. "What's inside this shell will give you a clue to what needs to happen next. *Pasensia a peyojo, ke la noche es larga* (Be patient, as we have a long way to go). *Tu korazon espejo* (Wait for your heart, let your conscience be your guide)."

I thanked her as I put the crusty nutshell into my backpack. Then the monkeys made a path for us to continue up the Rock of Gibraltar.

On our way up the mountain we met a robust hunchback who introduced himself as Rabbi Habibi. As we walked together, this gentle man with a strong voice told us about the Spanish Inquisition,[23] the forced *goluth* (exile, diaspora) of Spanish Jews and Moslems. He told us about the people of Gibraltar who have always been very friendly to Jews, and of his friend Americo Castro, the famous Spanish historian who declared: "Most people have forgotten that Iberia's ancestry is ½ Jewish, ½ Moslem, and ½ Catholic! That's who the Spanish people really are."

Just to be sure we'd be safe on our journey, Rabbi Habibi gave us *una kemiya* (amulet): a sprig of myrtle and a *hamsa*[24] to take with us for good luck and to give us courage!

"Zazu, your *neshama*, your soul,[25] is like an intricately knotted Persian carpet, weaving all who you will meet along your journey. You have the capacity to question and listen and act without fear."

I wasn't sure what he meant, but I asked him if he knew why the gypsies sang of ancient Sepharad. He told us that when he had been living in the caves of Spain he had learned from the *voivod*, the Roma chieftan, that the Roma gypsies are unafraid of *gadje* (strangers) since they themselves are nomads and are seen as strangers by others. The Roma felt deep empathy for the plight of the outcast wandering Jews, and expressed their melancholy in the *duende*, the deep emotion of their music and song.

"Inshallah! Ken se kema en la shorba, aspola al yagurt!" (If you get burned on the hot soup, blow on the cold yogurt!) Rabbi Habibi called out as the voices of the Romani faded into the distance. Cocomiso and I continued to climb the steep rock.

When we got to the top of Gibraltar, the mountain dropped abruptly, straight down to the sea. Peering over the edge, we could see just a sliver of the city below us along the shore. Mommia had taught me that if I breathe slowly and pay deep attention, unexpected magical things can happen; time and space—distance and scale can transform in unexplainable ways.[26] If we concentrated, far into the distance we could see Andalucian wine-makers stomping juicy grapes in a large vat—making sweet sherry in the town of Jerez, one hundred-thirteen kilometers north from where we stood.

Twenty-four kilometers to the south across the Mediterranean Sea, if we concentrated, we could see Moroccan farmers on tall ladders combing through olive tree branches. When I was a little boy while breastfeeding,[27] Mommia told me many stories about the olive-combers she had seen in Tunisia. Olive-combers wore a single sheep's horn on each finger and stroked the limbs of the trees, gently releasing the olives onto tight-mesh nets spread across the ground below. I realized the farther I could see into the distance of the landscape, the farther I could see into my own memories and imagination.[28]

I pet Cocomiso's soft ears, and we took a big breath together as we stood on the edge of the cliff. Now, as distance folded into itself, time began to expand—we found ourselves in two places at once. What the hairy heck?! Gazing across the shore, I could see what appeared to be a mesonychid,[28] the ancient ancestor of our friend the humpback whale who lived on land and then in the sea 50 million years ago!

Cocomiso looked around, confused—the mesonychid[29] looked like a big dog with flipper-like paws! "How can dogs and whales and humans all be cousins?" she howled in wonder and disbelief.

15

We ran down the craggy cliff toward our barnacled humpback as she playfully breached along the water's edge. Jumping onto her back, we held on tightly to her bubbly warts[30] as she carried us out to sea. A hop, skip, and a jump from the Rock of Gibraltar to Africa, we arrived in Morocco near the city of Ouazzane.

Ari, I must tell you about the desert festival of Hilloula[31] and the huge bonfires in the cemetery of the great *tzaddiks*.[32] But first, I've got to tell you about the Jewish pirates, the Jews of Spain and Turkey, the Middle East, North Africa, India, and the amazing histories that we never learned in school. We are not invisible, and we will not be forgotten or ignored!

Chapter Two
Pirates of the Caribbean

What a great adventure we had, Ari! All the stories my family has told me have come to life in my *haloms* (dreams)! Last night I dreamt about the Jewish Pirates of the Caribbean. *Tiya* (Aunt) Joya and *Tiyo* (Uncle) Saan had told me tales of the famous Sephardic pirate Moses Cohen Henriques Eanes who ran the biggest heist in pirate history![33]

"Wow, Zazu, the Pirates of the Caribbean were Jewish!?"

Yeah! A bunch of them were! Between the years 1100 and 1800,[34] many Jews became pirates, outlaws, and freedom-fighters because tens of thousands of Jews were brutally forced by the Inquisition to flee the Iberian Peninsula of Spain and Portugal or convert to Christianity, or be killed.[35] Jewish people had lived in Spain for more than 1000 years, before we were violently expelled from our ancient homeland.

In my dream, when we first met Rabbi Habibi from Gibraltar, he had recited ancient Ladino poetry, heavy with the melancholy of our diaspora. I remember his deep, hypnotic voice chanting: "*Montanyas yoran por aire* (Mountains cry for air); *Avlar kero, i no puedo, mi korazon sospira* (I want to speak, I can't, my heart sighs); *Quando sale la luna, nadie come naranjas* (When the moon departs, no one eats oranges)."

Sharing this same sadness and loss during the Spanish Inquisition,[36] swashbuckling, Ladino-speaking pirates ransacked the monarchy's flotilla on the high seas all across the Atlantic Ocean and the Caribbean Sea, often preventing Catholic missionaries from landing on shore and converting native people to Christianity. Rebellious Sephardic pirates really got their revenge against the Spanish galleons![37] They intercepted the Spanish Armada and looted gold from the ships of King Ferdinand and Queen Isabella[38] in retaliation for Jews and Moors being expelled from Spain.[39] Mommia told me that this history is an important part of the Age of Exploration and Colonialism, but we are not taught this history in school. Ari, I wonder why!

"So do I, Zazu! It feels like understanding how and why our histories have been forgotten and ignored would help us understand how and why animals and their worlds are being destroyed."

Cocomiso, the humpback whale, and I continued our expedition across the turquoise waters of the Caribbean Sea:[40] traveling to Hispaniola, Barbados, Curaçao, Jamaica,[41] Nevis, St. Croix, St. Thomas, St. Maarten, and St. Eustatius—(islands along the coast of North, South, and Central America)—the smell of salt water and the screeching cry of seagulls, always overhead.

We stopped at each island and visited the old *kal* (synagogues) and cemeteries, looking for familiar Sephardi names on tombstones: Perez, Lopez, Carbajal, Abravanel, and Rodriguez.[42] During our visits we met *mestizaje* (mixed) families of the Sephardic pirates who had married into the Taino, Galibi, Cibony, and Island Carib/Kalinago[43] people for the past five hundred years. The indigenous people and the Sephardim felt a mutual kinship. The pirates explained how their ancestors' hearts had ached for a landing place, a *querencia*,[44] a sanctuary, a home—what they called *Barcadares*. *Mestizaje* communities were born from these exiled pirates.[45]

Ari, one morning, swimming near the southern coast off the island of Jamaica, we found ourselves alongside the pirate sloop of Captain Moses Cohen Henriques Eanes. We had actually traveled from 2016 back to 1628!

Waving to us to come aboard from high above on the deck of his ship, he took out a leather pouch of tobacco snuff to sniff. Just then, a big gust of wind blew a wad of snuff out into the air. Spraying down on us, clumps of snuff tickled the nose of our humpback whale! She began to sneeze ACHOO out of her spout! "Oh dear," she said. "I sneeze and sneeze, and SNEEZE whenever I swim along the coast of big polluted cities… but usually not out here in the deep waters…." she explained in between sneezes…. "AACHOOO!" and with that Cocomiso and I were tossed, up, up, UP! into the air, landing on the deck of Captain Moses's ship.

"Well, *Bwènas dias!*" exclaimed Captain Moses. "*Buy roon!* (Welcome, come in!) *Keres komer kon mosotros?* (Would you care to dine with us?)"

We stayed for lunch and ate harrisa spiced couscous, sauerkraut,[46] and an okra *tagine* served in intricately decorated Lusterware[47] and Delft pottery[48]—bowls and porringers that the pirates had salvaged from their homes in Spain, before the rest of their possessions were stolen by the Inquisition.

As exiles, these old salts[49] yearned to put the pieces of their shattered lives back together. Eating from these vessels brought them closer to a sense of home, lost but not forgotten. Ari, as I listened to the pirates' many stories, I realized then that the reason for our odyssey was to search for the many meanings of 'home.'

Captain Moses' parrot had a lot to say about this:

"*El mundo se manea, ma no kaye* (The world shakes, but does not crumble); *Los Katalanes de las piedras azen panes* (The Catalans make bread from stone); *Kuándo una puerta sérra syen avren* (When one door closes, one hundred open) … SQUAWK SQUAWK! You think I talk a lot, huh? Try sailing across the ocean for months on end with a *graja* (crow) perched on your ship's mast!"

I noticed the parrot was wearing a knitted kippah.

"Captain Moses, I've heard about Jewish parrots—where did yours come from?"

"Oh! *mi papagayo djudio*![50] *Si!* She has traveled from the coast of Southern India where she spoke Judeo-Malayalam,[51] which is not to be confused with Judeo-Malay. I taught her Ladino, but she still loves her parrot songs—Judeo-Malayalam folksongs called kiḷipāṭṭə."[52]

As we listened to the parrot's rhythmic non-sequiturs and ate our *tagine*, we suddenly heard loud cannon fire exploding in the waters off in the distance.

"*Menèate àyde àyde!*" (Hurry up!)

To keep us safe, Captain Moses ushered us below deck. Our humpback whale plunged beneath the waves. In the belly of the ship, we met the crew's surgeon and sail-maker. The gunner ran past us up the stairs, skipping two at a time. He was heading to the crow's nest, the lookout platform near the top of one of the masts. Cocomiso stayed close by my side. The hull was crammed full of cannon balls, sharpened swords, daggers, *reals*,[53] and amber medicine bottles. Searching the sea through his periscope, Captain Moses mumbled:

"*No demandes ni al medico ni al jeráh, sino al ke pasa el mal*" (Don't ask the doctor or the surgeon, but the one who is suffering from the illness/Go straight to the source). Cocomiso and I looked at one another really confused! He explained to us that the gunfire was an aggressive warning signal from ships of the Spanish monarchy and the Inquisition.

"The Spanish monarchs," Captain Moses said defiantly, "King Ferdinand and Queen Isabella, like to pretend they have power over us no matter where we sail—to prove that we are no longer welcome in Spain, and that we must stay far away from Spanish shores. However, out on the high seas we are their masters, and their sailors fear us![54] They will not pursue us for long. We are safe out here. We can maintain our *kavod*, our honor. Perhaps one day our oppressors will learn that when they hurt one group of people they hurt all peoples, and themselves as well."

His parrot chimed in: "*Amostrate komo amigo en la ora mala* (Act like a friend in difficult times); *Una mano lava lo otra, I las dos lavas la kara* (One hand washes the other and together they wash the face); *El prove i el riko, todos se mesura por un negro piko* (Whether you are rich or poor you have the same grave)."[55]

Captain Moses reassured us, "Heed my parrot! Have no fear, *ke salgas salvo i sano* (You can get out safe and sound). You can return to your whale and to your journey." [56]
So we embraced our new pirate friends. "*Buendád!*" (thank you for your kindness and hospitalility).

They shouted, *"Hasta luego, entonces! Kamínos de léche y myèl!* (May you have a good and safe journey, roads of milk and honey!) …and remember: *Ken mete kara, toma marido!"* (Those who are gutsy accomplish the most!)

Cocomiso and I jumped back onto our humpback whale and swam as fast as the wind, back onto the open seas.

In the distance, I could hear Captain Moses' parrot yammering away: "*Kyen a la mar se kaye, de la espanda se detyène* (A drowning man will hang onto anything); *Un bwen pleto, tráe una bwena paz* (A good argument clears the air); *Sin mashkar, no se englute* (You cannot swallow without chewing/nothing can be accomplished without hard work); *El árto no kreye al ambierto"* (The contented person does not understand the person who is hungry).
Her final words of encouragement drifted over the green-blue waters: "*Kon pedos no se boyadeya wevos"* (One cannot paint eggs with farts).

Cocomiso furrowed her furry brow. We didn't know birds had gas.

Once again, I felt we were sliding through time as we traveled across the Caribbean Islands. Time appeared to be suspended between the past and the future in a continuous present. We seemed to be inside folded time, overlapping pre-history and the Middle Ages, all the way up to 2016! On top of the Rock of Gibraltar, looking down at the mesonychid, this weird time travel had excited me, but also scared me, and I had held Cocomiso close to my heart, wondering what was going to happen next. Now, our humpback whale sensed my fear and sang out a *cante hondo*, a deep song like a gypsy lullaby to comfort us.

We held on tightly to her and rode from the island of Hispanola, now called Cuba, south to Curaçao, and then through the Panama Canal across Central America to the Pacific Ocean. Exhausted and parched by the heat of the sun, we finally approached the sub-continent of India in the Arabian Sea. It had been a long journey, and after thousands of kilometers of listening to the songs of the whales,[57] I began to decipher their collective voice as a song of peace.

As communal animals, whales instinctively know we are all interdependent—all the creatures of the land and of the sea—all the creatures of the oceans, rivers, lakes, and sky. The whales alerted us to the crises that petroleum companies caused when they explored for oil by using massive underwater sound cannons that cause whales, dolphins, and other sea creatures to become deaf. Oceanic noise pollution can also be deadly.[58] Numbing underwater sound disrupts the whales' ability to communicate through echolocation.[59] We were immediately reminded of the threatening cannon fire we heard onboard Captain Moses Cohen Henriques Eanes' pirate ship, and again we saw the connections, right there in front of us, between power that destroys animals and the planet, and power that destroys people! As we had promised the macaque monkeys that we would intervene on their behalf, Cocomiso and I promised the whales that we would find a way as soon as we could to stop the underwater sound cannons that plagued them. The whales taught us one of their songs. As we held on tightly to our humpback whale swimming across the sea, together we sang the Song of Peace:

> "Oh, the wolf shall dwell with the lamb,
> And the leopard shall lie with the kid,
> And the cow and the bear shall feed,
> While the lion eats straw like the ox…"[60]

Chapter Three
The Oldest Jews on the Planet

Do you remember when we were babies, Ari, and my Daddia sang songs to me about my Great-Great Grandmommy Sarina's home on the Southwestern coast of India? She lived in the ancient village of Cochin, today called Kochi, in the province of Kerala, the 'land of temples.'

"Yeah, Zazu, I remember dancing to those songs—we had so much fun! The music reminded me of memories of my own family."

We arrived along the coast of India[61] just as the sun was rising. As we approached, we saw a hundred small fishing boats with big sails leaning away from the wind as fishermen set off for their early morning catch. With the force of her blowholes,[62] the humpback whale's geyser shot us up, up, UP!!! high into the air onto the sandy shore.

"LOOK!" cried Cocomiso, "that must be one of the sacred cows Daddia sings about!"

Sure enough, emerging from behind a venerable tree that had been split by lightening long ago, we saw a big grey Brahmin cow with long velvety ears and round brown eyes as big as giant figs. "*Dobrùto* (good morning), *safra* (morning greeting)," said the sacred cow in her deep soft voice, almost in whispers. "I will take you to visit your Great-Great Grandmommy. She's waiting for you. *Vyeja en kaza, alegria en kaza* (An old woman in the house brings joy into it)." So off we went through the forest of Kavalai and arrived at a village with children running and playing.

"Welcome, my dear Zazu, *vènga en bon óra*" (I'm glad to see you, please come in), called Great-Great Grandmommy Sarina as she hugged and kissed us. We helped her lay out many bowls and baskets of food on a long table shaded by flowering mimosa trees. She was so excited for our visit. I was so happy to meet her, my twelve *primos* (eight girl and four boy cousins), and my four aunts and uncles.[63] I saw myself in my cousins' faces and gestures! *Tiyo* Micah told us about the Jewish history of Kerala as the center of the Indian spice trade.

"Zazu, we are known as the *Malabar Yehude*, or Cochin Jews. Most of our Jewish community[64] has by now migrated to Israel and the United States, and only a few families remain here in Cochin. But our history in India is long and deep. Jews have lived here in peace without any hostilities. We arrived here long before the destruction of the first Temple in Jerusalem. Like Moses who parted the Red Sea to free the Jews from persecution in Egypt, Varuna, the Underwater God in Hindu mythology, parted the seas and revealed the state of Kerala where we are now sitting and eating together. Kerala offers freedom for many, many people![65]

"Our village follows the Jewish practice of *bal tashchit*, do not destroy or waste. Long before environmental movements, Jewish tradition taught how important it is to respect and care for the earth. Nature is *HaShem* (G-d). Nature and ecology are integral to Jewish life, just like *mitzvot* and Shabbat—how we interpret the Torah, pray, and celebrate our holidays. We must live in peace with people who have different beliefs, and live in peace with our land and its animals. We are all guests on this planet. Our commitment to *bal tashchit*, to caring for our environment, is a form of hospitality, and both ea personal and social commitment to non-violence. Connecting refusal to waste with non-violence was also one of Mahatma Gandhi's vows.

"The Talmud, our *melamed* (teacher) and our *matana* (gift), reminds us that the *mitzvah* (good deed) of hospitality is just as important as Torah study. This way of honoring God teaches us how to think about and share other people's feelings and our joyous and challenging responsibility to our earth. *Bal tashchit* is a form of compassion and empathy."

I remembered hearing that Indian rabbis had protested against the caste system for many centuries. *Tiyo* Micah smiled warmly as he spoke: "*Ande komen dos, komen i tres*" (Where two people eat, three people also can).

Ari, I wish you could have heard the many voices of Cochin! Besides Jews, there are Hindus, Christians, Muslims, Jains, Sikhs, and Buddhists who all live and work together, speaking many different dialects and respecting each other's different ethnic histories.[66]

Our humpback whale friend felt right at home on the Southwestern coast of India. She told us that whales also share intricate cooperation techniques,[67] and they speak in different dialects depending on where they come from. Since Cocomiso is a malamute husky, she loves to hear about teamwork. It reminds her of her days as a sled dog. She is excited about how we are all the same and different at the same time. The whale told us each whale tail, called a fluke,[68] has a unique shape, like individual fingerprints or snowflakes[69] that made up the snowdrifts Cocomiso loved to run through.

Cochin is like a paradise flowing with sameness and difference,[70] and even the synagogue is called Paradesi Synagogue of Cochin. Everyone is able to go to school, have jobs, and eat healthy food! The people of Cochin understand that *kitar I no meter, el dip ay ke ver* (when you remove and do not replace, you soon see the bottom). Their sense of long-term community reminded me of the renegade Spinoza and his 'declaration of cooperation,'[71] but I will get to that soon!

We sat together around a low table and ate quinoa salad with figs and mint, coconut and spices with dhal, fish curry, cucumber yogurt salad, and goat kebab with lots of lemon. After we gobbled the last bits, we nibbled on marzipan—a symbol of sweet life. When we had finished eating, my *primos* brought out tablas, dulcimers, and lutes. We played the instruments and all sang songs about magical rivers that run east and west.

After lunch, we played soccer until dusk. Orangutans[72] the color of sunlit turmeric joined us on the soccer field, tossing the ball into the air with their finger-like toes.

Ari, orangutans look like they have four hands with twenty fingers instead of two hands and two feet. We learned that these 'people of the forest' are almost extinct because of the worldwide trade in palm oil.[73] This group of orangutans were refugees[74] from Indonesia.[75] They wore a *hamsa* to avert the *nazár* (evil eye). A local *endul kadera* (magician, witch doctor, shaman, sorcerer, conjurer, charmer, whisperer, *baal shem, baal nes* who practices home remedies) had given them *en dúlko* (magic potion)[76] to protect the orangutans against transnational agribusiness.[77] We had all heard how Nestlé Corporation and PepsiCo.[78] destroy their forests by stripping their land for palm oil.[79] Palm oil is used to make chips crunchy, like Doritos. They plant huge palm oil plantations that are responsible for massive clear-cutting leading to deforestation. We saw more and more connections between environmental and human degradation. *Esta apegado komo la unya kon la karne* (They are inseparable).

    Not only are orangutans and other animals threatened to the brink of extinction, but we even met child workers who are trapped on the palm oil plantations in a form of modern slavery.[80] Producing gigatons of greenhouse gases, these plantations are corroding the Earth's atmosphere.[81] Who needs imaginary monsters or giants or evil empires when corporations like Nestlé[82] and PepsiCo (who share their own freaky form of conviviality), Merck and Monsanto[83] destroy everything in their path? Between three months and five years old, Mommia took me to Storytime in children's libraries all over the United States. Why weren't any real stories about 'good' and 'evil' ever read to us?!

    We spent the day playing soccer with our cousins and new friends, the orangutans. After a rough game, the orangutans showed us their homemade first-aid kit. They showed us how to chew up dracaena leaves into a paste that helps heal sore muscles.[84] Happy and pooped, we all fell asleep under the hanging roots of a banyan tree listening to the nearby croaking conversations among Indian Purple Frogs.[85] The humpback whale had also fallen asleep. She told us later that whales sleep by switching off one half of their brain at a time. I had also heard that whales dream—you could tell because of the way their eyes move back and forth while they sleep. Cocomiso thought it was strange that I had been surprised at that.

    Hours later, the eruption of orangutans woke us up. Their voices filled the forest with what my cousins, *mi primos*, said was their 'Long Call,'[86] a sound that even traveled far out to sea where our humpback was tail lobbing. We watched her as she flapped her fluke against the waves, and breached with her humpback friends off the coast of Cochin. We heard the whales' deep song—responses that echoed across the shore all the way to the forest's edge.

The burning forests in both Indonesia and Brazil can be seen from outer space.

"Two-thirds of the world's population will not have access to fresh drinking water by 2025."

There will be more plastic in our oceans than fish by 2050.

The "slow violence" wrought by climate change, toxic drift, deforestation, oil spills, and the environmental aftermath of war insidiously work their way into our daily lives.

"Bacteria are *evolving*. We should, too."

Every 60 seconds more than one million single-use non-biodegradable bags are thrown away.

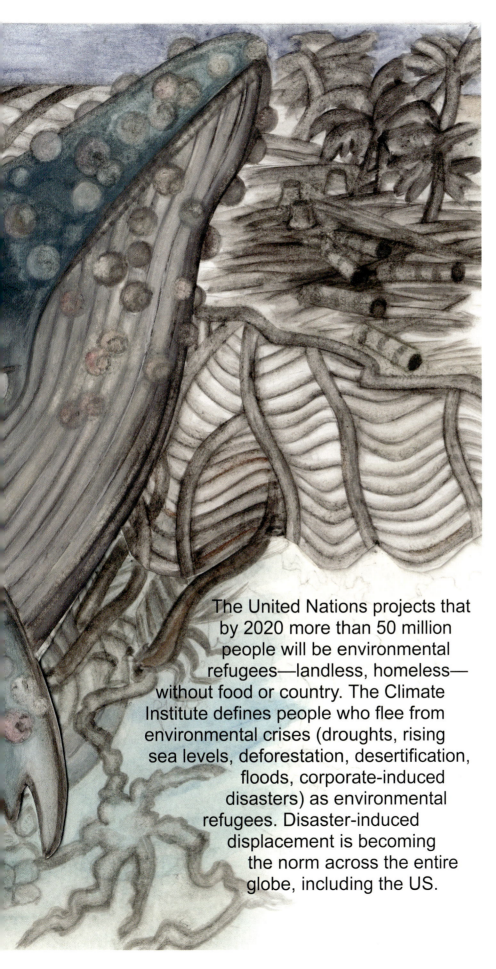

The United Nations projects that by 2020 more than 50 million people will be environmental refugees—landless, homeless—without food or country. The Climate Institute defines people who flee from environmental crises (droughts, rising sea levels, deforestation, desertification, floods, corporate-induced disasters) as environmental refugees. Disaster-induced displacement is becoming the norm across the entire globe, including the US.

It was so exciting to hear the orangutans and whales talk to one another and to see the whales' breach in response—rising up, twisting in mid-air, then slapping their enormous bodies across the water!

The orangutan's 'Long Call' actually reminded me of the deep, quavering sound of the shofar.[87] I thought how crazy it was that the sound of repentance should visit me now as I learned about how the homes and lives of these 'people of the forest' were in desperate danger. And on top of that, I had learned that only a free man[88] can be a *Ba'al Tekiah* (shofar sounder); but these vocal orangutans were anything but free.

Cocomiso howled in grief for the orangutans who, like the whales[89] and their other sea-friends, were suffering because of globalization, consumer demands, and corporate greed: "Our industrial societies caused these problems so it is our responsibility to stop them!"

Far in the distance, we could hear the orangutans' 'kiss squeaks.'[90] They had taught us how to use leaves to let predators know that they had been spotted.

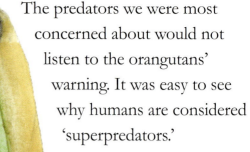

The predators we were most concerned about would not listen to the orangutans' warning. It was easy to see why humans are considered 'superpredators.'

I understood more and more that there was so much work to be done; that the only way to heal ethnic and racial divisions and the ecology of our global body is to see how we are all intermeshed. We all have to take care of each other.

Cocomiso howled: "We are not going to 'save the planet'[91] or fix these crazy problems that generations before us have scattered at our feet, but maybe, just maybe, we could feel empathy for those who are directly affected by our culture-of-convenience, and we can finally make a difference—make the bad less bad by refusing to be silent. We have got to speak up, spread the word, make sure that we are heard, make sure that everyone knows that these things are happening right here, right now!"

These creatures of nature somehow understand what has to change. Albert Einstein recognized this: "Look deep into nature, and then you will understand everything better."

We walked down the road to a cove along the shore where we could see the hundred fishing boats returning to Cochin as they do everyday at dusk, their decks filled high with fish![92] Villagers flocked to the shore to help the fishermen unload their catch. *Primos* Mira and Dhruv urged us to visit the Ganges River before leaving India so we could learn about the myth of Varuna. We hugged and kissed and thanked our family for their kindness, and waved good-bye: "*Namasté!* Come back to visit us again soon!"

Off we went to the Varuna River that led us to the sacred Mother Ganga—the river goddess, the 'river of life' that flows from the Himalayas at the headwaters where heaven and earth meet. The Himalayas are the highest mountains on earth that continue to grow higher as the subcontinent of India pushes northward. The Ganges flows from northern India, the land of the endangered white leopard and musk deer, southeastward to the Bay of Bengal.

Offering a blessing of agricultural abundance, the Ganges irrigates some of the most fertile soils on earth. Shiva diverts the potentially dangerous powers of the Ganges River from the Himalayas southward, dividing it into many rivers. These tributaries flow downstream until they join together again into the one mighty Ganga River.

A heavy, hot mist hung over the water as we traveled toward the city of Varanasi.[93] I remembered Mommia's stories about her visit there—among the thousands of alters for Lord Shiva, there was poop—everywhere![94]

Usually the Great Ganges is packed with tremendous activity and hoards of people. But arriving so early in the morning there was only a calm silence, except for an occasional lammergeyer bird and the mesmerizing voice of an apparition of the great political poet Rabinandrath Tagore,[95] whose spirit is suspended between India and Bengal, Hinduism and Islam. After his death, Tagore's ashes had been scattered over the Ganges in Calcutta in 1941. But now out of the mist, we could see his floating body as he meditated and chanted on the bank of the river. To our even greater surprise, he knew my name, and turned to us saying: "Zazu, listen carefully to my words—I want you to remember that the same stream that flows through your veins,[96] flows through the universe in rhythmic measure. In this land of fire and air you are a human estuary.[97] You are a body of water that is connected to the global cycle of water. We are all human estuaries, and must take care of the waters of the world so that we may all thrive.[98] We cannot forget that water supports everything that makes up our lives—humans, animals, insects, plants, the seas, rivers, mountains, the atmosphere, the air. Without water we are nothing at all."[99]

"Thank you, Babu Tagore, for speaking to me.[100] Your words are like the songs we sing in synagogue. Everything is bound together! The inside, the outside, above and below."[101]

As the sun set, Tagore's voice drifted through my consciousness, "On the seashore of endless worlds, children play."[102] He winked at me with a broad, mischievous smile, and then before my eyes, Tagore had evaporated into the thick wet air.

"But wait!" I needed to ask Tagore what should we do when the world begins to turn inside out—when the bottom of the ocean begins to turn into a desert,[103] when people become animals and animals become people.[104]

It was too late, I would have to keep asking my question. Again, I felt the elasticity of time. Space expanded.

31

I got a sense that the heavy mist gradually enveloping us may have been Tagore himself. He had reminded me that not only are all living things made mostly of water, we are part of its infinite recycling. Water is older than the earth itself. Like energy, water is neither created nor destroyed, it simply transforms; water is our ultimate manifestation of interconnectedness. We may be drinking the same water that fed multi-ocular animals 530 million years ago, or the same water a worm-like exvertebrate slunk through 390 million years ago, or an ancient crocodile splashed in 75 million years ago, or dinosaur pee, or the deepest, darkest ocean currents four miles below sea level, or a devastating tsunami, or what was poured into Cleopatra's bath.[105]

The almost microscopic water droplets began to feel like tiny grains. Cocomiso licked her jowls. I stuck out my tongue. Salt! The air was dripping with salt!

I let go of a deep breath and realized the salt had coalesced into a human figure that I could see hundreds of miles away. I was looking at Mahatma Gandhi kneeling at the edge of the Arabian Sea. Thousands of people stood in reverence behind him as he held a chunk of something stark white, a white that sparkled in the setting sun. Flashes of bright light reflected across the miles.[106]

In the midst of the crowd, TIME-LIFE photographers were clicking away. I heard someone yell: "Hail deliverer!" I realized then we were looking back to 1930. We were witnessing Gandhi's defiance of British law in his infamous Salt March to the Sea. The movement toward India's independence had begun![107]

Chapter Four
"...spooky action at a distance..."

Cocomiso and I wiped off salt crystals from our bodies and jumped onto the back of the humpback whale. Passing Gandhi and his rebellious followers, we continued on our expedition west across the Arabian Sea to the Persian Gulf, one of the most sensitive marine ecosystems on the planet.

Our ancestors were exiled 2,700 years ago, first to the city-state of Babylonia in Mesopotamia (modern Iraq)—and then here to this land, first called Persia, now Iran.[108] Several miles off the southern coast of Iran we were suddenly engulfed in a huge tangle of plastic debris as big as a small island.[109] The humpback and Cocomiso were able to extricate themselves quickly. Leaning off the edge of the whale, Cocomiso tried to help me pull plastic bags off my face. I couldn't breathe and was unable to loosen my arms and legs that were caught in ghost nets,[110] dragging me down into dark waters. The more I struggled, the deeper I plummeted into a *tehom* (abyss) of a plastic underworld.[111] The tentacles of a giant Nomura,[112] a monstrous iridescent jellyfish bigger than my GrandPapa Don, got twisted in the strangulating mess.[113]

For a moment I stopped struggling as several small fish swam into the mound of tangled garbage and began chewing away with their sharp beak-like teeth in an attempt to cut me loose. I could hear a distant voice: "The impossible missions are the only ones which succeed." I recognized his French accent immediately—it was the voice of one of my heroes, Jacques Cousteau![114]

He, like the fish, came to my rescue, keeping me calm and focused. Finally I was free to swim as fast as I could back to the water's surface. Cocomiso and the humpback held onto me. Overwhelmed with relief, we all began to laugh!

Wow, Ari! It turns out that visible trash is not the most dangerous pollutant. Microplastic pollution—tiny particles that we can't see—is even more damaging to our environment and to sea life[115] because it blocks our respiratory systems and bloodstreams as we breathe.

I remembered hearing from my Great Papoo about the *hakim*, the physician ibn Sina.[116] When I finally caught my breath, we decided to make a *ziarat* (pilgrimage) to find this wizard-like doctor. After our nightmare of struggling to free ourselves from ghost nets and plastic, we needed his advice more than ever. When we got to land, we traveled many kilometers with a donkey who chatted with Cocomiso, sharing many stories. Could this be the trusted donkey of Joha the Trickster?

We passed a Bedouin camel caravan drinking from a spring. The camels are called the 'ships of the desert.' Fragrances of orange blossoms and roses wrapped around us as we passed groves of tangerine, pomelo, sour orange, and sweet lemon trees. We had heard that sweet lemons have medicinal *koah* (power, strength).

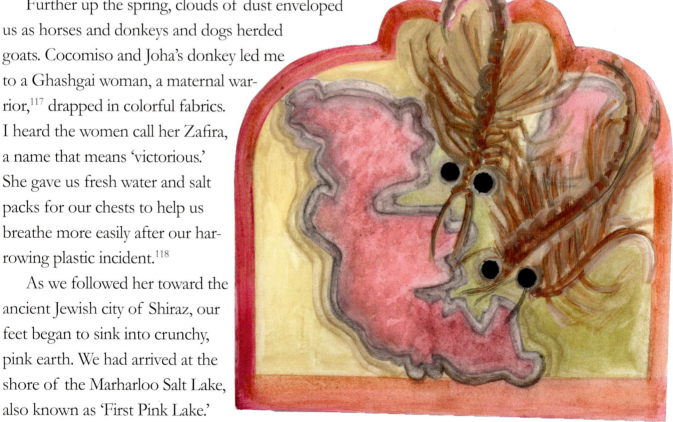

Further up the spring, clouds of dust enveloped us as horses and donkeys and dogs herded goats. Cocomiso and Joha's donkey led me to a Ghashgai woman, a maternal warrior,[117] drapped in colorful fabrics. I heard the women call her Zafira, a name that means 'victorious.' She gave us fresh water and salt packs for our chests to help us breathe more easily after our harrowing plastic incident.[118]

As we followed her toward the ancient Jewish city of Shiraz, our feet began to sink into crunchy, pink earth. We had arrived at the shore of the Marharloo Salt Lake, also known as 'First Pink Lake.'

Zafira explained in a Turkish dialect how the brilliant pink color was made up of brine shrimp —millions of tiny pink swimming bodies—the only creature that can live in such strong salt.[119]

"We are all halophiles! We love salt! It is deeply part of our spiritual life and rituals. If you focus your attention you will see halos everywhere. Halos surround every living thing, including salt—a living rock,[120] the only rock humans eat. And not just here, but everywhere…"[121]

With that, Zafira swung her arms wide gesturing toward the sky that was full of stars. How did night come so suddenly?

After our brine baths, we sat next to a fire as the Ghashghai elders told epic tales of their tribe's history. Cocomiso and I curled up next to the donkey. I was excited to share with our whale that we had met a people who migrate like whales do. They, like whales, love brine—a creature of the most dazzling, bright pink color that eats the whale's favorite food, plankton.[122] I remembered that the word in Greek, *planktos*, means wandering. I fell asleep thinking about luminescent pink whales wearing Ghashghai mirrored fabrics, migrating across land and sea on magic Kilim carpets.[123]

The animal hooves crunching into the salt woke me from my strange dream. I hugged Zafira: "*Chok teshekur ederim!*" (Thank you so much!)

"*Besimantór*" (good luck, praise be to God), she said as she kissed me on both cheeks and pet Cocomiso's soft ears. Zafira and Joha's donkey continued to lead us toward Shiraz where we said our final *allah is marlardik* and *gulle gulle* (goodbye) before the city ramparts. Just outside Shiraz, a herd of sheep blocked our path. As they slowly meandered past, we stopped and looked off into the distance. Once again, as in Gibraltar, vast distances magically transformed. Although we were hundreds of kilometers away, we had seen a kind of mirage—a mysterious form that seemed to move closer and closer to us. Far away, past Bab-e Anar, the Village of Pomegranates, we could see a male goitered gazelle[124] with its strange inflated neck.[125] Since our arrival in Iran we had seen this mirage. These gazelle live in the Khar Turan National Wildlife Refuge—the second largest biosphere in the world![126] This refuge is in the Semnan Province near Tehran—far north of our destination of Isfahan. The goitered gazelle reminded me of the camels Mommia told me she had seen while living in Tunisia. When I was little as I nursed,[127] she had shown me photos she had taken of a membrane that swells under the tongue of the male camel during mating season. She told me that it looked like a huge red balloon erupting out of the camel's mouth! And right here…well, miles away…was something almost as weird and beautiful! The Iranian male goitered gazelles' necks were so engorged! Joha's donkey told us that he and Joha could see the gazelle's swollen *garon* (throat) from as far away as Iran's eastern shore. They could see them from Hamadan in western Iran where Queen Esther and her cousin Mordecai are buried near gold glittering sand hills. The gazelles' necks could even be seen from as far away as the grave of the Prophet Daniel, who is buried in southwestern Iran. They were equally visible from ALL directions.

The donkey called this time-space mirage 'a conspiracy of magic!' This illusion of distance reminded me that what appears to be close is actually far away and what appears to be far away is actually close. Joha's donkey brayed in response. His jarring hee-haw felt urgent. Is this what Mommia meant when she told me that I was old enough to begin to understand how the choices I make, even back then as a four year-old child, impact so many people and things around me? She taught me that this huge responsibility we all share is exciting and can be full of love. Walking next to his furry-eared donkey, I began to understand how Joha the Trickster was reminding me of things I already know—ways of looking at the world that had gotten buried under years of school and socialization. Like with the gazelle, so close in the distance, I began to see how Joha was teaching me to remember by showing me the opposite of what I think I know.

Still with the gazelle in our sight, we arrived at the walls of Shiraz, a city we knew our family had lived in for centuries, but no were longer there. *Tiyo* Salomon, *Tiya* Marie, and their *ijas*, Aziza and Adina, had migrated to Paris from Shiraz in the 1960s. As far as we knew, none of our family remained. I was feeling dizzy and nauseous, and Cocomiso's eyes were aching and almost swollen shut from our near death encounter with the island of plastic trash. Zafira had warned us that the salt would bring the toxins to the surface; we would need help to get the pollution completely out of our systems (or as much as possible). If we went to one of the nearby synagogues, someone would surely help us find ibn Sina.

We entered the *mahaleh*, the Jewish ghetto where my family had lived many years ago. The rich smell of *kebab* immediately filled our nostrils. "*Shalomalekhem!*" said a voice on the wall above our heads. It was a young girl looking down at us who was about my age. I asked her if she knew how to find ibn Sina. Waving for us to follow her, she led us across mud-covered roofs connecting the houses of the *mahaleh*. We jumped from one roof to the next above the cobblestone maze of alleyways, canopies, and arches. Onion bulbs and salt crystals to keep away bad spirits hung on every door. In the narrow streets below we saw women wearing cowrie shells that looked like sleeping eyes. We saw scarab amulets,[128] and square gold pieces encased in salt to deter evil.[129] The *ayin ara* (evil eye) symbol, intended to reflect away evil, was everywhere—pinned to children's clothes, hanging in windows, painted on walls. In the distance we could hear a trilling noise—collective voices that we knew were supposed to draw out evil and protect the city's inhabitants.

A shrouded crouching figure called up to us: "*Mas ke te koma boka de leon, i no ojo de benadam*" (More than the roar of a lion is the evil eye of a person). We heard children in the streets yelling in Judi, Judeo-Persian, the language spoken only by Shirazi Jews. I understood them to be calling to me: "*Khebeen, khesheen?*" (How is your health?) As we moved deeper into the maze, I felt the folds of time expanding once again. I understood we were traveling back in time to meet ibn Sina. We were simultaneously in both the 10th and 21st centuries.

Instead of a synagoge, the girl led us to a restaurant that looked like a shimmering cave. It was made of salt! She put her hand on my chest and told us how the powers of salt could heal my sore lungs. The Salt Restaurant[130] was designed to look like the local salt mines. Before us sat ibn Sina, writing at one of the tables handcrafted from rock salt. Cocomiso started licking the walls of salt. I thought a little licking was okay since the salt was held together by its own natural gum covering, not a toxic resin or formaldehyde. The restaurant owners didn't seem to mind—we were definitely not in the United States.

"*Me da mùcho alegria de konoserlo* (Very happy to know you). *Páncho y áncho* (At your pleasure)."

Ibn Sina had heard about our encounter. To prevent infections[131] from being caught in the ghost nets, he gave us ground beetles to eat, and instructed me to go to the *haman*, the public baths. I was to meet them after my cleansing when the sun had reached its zenith on the celestial sphere. Cocomiso then followed ibn Sina up the spiral salt staircase, licking each step as she went.

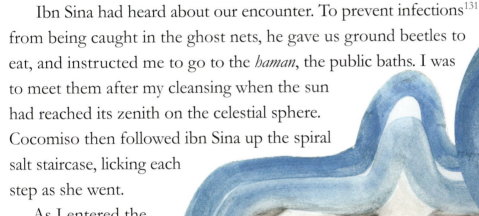

As I entered the *haman*, I was given a sour cherry drink and little Persian apricots that melted in my mouth. In the wet darkness I could hear a child excitedly whispering: "*Mava! Mava!*" (Mama! Mama!). I remembered how Mommia had told me about *les bains Maures* (the Moorish Baths) in Tunisia.

Her description of the Muslim Tunisian women decorated with green-dotted tattoos on their foreheads and wrists to relieve pain (the tattoos must have been located on acupressure/acupuncture points) and ropes of hennaed-hair high on their heads sitting cross-legged on stacks of Persian carpets exactly mirrored these older Jewish Iranian women who I passed as I entered the men's section of the *haman*. It felt weird and reassuring to see through Mommia's eyes so vividly. I had the feeling that Joha the Trickster had something to do with this.

Ibn Sina had given me amber[132] to rub while I was in the baths. He told me that resin is the result of a tree attempting to heal itself; and, amber is fossilized resin. Because trees all over the planet were dying, amber's healing properties had become even more powerful. To draw out its antiseptic properties, ibn Sina instructed me to wrap sun-dried camel *goh* (dung, excrement)[133] where the nets and plastic had torn my skin. As I coated my arms and belly with camel dung, I remembered Mommia's story of her travels in Belize where she ate the most delicious chocolate prepared by Mayan's who use jaguar dung to fertilize their cacao plants.[134] I definitely would have preferred eating chocolate to being wrapped in poop.

But, I felt reassured by what ibn Sina had told me: "Zazu, if you respect the earth, she will take care of you—her flesh will protect yours. Dirt is a living, breathing skin; dirt is the skin of the earth.[135] It is the matrix of life. Cow, camel, dog, human—all kinds of animal dung is the essence of dirt—its very origin; the dung microbes in dirt are vital to the biosphere; dirt is a process that turns gar-

39

bage into life; the process that turns garbage into a *bostán* (garden) is central to our survival; just as we came from dirt,[136] we depend on dirt to purify and heal the systems that sustain us.[137] Dirt teems with convivial communities."

I let the camel dung do its job. When I joined ibn Sina and Cocomiso, who was now all fluffy and had fully recovered from our battle with the ghost nets, we mounted a camel, Cocomiso ran alongside, and we continued our journey to Esfahan[138]—the city that was ibn Sina's home when he had been alive 600 years ago. I was grateful to the local camels for many reasons!

Ari, when we finally arrived in Esfahan we could still see the gazelles! I asked ibn Sina how this was happening—another wacky moment where the strangeness of scale and magic conspired[139] to help us see the world around us—alert and amplified!

I remembered something Einstein said about quantum entanglement: he referred to it as "spooky action at a distance." This was how he explained how wormholes link separate points in space-time. Shortcuts through the universe connect these pairs of quarks—the building blocks of matter.[140]

Ibn Sina was sharing the same idea but in a different way: he reminded us how important and exciting it is to find connections in the most unexpected places. Looking at me intently he said: "Let your imagination take you wherever it wants to go…fly away on thought-experiments.[141] Time and space are not independent; they form a time-space fabric."

Ibn Sina's words again reminded me of Einstein when he said: "Imagination is knowledge…"[142] Pierre Rabhi echoes this commitment to the law of attraction: "Can we look at a desert and see an oasis?"[143]

Maybe Joha was somehow connected to our physician apparition, who was escorting us from one historically Jewish Iranian city to the next.

Isfahan[144] is the ancient city once known as *Dar-Al-Yahud*[145] ("House of the Jews," in Farsi), and fabled for its lush, turquoise carpets and intricate tiles that adorn the synagogues. Heading across the city, we saw Jewish women gathering in the direction of the *souk*, their heads covered with flowered scarves.

We entered a teashop to drink yellow date tea from a *samovar*. After performing the *taarof* rituals before eating together, we spread the *sofreh* (tablecloth). Breakfast was long overdue! Ibn Sina offered us chunks of cucumber and watermelon, flower-essence drinks, and chickpea sweets. "Please indulge yourselves! *Todo ke tyenene amber, venga y komen.*" (Let anyone who is hungry, come and eat with us).

We devoured *shamee* (sesame oil and turmeric, grated potatoes, ground beef, eggs), mung and fava beans, cow intestine and stomach stuffed with rice, split yellow peas, and cilantro. We topped it all off with such yummy pastries: *koloocheh, zulbia* dipped in honey saffron syrup, and pistachio *masghati*. Ibn Sina gobbled as much as we did—I had no idea that dead people liked to eat so much!

Ésta komida es parachupar los dethos! (This meal is finger-licking good!)

As we were leaving *Dar-Al-Yahud*,[146] ibn Sina invited us to visit the Hapt Tappeh catacombs, near the Tomb of the prophet Daniel,[147] in the ancient city of Susa. He told us that this is where we would continue our healing. Cocomiso stayed close by my side as we entered The Rotting Room. The cavernous space reminded me of what Mommia had described on her visits to the coalmines of Appalachia. It was pitch black! Much darker than a moonless night sky! Ibn Sina's torch lit our path. We passed stacks of skeletons, and saw petroglyphs with cuneiform inscriptions in Akkadian of the Elamite kings. I traced my fingers across the surfaces of interlacing blue, red, orange, yellow, gray, black, and white geometric patterns—mosaics made of bone, bronze, and lazulite.

Out of the corner of my eye, I noticed a hooded figure hovering near the arched openings of one of the catacomb's tunnels. As we moved in her direction, she leaned forward and whispered mysteriously into my ear "Zazu! Remember the *Ummah*…"[148] Instantly, I imagined the catacombs in Toledo, Spain. And as I looked into her deep dark eyes, I could see images of Toledo's underground cemetery[149] of the Jews, where rich and poor were buried together. The tunnel walls, ceilings, and corners of the Toledo catacombs were etched and drawn with the unmistakable symbols of the menorah, date palms (the Jewish symbol of resurrection), peacocks (symbol of creation), flying horses, and oddly, cupids. The hooded figure closed her eyes, and the images of the Spanish catacombs disappeared! We emerged from the cave, blinking in the bright light.

"*Shalomalekhem!* Peace be with you, ibn Sina!"

"*Salaam Alaikum!* and *Mashallah!*" (May God preserve you from the evil eye!)

Then he too disappeared.

When we looked around to see where we were, Cocomiso and could still see the grazing gazelles.

Holy cow! We were traveling through a qanat (or was it the Paris arcades?), a kind of quantum entanglement—pairs of quarks strung together by tunneling wormholes!

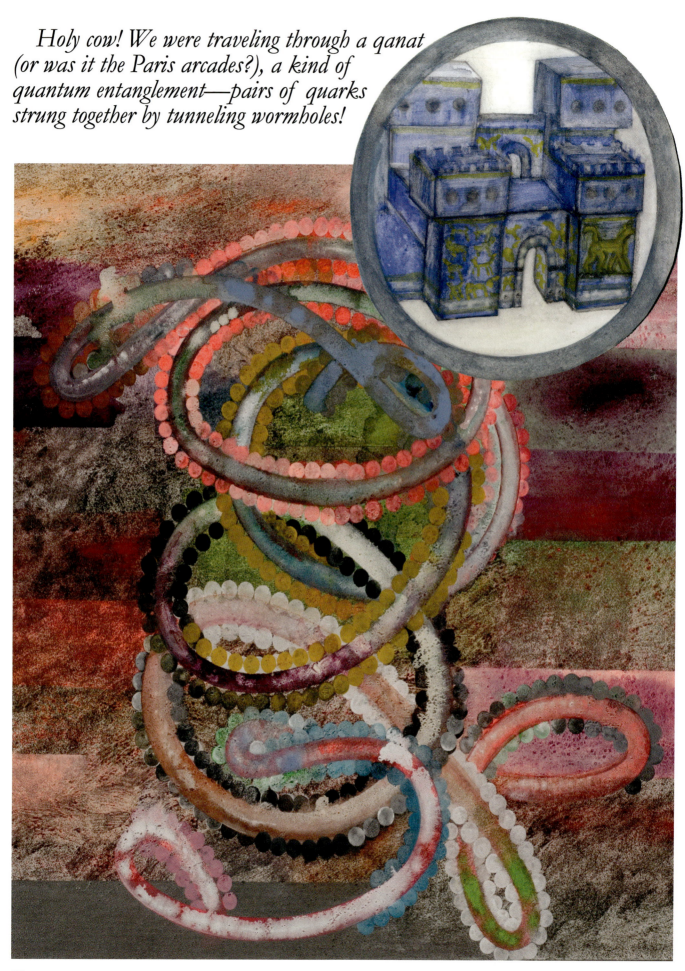

Chapter Five
"It takes a village…"

I realized we had been traveling through a system of *qanat*,[150] deep underground tunnels throughout the Middle East.[151] These had been dug into the earth to bring water from the mountains to the desert—strange and bewitching patterns that reminded me of constellations and mosaics. But, water is so scarce everywhere that these ancient subterranean aqueducts had been transformed into graves. We were finding out that so many waterways that once supported all kinds of life had almost completely dried up.

Outside the Rotting Room at the border of the ancient *qanat*, Cocomiso got a little edgy. She was behaving strangely. She began to dig and dig and dig. I thought she was looking for human bones from the catacombs, but she actually dug up what looked like a fossil —a mosaic of some kind of animal-reptile that looked like a dog, or a big cat! We weren't sure if it was a real fossil or had been hidden there by Joha the Trickster. Suddenly, it opened its fiery mouth, speaking directly to Cocomiso:

"I am not you. I am a mushhushshu[152]
I am a dragon—have you heard?: part serpent, part bird[153]
I live as-both; in-both earth and air, water and land, in Iraq and Iran
I cannot be seen for I breathe the in-between.
But you, dog and boy, know that I am here once you leave our atmosphere
I will speak with candor: my home was split, and now, you must find the amber…"

What in the world was this scaly creature saying? Were the *mushhushshu*'s words connected to Ladino 'rhyming songs?'[154] Cocomiso was listening intently. She looked a little perplexed as she unraveled the *mushhushshu*'s words. It continued:

"Those who are deaf to history say it is a sham,
even though Iraq was the birthplace of your Patriarch Abraham
Since you found me, I can finally return to my home in Iraq
I will carry you through as we explore each and every cranny and crack
we will travel across Ancient Mesopotamia,
the land that lies between the two great rivers that now lack[155]
Across the Tigris-Euphrates Valley river system we go
Since you found me in the spaces between the sand grains,[156] I know…"

We soon arrived at Babylon's Ishtar Gate, adorned with dragons and canine-like creatures.[157] When I asked the *mushhushshu* how the Mesopotamian King Nebuchadnezzar could build a tribute to Ishtar the Goddess of Love *and* destroy Jerusalem,[158] it snarfled:

> "Ishtar is not only the Goddess of Love,
> Ishtar is the Goddess of War
> Festooned between the Tigris and the
> Euphrates were the many hearts she tore…
> I do not care that I have no dragon's liar, but
> this is my home so I no longer have to roam
> Once inside the gate
> It is my fate to return
> to my original fragmented state
> But before I shift, remember
> we can only heal the rift…"

The *mushhushshu* interrupted itself and sputtered:

"a colony of beavers…a colony of aspens…a murder of crows…a flutter of butterflies…a zeal of zebras…a parliament of owls…a covey of quail…a string of ponies…a knot of frogs…a mob of kangaroos…a troop of macaques…a bloat of hippopotami…a caravan of camels…a comfort of cats…an opera of canaries…an exaltation of larks….a quivering of cobras…a bouquet of hummingbirds…a leap of leopards…a mischief of mice…a yoke of oxen… a sounder of warthogs…a raft of otter…a galaxy of starfish…a murmuration of starlings…a raffle of turkeys…a mess of iguanas…a charm of hummingbirds…a watch of nightingales…a herd of gazelle…a bale of turtles…a bed of urchins…a pod of whales…a crash of rhinoceroses…a walk of snails…a nest of vipers…a whoop of baboons…an embarrassment of pandas…an aurora of polar bears…a shiver of sharks…an ostentation of peacocks…a wake of vultures…a stand of flamingos…a stand of trees…a gaggle of geese…a hum of bees…a streak of tigers…a smack of jellyfish…a brood of beetles…a team of ducks…a school of fish[159]…
a village of…"

With that, the *mushhushshu* re-disassembled— becoming a mosaic once again.

A village of…? OF? Of what? A village of people? I remember after Barack Obama was elected President, I heard that idea a lot: "It takes a village!"[160]

Why the list of collective animals?[161]
Was our babbling dragon friend reminding
us of *Convivencia*? Of communal symbiosis?
Of reconnecting through the Commons?

Cocomiso began to howl. It hit me of course that she was a pack animal and maybe longed to return to her friends running through the snow. She found relief from the desert heat and the fire-breath of the *mushhushshu* by rubbing against a shady palm tree.

We pulled ourselves together and found the town of Hillah, not far from the ancient site of Babylon and the Gate of Ishtar. My *khaleh* (maternal aunt), *Tiya* Zubayda[162] *Khanoum* (affectionate term that follows someone's name) cried when we entered her jewelry stall: "Oh, such a *simka*!" (happy event!)

After we got settled around the *tanoor* (clay oven) and drank from incantation bowls decorated with spirals,[163] I asked her about the many things we had learned on our journey with the talkative dragon. She explained how Iraqi Jews were the first Diasporic community outside of Judea—called the 'Babylonian Diaspora' back in 5th century BCE. Our ancestors settled in Iraq over 2,700 years ago, 600 years before Christianity, and 1,200 years before Islam.[164] Yet now, Baghdad's Jewish quarter in *Taht al-Takia* no longer exists; most traces of Jews living in Iraq have disappeared.[165] Our histories across the entire Middle East are rapidly being erased. *Leshos de aki ma serka de korason* (Far from here, close at heart).[166] I felt a huge sadness as I listened to *mi tiya*.

"The Tigris and Euphrates rivers were very different then. We called them Prat and Hidekel—their *Lashon Akodesh* (Hebrew) names. They had not yet been stripped and stolen and poisoned.[167] Truly a land of milk, honey, and opportunities for all, the river-life nourished us in its abundance. Like the Jews, the Ma'dan, also called the Marsh Arabs, have suffered greatly from the ruin of the rivers."

"Yes! When we were traveling with the *mushhushshu*, we passed a father and son poling a *mashoof* (dugout canoe). They told us how Sadam Hussein[168] had diverted and polluted their waters."

"Not just during the reign of Hussein,[169] but throughout history, both the Jews and the Ma'dan have had to be extraordinarily adaptable. *El yerro del doktor, la tierra lo kovija* (The mistake of the doctor is covered by dirt). The Marsh Arabs live in floating homes made of reeds on these rivers—the reed is a symbol of adaptability. Our histories tell us: *segun el tiempo, se abolta la vela* (according to the weather shift your sail). That is often seen as being weak—but we know better. Adaptability makes us both vulnerable and strong. We Sephardim are like the *sasnikos,* the fish-chameleon who lives in the river, at the border of the sea, *neti-neti* (neither this nor that), *ni agua, ni vino, ni buza* (neither here nor there), *trokar kazal, trokar mazal* (a change in location, changes one's fortune or fate).

"We are like the brittlestar whose survival depends on its capacity to pay attention.[170] Like its cousin, the sea slug,[171] we have no *kelipe* (pretension, outer shell). *Mas vale saver, ke tener* (It is better to know than to have)."

I realized her eyes were darting back and forth between Cocomiso and me.

"*A dyo sánto!* (Oh my God!) You are *kortado por la mizma tijera*! (Two of a kind!) You know, Zazu, you and Cocomiso have exactly the same color eyes, the color of *anbar*."

Tiya Zubayda told us that anbar is the Arabic word for amber[172] and also the Arabic word for whale![173] She jumped up and unhooked the mezuzah hanging by the beaded entrance. On its underside shining like a tiny flashlight was a bright blue bug—a beetle[174] of some kind. It was a perfect shape and a perfect brilliant color.[175]

"*Mashala, allah kerim. Loores al dio!*" (an expression of extraordinary joy)

Tiya Zubayda was breathless; her eyes filled with tears: "This firefly beetle entombed in amber[176] is probably around 50 million years old. It reminds me of the lush turquoise color of the alter carpets in the Persian synagogues I visited before we moved to Baghdad as a child. *Mi vieja Tia* gave this mezuzah to me. It has been in our family for hundreds of years. It reminds us that with all the forms of suffering Jews have endured, each suffering has embraced it's healing, its hidden light that cannot be extinguished—this is part of what it means to live as Jews.

"Amber protected us when we were first in exile as captives under Nebuchadnezzar, just as it protected us from radiation during the Iran-Iraq War in the 1980s. They say amber is hardened rays of sun. I burned powdered amber during your *primo* Zaman's childbirth because it helps in labor and prevents excessive bleeding. We have used it in our rituals to remember the ancient knowledge of our ancestors and to help reconnect with our many past lives. *Tfu, Tfu, Tfu!*[177] Amber brings balance back because it helps us remember our relationship with the earth."

I held her hand holding the mezuzah. "It looks like there is a star shining inside the beetle. Where is the light coming from?"

"Adaneyate! (Persevere with an eternal light like concentration camp survivors). That, *kerido* (dear) Zazu, is bioluminescence![178] Fireflies make carbon magic that looks like stars in the Milky Way. When they take a big breath their light turns on. Breathing creates light. The light fireflies breathe uses electricity more efficiently than any form humans have yet learned to create.[179] But beware! We cannot assume that what we see is what there is: the female firefly's light is used both for creation *and destruction*—attracting her mate and then devouring him. Those who live in exile understand this predatory deception too well. Our hosts too often trick us when we are attracted to their light.[180]

"Some people think Ladino is a fossilized language, like this beetle preserved in an amber deposit, forever unchanging, but it is not. Ladino is alive; it is like this *shofar*.[181] Our relationship to this ram's horn is our breath. The interaction between human and divine—our coexistence—brings us beauty and joy. Like the bending and adaptability of a reed, the spiraling bend in a *shofar* reminds us that everything is always changing, offering multiple perspectives. The *shofar* links us to the divine; it reminds us of our commitment to humility that allows us to look at relationships among many things."

"Yes, yes! We can adapt and continually transform ourselves, but what if we constantly get caught and stuck and caught and stuck, like the story of G-d showing

By 2030, one billion people are expected to get electricity for the first time.

Abraham a ram whose horns get stuck while trying to tear himself free from one thicket, and then becoming entangled in another and another?[182] This is actually happening right now to rams where I grew up! The desert bighorn sheep are endangered in California, and solar energy plants are making their situation worse. Because of poor location choices, solar power is being developed in ways that actually harm the animals and their environment. There is not a clear division between clean energy and dirty energy/dirty power—clean isn't always clean."[183]

Si, Zazu! De la bará to emprovisó mi padre (Bargains aren't always bargains). Our Sephardic ancestors understood these kinds of contradictions! Even if we find great alternatives to fossil fuels, Jurassic poop, what if renewable energies become big business and just maintain our addiction to consumption and convenience-culture? Replacing tar sands or oil-drills or coal power plants with megalithic 'green' energy is not the solution—it just masks the original problem—confusing 'freedom' with free-market and free-enterprise.[184] Industrial-sized[185] solar energy development is stripping the land bare—ravaging the already extremely vulnerable wildlife."[186]

"You are so right, *Tiya*. We have this crazy idea that anything 'green' is good—but we know that there is no clear-cut good and evil. How we compensate for the damage we have created can sometimes be more harmful than the initial wound.[187] What happens when the very solution causes more problems than the original problem it was supposed to fix?"[188]

This was a riddle for Joha to unravel.

"You can't really judge a mosaic if you don't look at it from a distance. If you really get close to it you get lost in detail. You get away from one detail only to get caught in another. Perhaps, Zazu, what you have been seeing until now was not the sand, but grains of sand.[189] *Ke bívas komo la agua!*" (May you live as abundantly as running water!)

Tiya Zubayda took my hands in hers: "*Dame te bezarè tu mano*" (Now you're talking! /Amen! / Let me kiss your hand).

Chapter Six
Mashallah!

We continued our adventure through the Persian Gulf, the Strait of Hormus, through the Arabian Sea, up the Red Sea, through the Suez Canal, back to the Mediterranean, and then north to the Aegean Sea. As we swam past Egypt, Israel, and Palestine, we heard the rapturous voice of Uum Kalthoum,[190] The Star of the East, blasting from loudspeakers all over the city of Cairo—Uum is beloved equally by Jews[191] and Arabs across the Middle East.

Ari, the perfection of her voice even roused the philosopher, astronomer, scientist, physician, Maimonides,[192] from his temporary grave[193] in Fustat,[194] who is known as the *haNesher haGadol*, the great eagle. As this majestic raptor flew low over the sea just above our heads, he called out, *"Ke haber, mi ijo!"* (Hello, my son!)

I was so excited to meet him!

"Zazu, are you going to Hilloula, to *ziara?"* (pilgrimage to a cemetery to commemorate the dear departed).

"Ya skapi! (Yes!)"

"Bravo! Your *hut spa* (audacity) and *hohma* (wisdom) will guide you and your companions. My brilliant friend and *apikorós* (heretic), Baruch Spinoza, will meet you there. He has a secret to tell you, Zazu."

"Ora bwèna!" (when one is surprised, one exclaims *Ora bwèna!*) A secret from Spinoza? I can't wait!

"Zazu, *en mi viejes* (in my old age), —I have been dead for hundresds of years, I have longed for a renewed *Convivencia* (conviviality—referring to the Golden Age of Spain during which Jewish and Muslim literature, science, and arts flourished). How can we move the world to make a new *tikkun olam*? I think we need to show our people how our differences can make us stronger and work together like the limbs and organs of the human body.[195] Remember that humans are made from the same five elements of the earth. Search within yourself—that's what the Kabbalistic Tree of Life teaches us."[196]

This was the first time I began to deeply get a sense of how my body is connected to all bodies—how the macrocosm is rooted in the microcosm of the human body. I felt a shiver of excitement thinking about this crazy beauty.

I would soon be seeing how another tree of life was being torn from humans…

As voices on land grew louder and more frantic, Maimonides evaporated into the salty sea air. A jumble of voices came tumbling across 50 miles of dry land, past the shore, where we held onto our humpback floating in the Aegean Sea, off the western coast of Turkey: "*Hadi, buldozerler geliyor! Hadi, buldozerler geliyor!*" (The bulldozers are coming! The bulldozers are coming!) We had heard from Joha's donkey that a coal company was planning to destroy more homes and olive-growing land. Power! More coal-fired power plants![197] As we neared the tiny town of Yirca we saw fields ringed by barbed wire that kept the Yirca villagers off their own land. The olive tree, both a symbol of peace and of cultural livelihood was being destroyed. We heard stories that in the middle of the night the coal company had ripped 6,000 olive trees out of the ground. Everything—the entire village, every garden, all the olive groves[198] were covered in coal-ash.

Our new friends, Akin and Hamide, told us stories of their neighbors diagnosed with cancer. This husband and wife team had been part of a protest where two-dozen Yirca villages tried to block bulldozers.[199] As she began to tell us about the Physicians for Social Responsibility, Hamide started coughing, and Akin had to take her away to rest.

"Remember that Cocomiso! The Physicians for Social Responsibility! We have to work with them when we return home." Cocomiso was panting heavily—too hot under her thick husky fur. Between the ash coating the air and the treeless expanse, it was hot![200] I couldn't help thinking of what is happening right now in California with the drought and the crazy, crazy fires burning whole towns to the ground! How could anyone doubt our climate was going through dangerous changes?![201]

We later learned that Akin and Hamide's cousins from Istanbul had been killed in an avalanche of trash. Wow! Climate change and coal power plants were just the tip of the iceberg—an iceberg that was quickly melting! Corrupt politicians and convenience-obsessed Western consumers seemed to be at the root of this recent Turkish disaster.

We continued our journey inland toward Izmir, also called Smyrna in ancient times. We could see how Turkey is the border between Europe and the Middle East, where EAST meets WEST! Izmir was the home of the ancient Greek storyteller, Homer[202]—such an old city, at least 8,000 years old! Like Cochin, Izmir is along the sea. There are sweet-scented fruit trees and flowering bushes everywhere. Cocomiso was so *ojo árto* (someone who is content) to see all the donkeys carrying farmers with their huge baskets of ripe eggplants, dates, and pomegranates. So much activity, Ari…like a swarm of bees.

Great-Grandmommy Rachel greeted us at her front door with hugs and kisses, thirteen times[203] on both cheeks, and then kissed a triangle amulet made of chickpea.

"*Hanoum*, Zazu, *mi alma, mi vida, mi pecaño tavşan, buyurùn* (Hello! Darling Zazu, my soul, my life, my little rabbit, please come in!)"

"*Chok teshekur ederim* (Thank you very much!) *Bendichos manos!* (A guest's remark to a hostess: bless your hands) *Hosh bulduk!* (I'm glad to be here!)"

As we listened to the melodic sounds of Ladino, she told us about growing up in Turkey and how most of her family had since moved to Africa and North America. We talked about the sweetness of life in Turkey, and its unique history as the crossroads of Europe, Africa, and the Middle East. We sat under the shade of a mimosa tree, drinking fresh lemonade with mint and rose water and eating my favorite food: Anchovies! *Hamsi* is a Turkish speciality: fried anchovies dredged in *findik* (hazelnut) flour. We also gobbled the most delectable *keftikas* (lamb), *sahlep* (ground orchid root), and *bamia* (okra in lemon and tomato). Nearby we could hear the Muslim call-to-prayer. Before going to sleep, mesmerized by the voice of the muezzin, we devoured more *zeytinyaghalr* (cold vegetable dishes), *sutlatch* (rice pudding sweet with raisins and saffron), and drank pomegranate wine. I asked Great-Grandmommy Rachel if she knew where the olives had been grown. She told us that even though Turkey was the world's second largest producer of olives, she couldn't get local olives because the coal-power plants had taken over; these olives had been imported from Tunisia.

Back at home, I had asked Mommia many questions about Turkey. When I shared these questions with Great Grandmommy Rachel, she had lots to tell me. She looked deeply into my eyes with eagerness to know who I was now, so grown up. She showed me photographs of my Granddaddy when he was a baby wearing a turquoise beaded amulet and *hamsa* pinned to his diaper. Great Grandmommy was delighted to share tales about how she and her friends frequently visit a nearby *taverna* to watch belly dancers, always dancing along with them. She told us about Turkish and Arab women, both Muslims and Jews here in Turkey and across North Africa and the Levant, who ululate with their tongues and their uvulas when they are really happy or really sad.[204]

We were delighted as she began to ululate for us! We laughed and laughed at how her voice made such a strange, loud sound: *Kililili! Ullillee! Kililili! Ullillee!* I liked that sound. It was really so loud and high pitched that it sounded like a flock of shrieking tropical birds. It even sounded like the alarm of fire engines! Along the shore the humpback whale responded with her own deep whale sounds. Usually only male humpback whales sing their magical songs, but our humpback whale was so inspired by Great Grandmommy's ululations that she had to join in too! And then Cocomiso began to howl! Total chaos!

"Zazu, you must continue across the Aegean Sea to the island of Rhodes[205] where your Great Papoo Aron the Alchemist was born. But first, stop in Salonika, where Jews, Muslims, and Christians all spoke Ladino. Remember that the Nazis killed our entire family who had lived there. Also remember that our memories and love of justice keep the Jews alive; let your mourning be filled with song: *Kililili! Ullillee! Kililili! Ullillee!*"[206]

She gave me seven of her gold bracelets to give to Mommia for our return home, and sent us on our way with my backpack full of *yaprak* (stuffed grape leaves), *ajada* (cucumber relish), *soup à la reine/ avgolemono soup* (egg lemon soup), *mousaka melitzanes* (eggplant salad), *kuchundooria* (beet relish), *toombala* (artichoke hearts) and *fideos* (golden brown thin pasta) with peas. She didn't forget the *membrillo* (quince) or *kitra glykisma zacharomeno* (candied grapefruit rind)—my favorite snack besides anchovies!

"*Barbinhah!* (G-d Forbid!) that you should have an empty stomach! Bite your tongue! Spit over both shoulders!"

We kissed both her hands. "Come back soon, Zazu *kuzùm* (my little lamb). *Dulsùra syèmpre* (Sweetness always!) *Qué no me mancas nunca!* I will miss you so much!"[207]

So we kissed Great Grandmommy Rachel *allah is marlardik* (goodbye) and promised to return to her soon. Off we swam on our singing humpback whale, with Cocomiso howling in unison all along the way. Both sadness and gratitude filled their voices.

When we arrived in Salonika, my *Tiya* Reina, Great Papoo Aron's eighth sister, led us through olive groves and wheat fields into the city—a faint shadow of what it had been as the 'Jewel of Sephardic culture.' Before the fires destroyed the city and before the remaining Jews were killed in the Holocaust, Salonika had been a flourishing intellectual community of scientists, poets, artists, and writers. *Tiya* Reina introduced us to Rabbis Perera and Abulafia who prepared medicinal *kameot* with healing herbs of garlic, cinnamon, cumin seeds, and salt to protect against the evil eye. At the Yochanan ben Zakkai Synagogue, we met *Romaniote*, Greek Jews whose families had lived in Salonika since 316 BC. They told us many tragic stories of Thessaloniki Jews.

As we swam away, Tiya Reina and the *Romaniote* called out to us: "*Si los aniyos kayeron, los dedos kedaron!*" (If we lost our rings, we still have our fingers / Don't give up!)

As we approached the black stone beaches of the Island of Rhodes, I remembered Mommia's tales of the ancient Colossus of Rhodes,[208] one of the seven wonders of the world!—a giant bronze statue that straddled the entrance to the port of Rhodes, protecting is citizens from invaders. As we passed the Colossus, I heard a voice, but saw only on a distant shore a young girl looking out to sea. Her faraway voice said to me, "Zazu, I am your friend, Emma Lazarus.[209] Like you, I fought for others to breathe-free." Her black hair turned into a bird, and flew away as her body slid into the sea. A shiver moved up my spine.

"Oh, Zazu, it's crazy that no one knows that Emma Lazarus, a young Sephardic woman, was the poet of The Statue of Liberty's huddled masses!"

"Yup! White culture has erased so much. And, let me tell you what happened next."

Dashing first across the hot black pebbles of Rhodes' beach, we entered the walled city and arrived at *La Calle Ancha*[210] on the way to the synagogue on Dossiadou Street. The Jewish Quarter of Rhodes is located inside giant stone walls of the eastern section of the Old City, *el viejo villa.*[211] We arrived at the Kahal Shalom Synagogue that was very much like our synagogue at home. It was also like those we had seen in Cochin and Izmir. There were many Turkish rugs laid over stone mosaic floors. The wooden bema stood in the middle of the room with the women's balcony above. Hundreds of brass lanterns hung from the ceiling, swaying gently with the breezes from open doors.

Rabbis de Sola Pool, Cardoza, and Turiel, three elderly *hahám* (Sephardic Rabbis) with beards down to their knees, walked toward us with arms open in welcome. "*Baruh aba!*" (Welcome!)

"Rabbis, will you tell us about life here in Rhodes?" They remembered my Great Papoo Aron the Alchemist and his nine brothers and sisters (*hermanos y hermanas*) from school at the Alliance Française Israelite Universelle. Their families had lived in Rhodes for over four hundred years, and some had arrived here over a thousand years ago! Together, we walked across the island where we saw ancient stone buildings, beautiful minarets[212] and Islamic mosques. We ran across the beaches of Kalitea and the ancient forum of Lindos. In a crowded bazaar we experienced thousands of different types of olives, spices, and strange fish that were unlike anything we had ever seen before. We touched brightly painted ceramics and delicately embroidered cloth. Mommia had told me about Great Aunt Esther who is 100 years old and still loves to talk about her childhood in Rhodes. She tells us about the sea lions that play off the shore early every morning, and the monarch butterflies[213] that live in the Petaloudes Valley (Valley of the Butterflies). Her eyes fill with tears of joy as she describes these bright orange and black-winged creatures. Monarch butterflies envelop hundreds of moist Oriental (Turkish) Sweetgum trees[214] that give off a scent that seduces the stomachless butterflies. They have co-existed in this symbiotic relationship for millions of years. The Rabbis were delighted to know Mommia had shared such wonderful memories with me.

We walked along the Boulevard Mandrake by the sea where families stroll arm in arm in the evening, listening to music and singing songs together in Ladino, Italian, French, Turkish, and Greek. We talked with the three Rabbis for long hours until the sun began to set. Under the stars, we visited my Great Papoo Aron's birth home where he learned from his mother how to use herbs, oils, and essences for health and healing. And we even climbed a ladder up to the roof to see where, as a boy, he had carved his name in stone: "Aron Amato – 1920."

We told the Rabbis that after migrating to the US, Great Papoo Aron had a Botanica in Spanish Harlem in New York, where people from all over the Caribbean and Latin America visited him to heal their bodies, hearts, and souls. Like many Sephardi men, Papoo wore a *fez*, a red felt taboosh with a black tassel. He spoke to his customers in Spanish and sometimes Swahili[215] and he prepared potent *kameot,* medicinal amulets, with herbs and oils to ward off the evil eye[216] and to invoke the help of protective angels. Like the great Sephardic and Muslim physicians before him, Grand Papoo concocted healing unguents and perfusions.

Somehow they knew this and responded: "Your Great Papoo Aron wanted to help heal what had been broken. He lived *tikkun olam*, and everyone who met him loved him because of his kindness and his generous heart. Zazu, you are a *viajéros valyente* (brave traveler). Remember, *lo ora mas eskura es para esklareser* (when things seem darkest, then comes the light). *Dios que te guadre…. Bivas, crescas y enflorescas como el pexe en el agua fresca*" (May G-d watch over you. …May you live, grow, flourish like a fish in fresh water). The long-bearded peripatetic philosophers blessed the *hamsa* that hung around my neck and my sprig of myrtle that I still held in my hand.

Off we went on our humpback whale, swimming back across the Mediterranean to Ouazzane, Morocco[217] for the Hilloula celebration.

Ari, I told you about Hilloula at the beginning of my odyssey. Now we have finally arrived.

Chapter Seven
Quantum Entanglements

The city of Ouazzane was so colorful against the rolling Rif Mountains! We entered *el viejo villa*, known as the *mellah*, or Jewish quarter, and saw walls of interlocking magical patterns—the Moorish tiles of infinity.[218] Like the Persian mosaics in Isfahan and the Ottoman tessellations in Istanbul,[219] we were surrounded by ceilings and floors of *zellige*[220] and intricate inlaid wood. Stucco houses were painted bright azure blue to ward off the evil eye. We learned these were very old customs of Jewish and Moorish communities all over North Africa and the Middle East.

We passed Maimonides' home on our way to the labyrinth of crammed alleyways where merchants sold Berber ironwork, local textiles, leather goods, filigreed gold and silver jewelry, gleaming copperware, sweet and spicy aromatic foods. Everywhere we heard people speaking Arabic, French, Berber languages including Judeo-Berber, and *haketia*.[221]

Cocomiso and I arrived just in time for the Hilloula festivities! We went to the home of my favorite *primos*, Tehilla and Naim. Tehilla wore a turquoise and red headscarf called a *hijab*, and Naim wore a long white robe called a *djellabah*. The scent of orange trees filled the air. They, like thousands of other Jews who live among indigenous North African Berbers, were preparing for Hilloula. Moroccan Jews from all over the world make pilgrimage each year during *Lag Ba' Omer*[222] into the desert of Ouazzane to visit cemeteries and celebrate the lives of their beloved rabbis who are called *tzaddim*,[223] including the exiled 18th century Rabbi Amran ben Diwan.[224]

Near the tombs of their *tzaddikim* known for miraculous powers after death, families live in big tents and share traditional food.[225] They camp out under the stars for a week of prayer, meditation, studying the sacred Zohar,[226] song and dance, and lighting bonfires for all the miracles of their rabbis. We prayed for healing, a sense of communal belonging, a reconciliation with the earth.[227] We expressed our deep, deep gratitude for the spirit of the universe. Muslims do this too!

Everyone was excited as bonfires burst with flames, celebrating the great Rabbi Rashbi.[228] Tehilla and Naim told us that Rashbi was persecuted by the Romans and forced to hide in a cave for thirteen years. During his exile, Rashbi wrote the mystical Zohar. The Zohar[229] is a spiritual text that channels the energy of Biblical mysteries, revealing the secrets of the Universe—every dimension of our world and our multiverse.[230] This book is written as a recording of spiritual energies, and it is the foundation for the Kabbalah.

Suddenly I made another connection: when Mommia read to me Arundhati Roy's *The Cost of Living*, she said: "All we can do is to change [history's] course by encouraging what we love instead of destroying what we don't."[231] As we visited Rabbi Rashbi's grave, I began to shiver. This is what we must do.

This wasn't only about being at a *keve* (burial plot) in the *midbar* (wilderness, desert) and chanting *besibur* (prayer said with a minyan) for a *nes* (miracle) or *niflaoth* (miracles). This was also about our deepest sense of being *agradesido* (grateful) while sharing a communal sense of *avtana* (hope) in order to take immediate action.

We prayed to our revered tzaddik for an end to profit-driven biocide; we prayed for an end to the monoculture of the mind;[232] we prayed for ecological intelligence to help us figure out how to encourage people to connect the dots between environmental justice and human rights, and act together to stop the suffering of people whose lands and water are poisoned and stolen; we prayed for a transition from a global extraction economy to a global regenerative economy; we prayed for zero-deforestation agriculture and product chains, ethically shared seeds,[233] proper poop-use,[234] an end to the epidemic of bee colony collapse, and for a miracle to release the turtles, whales, dolphins, dugongs, and manatees that had been caught and were dying in huge illegal drift gillnets[235] along their migration routes, connecting the Mediterranean Sea to the Atlantic Ocean.

From the cemetery at Hilloula we could hear many whales' songs of mourning. They were caught in the gillnets and feared for their lives! We needed a miracle to help activists convince tralling companies to release thousands of sea creatures that are trapped and killed.[236]

We silently spoke to Rashbi asking him to help us stop massive underwater sound cannons that cause sea creatures to go deaf.[237] We prayed that the SeaVax would do the work it needs to do. These solar-powered ships could potentially clean up the entire Pacific Garbage Patch in the next ten years.[238]

"Please help us solve the crises of the baby macaques, orangutans, monarch butterflies and their sweetgum trees, the whales and other sea mammals!"

I realized that a search for home was at the root of all these prayers. Home, I now understood, was a lived and shared opening to global interconnectedness. What if at the same time we could stop some of the really bad things corporations are doing, we could also figure out ways to fix, or at least lessen, some of the problems they have created. We can stop these crimes against nature if we can understand the connections between *bal tashchit* and *tikkun olam*—between caring for people and caring for the environment, for what Mommia calls our social ecology.[239]

Praying bodies swayed with the rhythm of flickering flames. At first they were absorbed in a *niggun*, a traditional chanting that expresses what is impossible to say in words. They began to spontaneously murmur: "*Ab...ra...ca...da...bra! Ab...ra...ca...da...bra!*" Little by little I understood their chant: *Abracadabra!*

They were praying for Jews to acknowledge one another's differences! They were praying for Jews to remember who we all are as a diverse people—like the Ethiopian Falashas[240] and Crypto-Jews[241] whose Judaism is so often ignored!

Grand Papoo Aron practiced *Abracadabra!*²⁴² I remember how he paid attention to the logic of nature, using herbs and oils to heal the hearts and bodies of the sick. He had been performing *Abracadabra!*

Tehilla, Naim, Cocomiso and I stood at the edge of a million miles of sand dunes, endless sand shimmering with grains of so many different colors: red, gold, silver, purple, and brown. We could hear the far-away echo of the Western Sahara²⁴³ sand slipping; a terrifying and mysterious drumming, almost a hollow screeching sound. This chorus of the dunes²⁴⁴ was so much like the whales' songs! Magic crossed borders, reminding us how definitions of what we think we know are always shifting.²⁴⁵

A Berber woman who called herself Ziba was draped in a black chador and offered me a basket of mesh-mesh (ripe apricots), sour cherries, bananas, raw eggs, almonds, and olives that we devoured—all food that has magical powers. She whispered an incantation into Cocomiso's furry ear.

It was a *lechishah*, a deep murmuring sound. Cocomiso began to wag her tail furiously, let out three long howls, and then sat down on my feet, almost pushing me over as she leaned against my legs. She then nudged me over to a big pile of camel poop not far from where we stood. Picking up a dead dung beetle,²⁴⁶ I heard Joha the trickster laughing—or maybe it was the sound of shifting sand. The shape of the dung beetle's little horns looked so much like gazelle horns.²⁴⁷ Was Joha in cahootz with Al-Ghazal, the 11ᵗʰ century trickster known as 'the Gazelle?' I showed it to Cocomiso, and right then, right there in my hand, the dead dung beetle transformed into a living iridescent turquoise scarab!²⁴⁸

"All flesh is grass." "Decay bacteria work for us and against us—providing fertile soil, but also potentially spoiling food." "Sand gives birth to water." "Dirt is the skin of the earth; dirt is a process that turns garbage into life." "Deadly waste and abundant life-giver." "There is no such thing as waste until it is wasted." "2/3 of our household waste can be composted." "Organic refuse is stored solar energy." "The microcosmos mirrors the macrocosmos." "As above, so below: root diversity echoes green diversity." "La'am" "Khepri" "The same stream that flows through your veins flows through the universe in rhythmic measure." "Poop helps hold the cycle of life together." "Bal tashchit, do not destroy or waste."

"Water, water everywhere, but not a drop to drink."

"Acidification of ocean = Desertification of land."

Chapter Eight
Between the Scarab and the Dung Beetle

I remembered Captain Moses Cohen Henriques Eanes' bo'sun,[249] the one-eyed, two-legged pirate, gently warning us: "What's essential is invisible to the eyes."[250] I suddenly understood what he meant! I remembered something Mommia read to me from Chimamanda Ngozi Adichie when I was little: "When you love somebody, really love somebody, you start to see the world through their eyes."[251]

Questioning what we think we know is an act of love; love means being open to the unknown. We think sand is one of the driest substances, yet under particular conditions it actually can produce and hold moisture.[252] We think that snow is one of the coldest substances yet under certain conditions, it actually can insulate our bodies.[253] Sand reminds us of what we don't know.[254] Sand reminds us of what we can't see.[255] Did Spinoza once say something about how our eyes don't see, but the eyes of our mind *do* see?[256]

As the scarab tried to crawl up my arm, Cocomiso got so excited she jumped up and knocked it onto the sand. Instantly, the scarab turned into a small pile of salt. Salt! Ibn Sina's voice floated past the 'singing wells,'[257] across the shifting dunes: "Magic is our everyday worlds looking back at us." GrandPapoo used to tell Mommia: "Magic is a respected art, a balance of contradictions."[258] *Yetser hara*, the bad and good combined, *la'am,* the yes simultaneous with the no! Maybe this was part of our co-evolution with water…and maybe our co-evolution with waste—or what we think is waste. There is no such thing as waste until it is wasted.[259]

I could hear Joha's voice chuckling across the desiccating winds; he was challenging me to a *game of salt*:[260] "The past is this: Jewish ghettos throughout the Middle East share a name that refers to salt. In Fez, Morocco, the Jewish quarter had been built on a salt marsh, a *mellah*.[261] The future is this: 'Water, water everywhere…but not a drop to drink.'[262] People fear oceans and rivers that were once our allies,[263] and now as water becomes more dangerous to drink and bathe in and sea levels continue to rise, it seems as though oceans and rivers have become our enemies. But we know it is not the water that is hurting us, we know it is the corporate stockholders, lobbyists, the think-tanks, the 'experts,' and transnational giants whose deceptions feed economic and ecosystem collapse.[264] We know it is peoples' fear of change and their consumer-addiction to convenience-culture that continue to heat our planet.[265] Because of global warming,[266] desertification is engulfing the planet. Oh! The earth dry as dust![267] At the same time, ocean levels are rising, and that means we will have lots and lots of salt."

He continued, "The Latin words for 'salt' and 'wisdom' are the same. Salt itself is an amazing symbol of what we can do when we work together; salt is a symbol of conviviality, of working together for the best kinds of transformation. The combined elements of salt form a truly wondrous team, but on their own, they can be lethal!"[268]

It was this Möbius-strip like idea of *both/and* that Joha wanted me to play with. I felt inspired by his trickster-approach to problem-solving. If salt deters evil (used in amulets), is so good for our health, can be made into low-cost beautiful buildings[269] that actually absorb city smog, and is a local resource[270] found in abundance,[271] then could we learn from the Saharan oasis of Taghaza made entirely of rock salt?[272] Could we find a way to ethically desalinate some of the ocean[273] to build eco-cities of salt in its natural colors of red, pink, orange?[274] What if Joha's salt challenge was somehow connected to poop—to changing our relationship to poop? Could we learn from the dung beetles? What if we could take a social permaculture approach that promotes zero-waste in which all by-products are re-integrated into use-systems? This game of salt, a game organized by the symbiotic possibilities of poop-use, would be examples of *bal tashchit* in action—the result of *tikkun olam* as a living-collaborative process.[275]

Ari, I looked around and saw that dovening bodies were in ecstatic meditation—the crowd had begun to levitate! The low murmur of chanting accumulated in an uncanny frequency that began to lift all of us higher and higher off the ground! We were forming a collective vibration, a *Shema* that could be heard drifting over the Mediterranean waters toward Iberia.

As we hovered among the devotees, I threw my sprig of myrtle into the fire. Through the smoke, I could see a mysterious man, an apparition. I knew that I knew him, but I also knew that we had never met before. As the smoke cleared, this figure, this hallucination, became two separate beings—and then re-formed as one[276]–just as *Hashem* had done with Adam and Eve.[277] The figure appeared to be both Spinoza[278] and Rashbi, or was it our Sephardic mystic Moshe de Leon?[279]

New Gourna Village, Egypt, Hassan Fathy

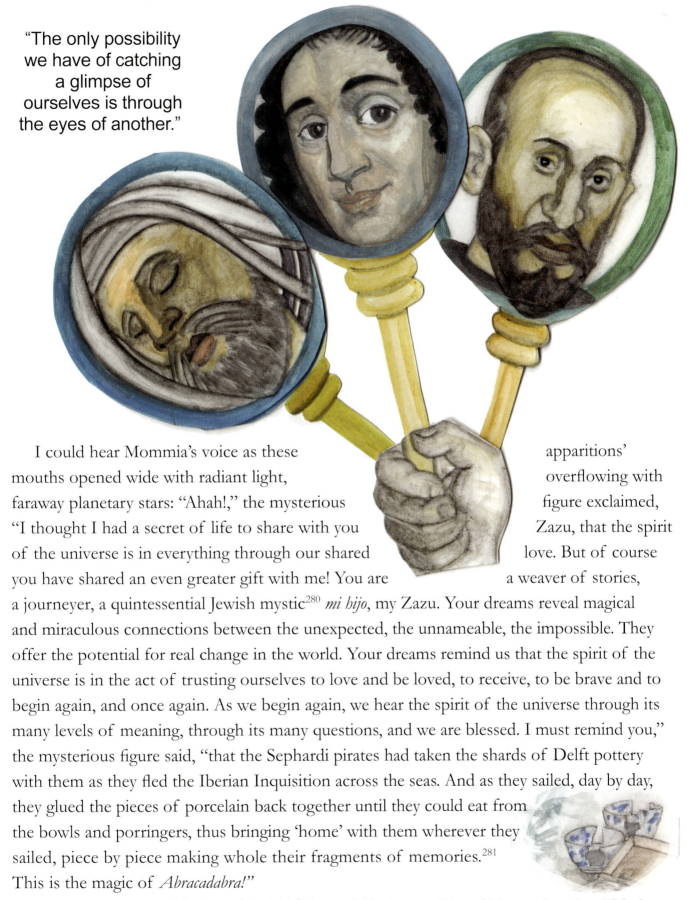

"The only possibility we have of catching a glimpse of ourselves is through the eyes of another."

I could hear Mommia's voice as these apparitions' mouths opened wide with radiant light, overflowing with faraway planetary stars: "Ahah!," the mysterious figure exclaimed, "I thought I had a secret of life to share with you Zazu, that the spirit of the universe is in everything through our shared love. But of course you have shared an even greater gift with me! You are a weaver of stories, a journeyer, a quintessential Jewish mystic[280] *mi hijo*, my Zazu. Your dreams reveal magical and miraculous connections between the unexpected, the unnameable, the impossible. They offer the potential for real change in the world. Your dreams remind us that the spirit of the universe is in the act of trusting ourselves to love and be loved, to receive, to be brave and to begin again, and once again. As we begin again, we hear the spirit of the universe through its many levels of meaning, through its many questions, and we are blessed. I must remind you," the mysterious figure said, "that the Sephardi pirates had taken the shards of Delft pottery with them as they fled the Iberian Inquisition across the seas. And as they sailed, day by day, they glued the pieces of porcelain back together until they could eat from the bowls and porringers, thus bringing 'home' with them wherever they sailed, piece by piece making whole their fragments of memories.[281] This is the magic of *Abracadabra!*"

As the apparition of Spinoza/Rashbi/Moses drifted away, I heard his gentle voice, "*Muchas gracias*, Zazu. *Hasta luego*. We will meet again in your dreams. *Al vermos* (Until we see each other)."

"Wait! Señor Spinoza/Rasbhi/Moses de Leon! There are people I want you to meet!"

As light began to drift into darkness, a second figure appeared. Like the Shekinah of the Zohar, composed of both male and female,[282] one side of this new apparition materialized as a woman dressed in clothes from the 1940s and the other side as a man in a wheelchair. They were the pioneering environmentalist Rachel Carson and the contemporary physicist and cosmologist Stephen Hawking.[283]

Carson's gratitude for our earth inspired her revolutionary commitment to expose connections between how chemical industries poison both Planet Earth and the human body.[284] Hawking reminds us that everything we need to know already exists within us, just waiting to be realized. Hawking's ideas parallel Nader Khalili's[285] who said, "Everything we need to build is in us, and in the place."

"Señor Spirit, (Spinoza/Rashbi/Moses), I thought you all would have a lot to talk about!"

Like the living principles of Judaism, Carson, Hawking, Khallili, and Rabhi show us how individual people committed to *tikkun olam* and *bal tashchit* really can make a difference. They are *Ben Adam* (righteous persons).

"*Salaam! Shalom Alehem!*" (Peace be with you!) I called out to them.

My words echoed back to me as "*Abracadabra!*" The mysterious figure of Señor Spirit, contracted and expanded, gradually transforming into a woman's face I thought I recognized…Yes!

Habitat 67, Canada, Moshe Safdie

She was the same woman from the catacomb caves in Iran—the hooded figure who had whispered to me about remembering the *Ummah*. Cocomiso recognized her voice.

As before, she spoke in a language I had never heard, but somehow I still understood her words: "Remember the Talmudic idea: 'She who saves one life, saves the entire world.'" As she spoke, her face slowly transformed into someone I had seen pictures of in Mommia's books. She had told me about women who started underground escape networks for persecuted people—women like Noor Inayat Khan,[286] who survived WWII as long as she did because of her belief in the imagination and her extraordinary commitment to human rights, and like Harriet Tubman,[287] called Moses by her fellow slaves, who manifested in the Underground Railroad: "Every great dream begins with a dreamer!;" women like the two standing before me now! Doña Gracia Nasi and Sol Hachuel! Doña Gracia Nasi developed a secret escape network that saved thousands of her fellow conversos from the brutalities of the Inquisition.[288] Sol Hachuel, a Jewish female saint who was revered by Muslims and Jews, defied forced conversions in Morocco in the 19th century.

Her image continued to change! Transforming before my eyes into these freedom fighters, she, actually they, imperceptibly began to fragment into a collection of more multiple faces. What originally looked like shards of a broken vessel became a magnificent, shifting kaleidoscope—what I recognized as the sculpture I had seen in Oakland, California, The Champions of Humanity—twenty-five human rights' activists, environmental justice fighters, artists, and humanitarians committed to creating a just and peaceful world, is an amazing representation of *sedaka* (acts of righteousness, charity, justice). The Champions of Humanity is a massive bronze sculpture commemorating 9-11, built a few blocks away from our home where we were born in Oakland—do you remember, Ari? We visited that together when we were little kids.[289]

"Zazu, yes! So many people from the Occupy Movement organized there! Our moms marched together—they carried us for hours during those Occupy rallies."

Ha! Yes! I remember those 'Occupying the Future' signs we held.

Back at Hilloula, with full bellies and wild images dancing in our minds, we watched along the shore as the humpback whale breached her enormous body across the Mediterranean Sea. She spouted fountains of water through her two blowholes—twenty kilometers up into the air!!!

We all felt such tremendous peace and even joy as we chanted *Modeh Ani*, a song of devotion and gratitude to our ancestors[290] who have shared traditions with their children for over 5,000 years. Through our adventures we shared the magic of the everyday!

"Hilloula! Modeh Ani!"

All was quiet as we left the continent of Africa and headed back to the United States—to our home. Just as the sun was setting, an enormous wave swept over our heads. Shaken and soaked, but still holding onto the warts of our humpback whale, I touched my neck to feel for my *hamsa*—for good luck. It was gone! The sea had taken my *hamsa*. Cocomiso told me this was a good sign and not to worry. She reminded me about something we had learned when we first embarked on our journey: it is good luck to lose your evil eye protection in a body of water; its job is finished when it is gone.

I remembered that Mommia had lost her evil eye earring while swimming off the coast of Mojacar, Spain. Again, I knew she was with me on our odyssey. I could really feel: *la madre es madre, y lo demas es ayre* (there is nothing to compare with a mother's love).

Chapter Nine
Worms and Germs

Suddenly our whale 'spy hopped'[291] up, up, UP!!! Usually humpbacks use their enormous flipper hands for balancing and maneuvering through the water, but when our humpback started to climb higher and higher, we saw that she was actually using her huge boney hands as wings[292] to propel us vertically into the sky!

Our aerial views looked like mosaics that extended forever and ever. As we shot up higher, we saw hundreds of Moroccan carpets laid out across the old city of Marrakesh. Their intricate colors and patterns looked like Persian paintings. To the East, we passed ripening striped fields of grain across the floor of Lebanon's Bekaa Valley.[293] We caught a glimpse of the setting sun glimmering on the cupola of the Dome of the Rock in Jerusalem.[294] We could see Burj Khalifa, the tallest human-made structure in the world: the 163-story building in the emirate of Dubai. To the Far East, we saw Arbil, the capital of Iraqi Kurdistan—one of the oldest continuously inhabited cities on earth.[295] To the West, we saw vast waves of sand drifting across the Sahara—even so far up in the sky, we could hear the eerie booming, singsong sounds of the shifting dunes. When we reached 10,000 feet (3,000 meters), the North Jafurah desert near Kammam, Saudi Arabia[296] looked like Arches National Monument back in Utah.

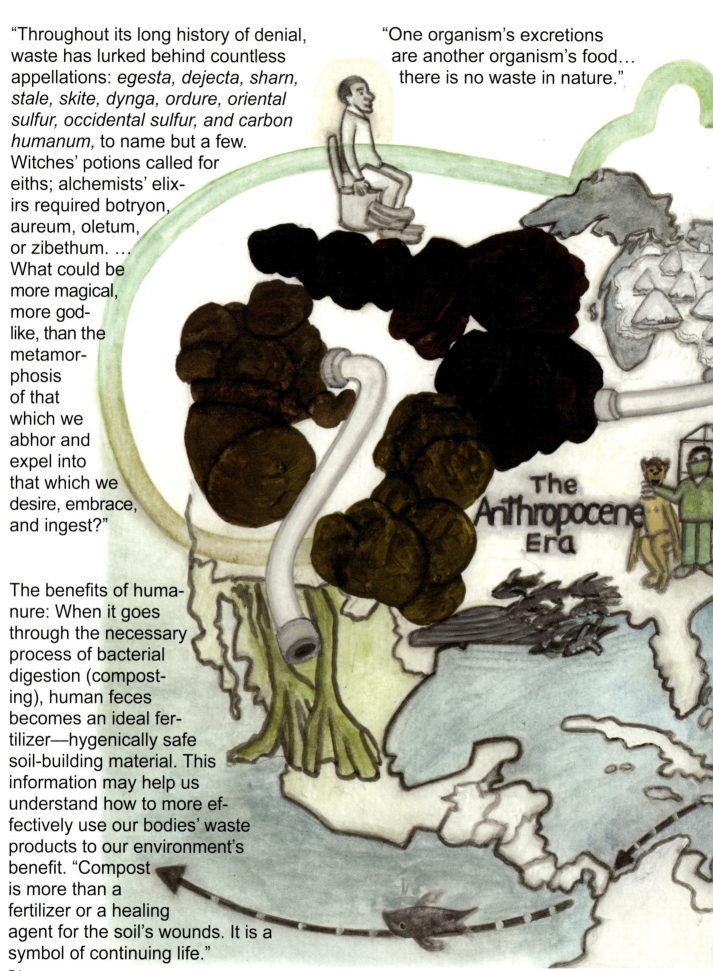

"Throughout its long history of denial, waste has lurked behind countless appellations: *egesta, dejecta, sharn, stale, skite, dynga, ordure, oriental sulfur, occidental sulfur,* and *carbon humanum,* to name but a few. Witches' potions called for eiths; alchemists' elixirs required botryon, aureum, oletum, or zibethum. … What could be more magical, more godlike, than the metamorphosis of that which we abhor and expel into that which we desire, embrace, and ingest?"

"One organism's excretions are another organism's food… there is no waste in nature."

The benefits of humanure: When it goes through the necessary process of bacterial digestion (composting), human feces becomes an ideal fertilizer—hygenically safe soil-building material. This information may help us understand how to more effectively use our bodies' waste products to our environment's benefit. "Compost is more than a fertilizer or a healing agent for the soil's wounds. It is a symbol of continuing life."

"At death, human bodies often contain enough toxins and heavy metals to be classified as hazardous waste. Similarly toxic are the bodies of whales and dolphins washed up on the banks of the...shores."

HORN FLIES
BACTERIA
DUNG BEETLES
VULTURES
FLEE
TOXIC CORPSES

The Portuguese man-of-war is not one creature, but a composite of four kinds of polyps (thousands of tiny animals that live together—an expression of conviviality). Each colony of polyps does a different job: floating, stinging, digesting, or reproducing. Perhaps it is a peculiar twist in our story that a cousin of the jellyfish, the very symbol of global warming effects arising from our free-market consumer, biophobic frenzy, actually demonstrates a model of collaborative behavior to which the authors aspire.

"Sea slugs are a prime example of waste conviviality: they eat lethal jellyfish and then store the stinging cells for the sea slugs' own defense."

Shooting like a rocket from the coast of the continent of Africa into the brilliant night sky, we passed a diving, whirling, swirling, spiraling congregation of fire beetles[297] on their way to the bonfires of Hilloula to mate and lay their eggs.

As we passed this throng of humming and drumming, the beetles flung a perfectly round ball of poop over to Cocomiso. The ball of poop had a map etched in it! Their cousins, the dung beetles, had carved directions on a sphere of dung! Dung beetles use the stars of the Milky Way[298] to navigate as they roll their balls of poop across the earth,[299] and they knew we would need help to find our way home through the cosmos.

Cocomiso stuck her muzzle in my backpack. She rooted around and pulled out the nutshell encasement the mama macaque had given us back at the Rock of Gibraltar. I understood that now was the time to pry it open. A rich, earthy, kind of unpleasant smell seeped out.[300] The three of us immediately knew what this was—poop. Unlike the poop map that had lost its poop-aroma because it had dried out, this poop appeared to be fresh.

The humpback explained, "YES! I heard rumors that the United States was soon going to be buried in poop—poop of all kinds: human, animal, insect. Some old whale friends told me they saw swarms of dung beetles fleeing the North American continent because they could no longer bare to eat the poop from the United States. The dung beetles cried that the poop was contaminated with GMOs, pesticides, vaccine-adjuvants, hospital hazardous waste, flame retardants,[301] endless chemicals and pollutants—the dung beetles, who have survived for 30 million years, knew better than to eat what had become an industrial toxic soup.[302]

"Not only is North Americans' poop chemically toxic, but when people living in the US die, their bodies are now toxic[303]—so they can't decompose, because nobody wants to eat them—no dung beetles, no vultures, no horn flies, not even the bacteria.[304]—they are fleeing too."

Then our mammal cetaceous friend began to cry:

"Now I understand—many of our beached whale and dolphin friends' dead bodies are also filled with chemicals.[305] If nothing eats our bodies, we will no longer be a part of the cycle of life; we will all be separate, forever isolated from one another. The shores and lands are getting covered in unwanted dead bodies and poop."

A strange whistle hushed the humpback from her creepy story; a sound seemed to rise from the stars themselves.

I realized now why we were given two poops: one was a symbolic map of wet, smelly poop that had come from long ago, but was warning us of the future if we did not change; the other was a literal map of dried, odorless poop to help guide us in the present. But, the third poop, one that was neither wet nor dry, was the poop we did not yet have. It was the poop for a hopeful future.[306]

We took one last look toward our blue Planet Earth. Below the swirling white clouds,[307] we could see the plumes of smoke rising from the deforested lands.[308] We could see what looked like a giant glacier. This frozen sea was actually miles and miles of salt![309] I remembered a story about a breastfeeding volcano-goddess who unlatched her suckling babe. When her sore nipple popped out of its mouth, a deluge of milk mixed with her tears and flowed across the Bolivian Altiplano landscape creating the Salar de Uyuni salt flats.[310]

As we left the earth's atmosphere and its familiar magnetic field, our humpback was no longer able to navigate.[311] We were grateful for the dried, odorless literal map since we knew our voyage home through clouds of gas and stardust[312] would be challenging. I flashed back on the *mushhushshu*'s strange rhyme: "I live as-both; in-both earth and air, water and land, in Iraq and Iran. I cannot be seen for I breathe the in-between. But you, dog and boy, know that I am here once you leave our atmosphere. I will speak with candor: my home was split, and now, you must find the amber…"

It was all beginning to make sense! I remembered Borges' *Book of Imaginary Beings*: "We are as ignorant of the meaning of the dragon as we are of the meaning of the universe." Was this imaginary being trying to tell us that we are not looking at the universe, we are the universe looking back at itself? Was it reminding us of the Talmudic story of a man, who searching for God, meets himself?

Cocomiso read our poop-map to the whale as we entered into the primordial light of the starry cosmos. We knew our pirate friends would have gotten such a kick out of using poop to navigate unfamiliar skies. I had a feeling Maimonides the Astronomer was up to something mischievous. Or maybe Maimonides' cohort ibn Sina,[313] who among his 400 books and treatises, wrote *On the Reprimants of a Feces-Eater,* had something to do with this—with all this poop. Or maybe Joha was at the root of it all—his voice among the stars like it was with the sand.

If the Greeks believed that the Milky Way[314] was created when Zeus tricked Hera into breastfeeding his mortal mistress's baby Hercules,[315] and the Navajo believed that in his impatience with the Holy People, the trickster Coyote threw the bag of stars over his head,[316] then Joha could help us figure out the connections between the Milky Way's spiraling arms,[317] sand, salt, water, and poop—and what to do with those connections. Again I felt the pull between remembering that everything I need to know is within me and everything I think I know is up for grabs—ready to become something else at any and every moment.
The star sound became even more audible. Little by little, eerie sizzling galactic noises enveloped us. The stars flickered and hissed. I told Cocomiso and our humpback what I had heard about Kepler's Planet Sounds.[318]

The whale listened attentively using her jawbone.[319] She told Cocomiso and me that both the curious hisses and flutters of the stars and the slipping sands reminded her of one of her whale cousin's songs[320]—a whale who had lived to be over a hundred years old.[321] The humpback began to translate the message the stars were singing to us, "In a nutshell: you are holding precious poop—that of a 50,000 year old Neanderthal.[322] Return to your Mommia's home in the mountains where the Dalai Lama smiles.[323] You will remember you are what you eat,[324] And climb a family tree[325]—the harder they come, the harder the fall. And remember," the stars insisted, "Jiddu Krishnamurti warned your species: 'It is no measure of health to be well adjusted to a profoundly sick society.'"

The heavenly constellations[326] were singing to us in fragmented puns! This *mazalot* of the planets, moons, and stars suddenly appeared to be the mosaics we had seen in synagogues everywhere in our travels. We were on our way home with more questions[327] than answers—puzzle pieces that I knew some how connected, but I wasn't sure how—I just knew we had to fit them together if anything was going to change. I wondered, were the constellations shattered light looking for home?[328]

"Exactly, Zazu. In search of kinship and connection, exiles of the diaspora gather holy sparks hidden in every bend of the globe to restore what has been broken, to repair the world. We learn that this light already exists within us and is all around us just waiting to be realized. This is our shared *tikkun olam*."[329]

And Ari, look what I woke up holding this morning.

He reached out and a hamsa with an inlaid evil eye dropped from his hand—it was the one that had been swept away by the waves in his dream.

"Wow, Zazu, it looks like its job was not done after all…"

This is a true story.

thought·speed·action
build interconnected worlds
Zohar is the radiance,
awareness and potential

"Everywhere is the center
of the universe
where it all began...
the big bang expanding...
Everything we need to
know is within us,
waiting to be realized."

A Möbius* Chronology of Selected Geologic and

- Dung Beetles co-evolving with land animals **30 million years ago**
- Dorudon **37 million years ago**
- Whales **40 million years ago**
- Coral Reefs **50 million years ago**
- Mesonychids **55 million years ago**
- Hippopotamus (whale ancestor) **100 million years ago**
- Sahara Desert covered in lush vegetation
- Beetles **265 million years ago**
- Jellyfish & Sea Slugs **500 million years ago** waste-use food chain established; prey and predator co-evolve
- Cyanobacteria **3.6 billion years ago**
- Microbes, the oldest known ecosystem on earth **3.8 billion years ago**
- Earth **4.6 billion years ago**
- Solar system **5 billion years ago**
- Big Bang / Our universe begins **13.7 billion years ago**

*In 1858, astronomer August Möbius discovered the loop with no beginning and no end. "Like the Möbius loop, solid waste isn't a stream that starts in one place and ends in another, it's an unending loop of valuable resources." *Sustainability Institute, Penn State University* (as cited over the recycling/compost bins in the university library).

Human Events Preceding Our Petro-Chemical Era

2 million years ago

2016 Number of Sephardim granted Spanish citizenship = 0

2012 Spain grants Right of Return

March 19, 1497 All Jews forcibly gathered in Lisbon for mass conversion. Only a few escape.

December 5, 1496 Jews expelled from Portugal

November 10, 1492 Jews permitted to return to Spain on condition they convert to Christianity

March 31, 1492 Jews expelled from Spain

1478 Spanish Inquisition officially begins; Catholic Church tortures and kills tens of thousands of Jews; auto-da-fé (burning at the stake)

1391 50,000 Jews publically executed in Spain

prior to the riots of 1391 Spain's Jewish community largest in Europe

1000s–1100s Jews and Muslims coexist relative peace and productivity

ca. 711 CE First forced conversions of Spanish Jews and Muslims (under the regime of the Visigoths)

Homo Sapiens arrive

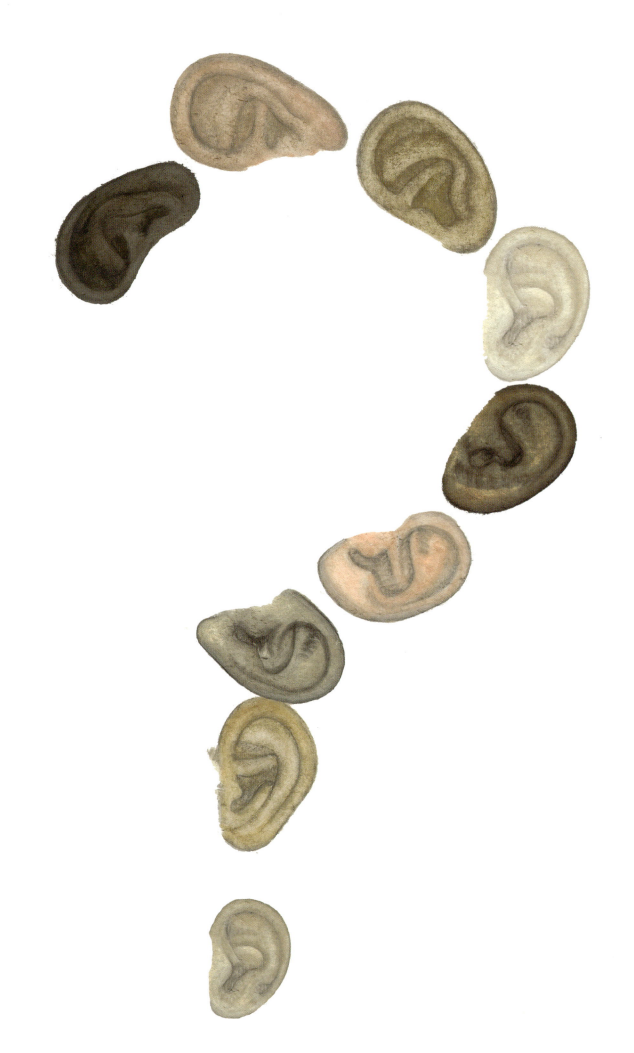

The 21st Century Arcades Project

1. We have chosen a humpback whale, a mammal, as Zazu and Cocomiso's travel companion for many reasons. These include: whales' cooperative feeding, nursing, and migration behaviors, whales' evolutionary physiology, their vocal communication, the brutal history of whale oil as the first major international fuel, and the current state of emergency of oceans and seas across the globe.

2. Sephardim were often traders and merchants, thus cartographers. Their language, Ladino, became the common language of the medieval silk trade routes. As mapmakers, they traveled by the rhythm of the tides and stars, trading figs, Madeira sugar, pearls, tapestries, and hides from the West Indies and glass and silk from Asia.

3. When asked his religion, Einstein replied: "Mosaic."

4. The ethnic category Arab Jew is controversial *not* because Arabs cannot be Jews and Jews cannot be Arabs as is mistakenly conveyed in US popular culture, but because many Jews inhabited Middle Eastern lands for thousands of years prior to Arab presence. Numerous scholars (including Loolwa Khazoom and David Shasha) distinguish between those Jews who arrived before Arab Muslims and those who co-existed with them once they settled. For example, Jewish communities have lived in Iraq (Mesopotamia) for over 2,600 years, 1,200 years before Arabs.

5. Sephardim has many different definitions. In her book *Sephardim*, Paloma Diaz-Maz defines the term to mean the descendants of those Jews exiled from Spain. Jane Gerber, on the other hand, includes the Jews in Medieval Spain as Sephardim. Then there is the Israeli definition, which includes all Jews who are not Ashkenazim. *Zazu Dreams* is an attempt to bridge this us-them divide. We define *Sefarad* (the Hebrew word for 'Spain') as the homeland where many Jews had lived since the destruction of the First Temple of Jerusalem in the year 500. *Mizrahi* (the Hebrew word for 'Eastern' or 'Oriental') refers to Jewish communities from North Africa and the Middle East as well as Central and East Asia. Mizrahi Jews include Persians from Iran.

6. On March 31st 1492, hundreds of thousands of Jews fled Spain. If within three-months they did not convert to Catholicism or leave Spain, they were threatened with torture and public execution; *auto-da-fé* (burning at the stake) was the most common and dramatic form of officially sanctioned murder of the Jews. The trauma inflicted from the Inquisition still impacts Sephardic communities today. A vivid example of the manipulation of Jewish bodies and psyches is the absurd 'Right of Return' in which the Spanish government's 2012 duplicitous invitation/apology to Sephardic Jewry to reclaim their citizenship as 'compensation' for the Inquisition. There have been *no* dual-citizenships actualized; no passports to Sephardim who were born in other countries have been issued because they need documented proof of their ancestors' identity. This bogus attempt to revive Spain's faltering economy is another example of institutionalized anti-Semitism. Our characters stay on the perimeters of Spain, focusing instead on the diaspora. We do not include the landmass of Spain as one of Zazu's destinations in order to emphasize the contradictions in the current invitation of The Right of Return. We are using this paradox as a symbol of the shattered vessel that remains broken, particularly in the search for home (www.forward.com/articles/191376/can-sephardic-jews-go-home-again--years-after/?p=all).

7. Pomegranates are a Rosh Hashanah speciality—symbolizing abundance. Middle Eastern Sephardic versions of *Genesis* emphasize a pomegranate, rather than an apple, in the Garden of Eden.

8. Lela Abravanal, who has collected over 600 Ladino proverbs and oaths, also known as *refranes*, shares that these idioms are 'the voice of our ancestors.' They are folk poetry, a collective wisdom of the Sephardim imbued with humor. For centuries, *refranes* were spoken by everyone: "young and old, literate and illiterate;" "they articulate the unwritten laws of how to see and how to be" (Ladino Day, 2014, Stroum Center for Jewish Studies, University of Washington).

9. Throughout our story, the characters hear and speak Ladino. Exiles of the Diaspora of 1492 wove Hebrew, Turkish, Greek, Italian, French, Portuguese, and Arabic into their 15th century Spanish. Ladino is the ultimate polyvocal, hybrid language—a reflection of the Diaspora; embracing difference. Rich with humor, songs, and poetic metaphors, Ladino has no set linguistic laws; grammar laws of Spanish do not apply. It is deeply connected to oral traditions; only phonetic pronunciations are used. Ladino is the language of the polymath Maimonides, the poet Yehuda Halevi, and the entire tradition of Kabalah (and the Zohar, its foundation). These sacred texts were written in Jewish Babylonian Aramaic—identified as one of the many layers of Ladino. Because of our vast diaspora, Ladino language gradually developed two overarching dialects. Oriental Ladino spoken in Turkey, Rhodes, North Africa, Egypt (echoing Castilian Spanish), while Western Ladino (closer to northern Spanish and Portuguese) was spoken in Greece, Macedonia, Bosnia, Serbia, the former Yugoslavia, Bulgaria, and Romania. Both dialects were also spoken in France, Israel, the United States and Latin America. The United Nations agency, UNESCO, publishes a Red Book of Endangered

Languages. Yiddish is listed as 'endangered' while Ladino is listed as 'seriously endangered.'

Our characters' search for home through language is also an attempt to build solidarity alliances with other ethnic minorities whose languages have been systematically obliterated—thus stripping and eventually erasing their cultures. In her documentary film, "Philosophy of the Encounter," Kendall Moore's main character goes on a personal intellectual journey during which she discovers the meaning of "mind colonization" from Kenyan, anti-colonial scholar Ngũgĩ Wa Thiong'o and his *Decolonising the Mind: The Politics of Language in African Literature*. Moore's characters discuss the institutional violence of such tyrannies: "Like Stuart Hall, he sees the loss of the authentic African self as having much to do with the loss of language. He would argue that psychological inscription begins with the attrition of the original language because it is both a means of communcation and a carrier of culture. The imposition of another language is a way for the colonizing and imperializing cultures to chip away at [other] culture and history."

In spite of its history of adaptation, Ladino will most likely be extinct in 30 years or less. Few Jews are even aware of Ladino's existence, let alone its demise. Although Yeshiva University is attempting to revitalize Ladino, most major American rabbinical schools have chosen to ignore Ladino. Additionally, Yeshiva University permitted a Hebrew Literature professor to call Sephardim "poor and uneducated" (David Shasha, "The Idiot Sephardim"groups.google.com/forum/#!searchin/davidshasha/idiot$20sephardim/davidshasha/HWE675C8-No/VxmT4bkxZlcJ). Prior to World War II, approximately 80% of Diaspora Jews were Ladino-speaking. However, an estimated 90% of all the world's Ladino-speakers were wiped out during the Holocaust (Lorne Rozovsky, "Will Ladino Rise Again?": www.chabad.org/library/article_cdo/aid/1085545/jewish/Will-Ladino-Rise-Again.htm).

Examples of the differences between Spanish and Ladino:

ENGLISH	SPANISH	LADINO
to fly	volar	bolar
red	rojo	kolorado
grandmother	abuela	vava, bula
answer	respuesta	repuesta
praise	alabanza	alavasyon
strong	recio	rezio
house	cazita	kazika
small	pekenyo	chiko
dark	oscuro	aliskura
teach	ensenyar	embezar
head	cabeza	kavessa
blessed	bendito	bendicho
crow, raven	cuerco	graja
dozen	docena	dozena
corner	esquina	rinkon

10. Mizrahim speak combinations of Arabic, Persian, Turkish, and Hebrew.

11. "Hebrew is a Semitic language, originating in the Middle East and North Africa. Originally, Hebrew had a different pronunciation for each letter. The Mizrahi community preserved the linguistic distinctions because they lived for thousands of years in lands where such sounds are common to all languages. The Ashkenazi community lost many of these distinctions after settling in Europe. Slavic and Germanic sounds are not compatible with many of the original pronunciations in Hebrew. Such characteristics as those be 'h' and 'ch,' 'w' and 'v' were lost. Today, 'standard' Hebrew taught in schools throughout the world follow a modified version of Ashkenazi Hebrew, where many letters do not bear distinctions. Though the Mizrahi accent preserves the pronunciations of original Hebrew, it is the subject of frequent ridicule in Jewish communities throughout the world" (Loolwa Khazzoom, "We Are Here, This is Ours," ed. Loolwa Khazzoom, *The Flying Camel: Essays on Identity by Women of North African and Middle Eastern Heritage.* New York: Seal Press, 2003: 236).

12. Like Sephardim, many Ashkenazim are also Jews-of-color, but a different kind. In contrast to the Ethiopian Falasha Jews who are historically Jewish-Africans, some Ashkenazim are Jews-of-color because one of their parents is black, Latino, or Asian, while the other is white Eastern-European or German Jewish. While 'Sepharad' refers to Spain, 'Ashkenaz' refers to Germany. Because Western culture attempts to categorize identities in unambiguous categories, Jews are often divided into the false binary: Ashkenazim or Sephardim. Many so-called Sephardim, such as Jews from Yemen, Kurdistan, Ethiopia, and Bukhara are actually not of Spanish origin and Ladino was not their family language.

13. For centuries, the Straits of Gibraltar has served as a bridge between North Africa and Europe, facilitating transcontinental travel and trade. It was a central passage for Sephardic refugees fleeing from multiple expulsions. Also, the Straits of Gibraltar mark a geological tectonic struggle between Africa and Europe that continues to form the Alps mountain range.

14. Bruno Bettelheim was a child psychologist who survived Nazi, Germany and focused on therapies for autistic children. In his *The Enchantment of Fairy Tales,* Bettelheim writes of the critical necessity of balance between 'good' and 'evil' in children's fairytales. He mourns parents' modern tendency to 'protect' children from any references to negative characteristics and disturbing social realities, believing that this protection undermines children's sense of selfhood. Bettelheim writes how children blame themselves for being 'bad' when they have no models that demonstrate the complexity of human emotions and behavior. Shifting this parental

compulsion to keep children 'safe' is central to our project. We aim to inspire parents to educate themselves and their children about ethnic histories and contemporary environmental, social, and political ecologies. Because the world's largest food company, Nestlé Corporation, negatively impacts so many different kinds of lives, we have chosen it as our fairy tale's 'villain'/monster/evil giant. Nestlé is also the most boycotted company on the planet. Reasons include child labor, starvation wages, and other human rights' abuses. Throughout our tale we revisit the myriad horrors that this corporate criminal inflicts on people, animals, and their environments. Throughout their travels, Zazu and his animal friends witness and confront these personal and global crises.

15. The fig is the first fruit cited in the Torah. It is eaten on the holiday of *Tu b'Shevat*, the holiday for planting trees, and is among the seven species that embodies the beauty and histories of Israel. The Torah tells us that when the Messiah comes, we will all "sit under a (grape) vine and fig tree and that no one will be afraid again" (Micah 4:4).

16. The Romani people, called Roma, are nomadic peoples from all over the world. We begin our story with reference to these migrating peoples because they *do not identify* with a homeland. They do not long to return to a homeland because they make their home wherever they are—not having ties to a specific territory or nationality is their way of experiencing and expressing their passion for freedom. In contrast, the Sephardim have fiercely yearned (*saudade*, from the Portuguese) to return to their homeland. We would like to point out the stereotype of the Romani people as musical gypsies. An example of a group of young Romanis struggling against this one-dimensional image can be found on through the Open Society Foundation: "We are physicians, not musicians…" (www.opensocietyfoundations.org/voices/these-roma-students-make-better-physicians-musicians).

17. Gibraltar had been Moorish for 750 years. It was originally called *Jebel Tariq*, meaning Tariq's Rock, and was occupied by Spanish Christians in 1462. A fleeing Jewish community found fleeting refuge there.

18. The legendary character Joha is a trickster (villain, fool, and wise man) in Sephardic oral traditions and folklore. As with tricksters from all cultures, polymorphism is the primary characteristic of narrative folktales about Joha. His double face of Janus plays out in the *both/and*: "History is like Janus; it has two faces. Whether it looks at the past or at the present, it sees the same things" (Maxime du Champ, *Paris*, vol. 6, 315). Joha is both victim and victimizer, cheater and cheated, trapping others while falling into traps. He meets imaginary characters as well as real people, such as Baron Rothschild and Hitler; sometimes he is likened to cultural heroes such as Maimonides or Rabbi Abraham ibn Ezra. Joha does not differentiate between humans, plants, animals, and objects, and he has a particularly strong relationship with his mother. Transformation and shifting identities are integral to how he engages with the world around him. Joha is frequently represented by *hakawatis,* Arab storytellers, as a Middle Eastern character (not specifically Jewish, and often Moslem) named Goha. He is a hybrid of Jewish, Persian, and Muslim, a multifaceted character found throughout the Sephardic Diaspora, medieval and modern Turkish stories, and the Islamic world. As it traveled, this literary tradition co-mingled with local folktales producing parallel stories referring to Abû Nuwâs on the eastern coast of Africa and in Iraq, and Giufà in Sicily. Nasr-a-din Hodja and Joha are two renditions that have merged into the modern Turkish character, Nasreddin. We hope our story will reveal many commonalities between Islamic, Persian, and Jewish histories—reuniting our common cultures by restoring historical erasures. One reason we are focusing on trickster folklore is because it is integral to the vitality of storytelling and oral traditions that struggle against forgetting. Many cultures' histories include the trickster; for example, Coyote in Navajo traditions, Brer Rabbit in African-American stories, the Judaic Biblical Jacob, and Loki in Nordic mythology.

19. 'Old World' Barbary Macaque monkeys (genus *Macaca*, scientific name, *Macaca sylvanus*) are the only wild population of the monkeys anywhere in Europe. Because they are the only macaque species living outside of Asia, they are in a form of exile. They are one of at least 20 different macaque species characterized by how they developed diverse ecological adaptations. Macaques are found in more climates and habitats than any other primate except humans. About 230 Barbary Macaques now live on the Rock of Gibraltar. In 1782, Ignacio López de Ayala wrote about the macaques in his *History of Gibraltar*: "Neither the incursions of Moor, the Spaniards nor the English, nor cannon nor bomb of either have been able to dislodge them." Because of their loss of habitat (industrial-scale deforestation and livestock over-grazing), the Barbary Macaque species is now listed as 'vulnerable' in the International Union for the Conservation of Nature's Red List of Threatened Species (IUCN). In accordance with tourist disturbances, macaques are systematically culled from their Gibraltar population. They are either killed or deported back to Morocco from where they were originally taken for tourist entertainment. Ironically, the macaque monkey is the national symbol of Gibraltar. We cannot ignore the colonialist histories echoing human environmental refugees (conversation with Christos Galanis, SEEDS: Somatic Experiments in Ecology, Dance, and Science, 2016).

Numerous species of macaques are used extensively in neuroscience research laboratories studying visual perception and other animal testing including toxicology tests, research on AIDS, hepatitis, neurology, behavior and cognition, reproduction, genetics, and xenotransplantation. The macaque species diverged from humans over 15 million years ago. Our fundamental differences limit macaques utility in preclinical studies, yet cruelly, they are still primary medical specimens (RC Kennedy, MH Shearer, W. Hildebrand, "Nonhuman Primate Models to Evaluate Vaccine Safety and Immunogenicity," *Vaccine*. June 15, 1997, (8): 903-8). See also footnote 116 for a discussion of the Persian Jewish pharmacist/ physician, ibn Sina, who explicitly stated that only the human body should be used for medical experimentations.

In the name of 'science,' animals' lives are too often exploited. We begin our tale with one of the most widely abused specimens of medical history, the macaque, because of our theme: do not believe what you think you see; we must approach ideas and actions from multiple unexpected perspectives.

Additionally, our tale questions the motives of industry-funded science. Globally, we are in the midst of a scientific fraud and retraction epidemic. Top medical journal editors have gone public to expose corruption in 'the science.' During a 2015 symposium on the reproducibility and reliability of biomedical research at the Israeli Rambam Health Care Campus (named after Maimonides), Richard Horton, the chief editor of *The Lancet* stated: "Much of the scientific literature, perhaps half, may simply be untrue. Afflicted by studies with small sample sizes, tiny effects, invalid exploratory analyses, and flagrant conflicts of interest, together with an obsession for pursuing fashionable trends of dubious importance, science has taken a turn towards darkness" (www.journal-neo.org/2015/06/18/shocking-report-from-medical-insiders/: *New Eastern Outlook*. June 18, 2015). (I do not condone the racialized language, but Horton's point is clear). Dr. Marcia Angell, physician and Editor-in-Chief of the New England Medical Journal (NEMJ) for twenty-years decries: "It is simply no longer possible to believe much of the clinical research that is published, or to rely on the judgment of trusted physicians or authoritative medical guidelines" (Ibid.). F. William Engdahl, science investigative researcher claims: "Corruption of the medical industry worldwide is a huge issue, perhaps more dangerous than the threat of all wars combined" (Ibid.).

Open Science Collaboration (OSC) has exposed the fabrication of numerous scientific experiment results—falsity published as fact in the most prestigious science journals (William A. Wilson, "Scientific Regress," *First Things*. May 2016.

20. Teeth-chattering or lip-smacking can be expressed to demonstrate dominance or friendly care-taking of infant monkeys.

21. In 2014, Dr. Ruth Decker of St. Louis started a campaign to stop cruel psychological experiments performed on baby macaque monkeys. Sponsored by The National Institutes of Health (NIH), scientists at the University of Wisconsin's primate research laboratory conducted experiments on newborn rhesus macaque monkeys through a procedure whereby macaques were taken from their mothers, put into solitary confinement, and subjected to cruel laboratory experimentation in order to induce anxiety. The infants are then killed and their brains dissected. Ironically, the goal of the study was to "unlock the key to childhood distress." Dr. Ned Kalin, University of Wisconsin's lead investigator, received over $30 million taxpayer to terrorize the infants, while no new treatments for human anxiety were discovered. To clarify, regardless of any 'discoveries,' the experiments were inhumane; that the results reiterate given facts simply makes the experiments more obscene. Through the efforts of Dr. Decker, Johns Hopkins University bioethicist, Jeffrey Kahn, and significant public outcry, this unethical research was aborted. They are currently petitioning Congress to request an audit by the National Academy of Medicine of all NIH-funded research on monkeys.

We begin our story with US society's pernicious addiction to Research and Development and its seemingly infinite reservoir of funding. The particular egregiousness of R&D on baby macaques presents an example of brutality toward other living creatures in order to prove something *we already know*: stress can be debilitating for babies and children—mammals of all species. We begin Zazu's journey with this morbid, yet true success story as an example of how individuals can make a difference for humanitarian, animal, and environmental justice. The baby macaque reference is an example of our theme: the interwoven relationships between people and animals, between people and biomes. *We believe that only by understanding how all forms of oppression are interconnected can we understand that all forms of emancipation are equally interconnected*. And, in order to achieve emancipation, we must work collectively—recognizing how we are all interdependent.

Nestlé claims that they do not use animal testing to develop their foods and drinks, (including coffee, tea, cereal and candy products). "However," states a Nestlé spokesperson, "animal studies are critically important to make advances in fundamental nutrition and health science." The British Union for the Abolition of Vivisection (BUAV) has called for an international moratorium on Nestlé's 'health' food product and ingredient testing on animals. Examples of Nestlé's experiments are too grotesque to include in these pages (www.express.co.uk/news/world/409256/Food-giants-accused-of-cruel-and-sickening-experiments-in-animal-testing-scandal.html; www.forcechange.com/67782/demand-nestle-stop-cruel-animal-testing/).

PETA, People for the Ethical Treatment of Animals,

states that 92% of drugs that pass tests on animals fail in human bodies. These drugs often simply do not work for humans, or if they do offer the desired results, they are often accompanied by dangerous side effects. Instead, testing these pharmaceutical products in a petri dish on cultured human cells is potentially more predictive for human safety than animal tests, and would be much less expensive, and clearly more humane. The obscene irony that Nestlé conducts vivisection experiments for human 'superfoods' (including 'friendly bacteria' probiotics and safe strains of E. coli bacteria, the cellular biologist's favorite guinea pig) corresponds with vast corporate greenwashing practices. This perversity is reminiscent of Nazi science experiments during WWII.

Again, they claim to not test on animals for cosmetics, but Nestlé owns about 30% of L'Oreal shares and Galderma (which is co-owned by L'Oreal and Nestlé) who conducts animal experiments outside the European Union— meaning, in countries that are not held accountable to animal protection laws (www.bwcsa.co.za/issues/vivisection#sthash.w3ARJ0SR.dpuf).

Internationally, families unknowingly support and/or are subjected to Nestlé's micro and macro-barbarism— products that are derived from not just cruel, but unnecessary experiments and injustices (ranging from their baby-formula campaigns to pharmaceutical Research and Development to their global illegal attempts to privatize water). We are choosing to focus on Nestlé the food giant because of its staggering hypocrisy—its claims to promote 'health' and the damaging role it plays in children's lives across the world. Nestlé's 'Health Science' division (that invested $70 million in their US Product Technology Center) sabotages peoples' health and land as it hypocritcally promotes "nutritional therapy innovation"— "the intersection of nutrition and healthcare." To clarify, I am defining health in this context as the effect of Nestlé products on bodies, and land, in view of how those products are produced (www.livescience.com/47747-nestle-adopts-humane-farming-policy.html).

A spokesman for Nestlé said that one of their research focal goals is to develop foods that help people with medical conditions such as bowel problems. Later in the story, Zazu and his companions will play with this fecal irony. Given Nestlé's history with and purchase of Pfizer's infant health division, 'Health Science' is clearly a euphemism for pharmaceuticals.

22.   Breast milk contains all the vital nutrients for beginning human development and gives foundational immunities that protect against disease and infection as the child grows into adulthood. Benefits of breast milk include treating Crohn's disease, HIV susceptibility, allergies, asthma, ear infections. Antibodies in breast milk suppress HIV1 in babies of infected of mothers. Although contested by some, new studies indicate that breastfeeding leads to higher IQ scores and higher education levels and earning among those breastfed up to a year, compared to those breastfed for a month or less. Tragically since the 1940s (and again a resurgence in 1988), due to aggressive marketing campaigns from formula (artificial milk) companies such as Carnation (a division of Nestlé) and Big-Pharma such as Merck & Co., many US physicians have pressured new mothers to become dependent on formula. Nestlé provides free formula following hospital-births—resulting in many babies who never even get a chance to start breastfeeding. Nestlé-hospital cooperation is rooted in unscrupulous misrepresentation and coercion. Women stuck in the weakest economic position are effectively forced to feed their infants formula. Formula can harm babies' digestive tracts and immune systems because it does not contain the natural antibodies that mother's milk provides. Formula can be extremely expensive, forcing poor mothers to mix it with too much water resulting in toxicity and malnutrition; the water used to dilute the formula is often not potable. Once a mother starts giving her baby formula, her own milk supply dries up, often an emotionally and physically wrenching process. Frequently, families can no longer afford formula, so they give their baby juice as an alternative. Juice is pure sugar, offering little nutritional value, inevitably leading to health problems such as obesity and ADHD. In 1977, consumers initiated an international boycott against Nestlé protesting its deceptive promotion of synthetic baby formula as a superior alternative to mother's milk. In 1984, the boycott forced Nestlé to abide by the World Health Organization's International Code of Marketing of Breast Milk Substitutes. The boycott was re-launched four years later when it was discovered that Nestlé continued to break the law. Another criminal disregard of the law is Nestlé's illegal water privatization in California 2015 (see footnote 155). The boycott is still in practice today against Nestlé's and its subsidiaries: Nescafé, Taster's Choice, Hills Bros, Cerealac, Nido, Fitness & Fruit, Appleminis, Cheerios, Chocapic Cornflakes (in some countries), Shreddies, Golden Grahams, Trix, Perrier, Poland Spring, Deer Park, Calistoga, Sohat, Vittel, Pure Life, Carnation, Libby's, Nesquik, Maggi, Buitoni, Milkybar, KitKat, Quality Street, Smarties, Oreo, After Eight, Lion, Aero, Polo, Toll House Morsels, Crunch, L'Oréal, Alcon Eyecare, Goobers, Mint Royal, Nerds, Oh Henry!, Rowntree, Rolo, Del Monte Real Fruit Bar, Minute Maid, Petit Gervals, Contadina, Alpo, Purina, Tidy Cats, Meow Mix, Mighty Dog, Friskies, Felix, Stouffers.

In 2012, Nestlé bought U.S. drug company Pfizer's baby food business for $11.85 billion—about 50% more than analysts thought it was worth only a few months prior to the sale. Nestlé has once again won the battle for dominance of the 'infant nutrition' (i.e., infant formula) market in rapidly growing emerging markets such as

China. The *Wall Street Journal* reported that according to analysts at Citigroup, China's $6 billion market will double to $12 billion by 2016. In order to maintain their manufactured consumer-base, the market has grown 20% every year over the last five years, 'feeding' 16 million new births each year. Nestlé's formal statement included: "…this acquisition underlines our commitment to be the world's *leading nutrition, health and wellness* company" (my italics) (blogs.wsj.com/source/2012/04/23/nestles-pfizer-deal-is-all-about-the-growth/). Because of their role in 'developing countries,' Nestlé's $30 billion global sales are growing annually by 10% (Ibid.).

Merck is the world's largest vaccine manufacturer and happens to publish *The Merck Manuals,* medical reference texts for physicians, nurses, and technicians. These include the world's best-selling medical reference: *Merck Manual of Medicinal Information,* containing insidious neonatal nutritional doctrine (www.merckmanuals.com/professional/pediatrics/care-of-newborns-and-infants/nutrition-in-infants). Congruently, The American Academy of Pediatrics (AAP) recommends exclusive breastfeeding for a minimum of six months. Although absolutely critical up to that point, six months hardly enables the infant to receive the full physiological or psychological benefits of breastfeeding (of course, ideally from uncontaminated breast milk, see footnote 109). According to the World Health Organization, "a modest increase in breastfeeding rates could prevent up to 10% of all deaths of children *under five.* Breastfeeding plays an essential and sometimes underestimated role in the treatment and prevention of childhood illness" (my italics) (G. Gaynor, "Breastfeeding advocacy," *Maine Nurse*. 2003: 5(2):13; D. Wright, "Progress review: Maternal, infant, and child health," 2007, www.healthypeople.gov/data/2010prog/focus16/; See also: JH. Wolf, "Low breastfeeding rates and public health in the United States," *American Journal of Public Health*. 2003: 93(12):2000–2010, and Emily E. Stevens, RN, FNP, WHNP, PhD, Thelma E. Patrick, RN, PhD, and Rita Pickler, RN, PNP, PhD ,"A History of Infant Feeding," *The Journal of Perinatal Education*. 2009 Spring; 18(2): 32–39; www.ncbi.nlm.nih.gov/pmc/articles/PMC2684040/). Breastfeeding rates had been 90% in the 20th century, but declined to approximately 42% in the 21st century. Replacing breast milk with infant-formula has resulted in serious health conditions: including atopy, diabetes mellitus, and childhood obesity (Ibid.).

Pharmaceutical and formula companies' advertising and production has had calamitous impacts on non-industrialized, neo-colonized countries—both in terms of infant-mortality and introducing an entire new breed of infant illnesses.

This discussion is by no means meant to stigmatize women who do not have the choice to breastfeed due to specific health or economic conditions (working mothers who cannot pump). What is paramount is informed consent. This includes women understanding the implications of how forced labor drugs (pitocin and epidurals) may reduce breast milk, thus altering the entire breastfeeding relationship between mother and newborn (www.mothering.com/articles/breastfeeding-success-affected-labor-drugs/).

Human breast milk contains human-made:

- Proteins
- Lactose
- Oligosaccharides
- Carbohydrates
- Triglycerides
- Fat-human milk fat (the beneficial kind)
- Oleic Acid which forms Hamlet that kills tumor cells
- Lipids
- Vaccenic acid
- Conjugated linoleum acid (CLA's)
- Oleic acid (anti-cancer substance that the mother passes on to her child)

Consistent with grotesque appropriatins throughout our Petrol-Chemical Anthropocene Era, there are currently 2,000 patents on human breast milk components. "Human Breast Milk is now under a Nestlé-Monsanto patent" (www.removingtheshackles.blogspot.com/2013/04/monsanto-nestle-patent-human-breast-milk.html).

23.   The Spanish Inquisition was both a culmination and a continuation of expulsions of Jews from the Iberian Peninsula and across Europe and the Americas. Historian Simon Schama tells us that the expulsions (beginning in the 12th century in England and continuing through the 16th century throughout Iberia) relieved Christians of their obligation to repay debts to Jewish moneylenders—often the only profession Christian governments would allow Jews to be (*The Story of the Jews*. PBS, 2014).

24.   The hand of G-d, the *hamsa*, like the myrtle sprig, fortifies the spirit. In Muslim contexts, the *hamsa* is referred to as the Hand of Fatima, and like other amulets, talismans, and fetishes, it wards off the evil eye—offering good luck, healing, fertility, protection, positive energy, while deflecting destructive emotions, like envy and hatred. Amulets also are used to gain someone's love. The five fingers of the *hamsa* are supposed to remind its wearer to use their five senses to experience and express gratitude to the spirit of the universe/ G-d. After the establishment of Israel, the dominant Eurocentric Ashkenazim looked down on the widespread use of the amulet that was seen as a sign of 'Easternness.' The *hamsa* has since become a trendy symbol and is now heavily commercialized throughout Israel.

In his post-colonial, magical realist novel, *Midnight's Children,* Salman Rushdie reminds us "the *hamsa* or *parahamsa* is the symbol of an ability to live in two worlds—the physical and spiritual world of land & water and the world of air, of flight" (New York: Penguin, 1980: 267). In Hindi, it is called the *Humsa*. Whether *hamsa*, Hand of Fatima, or *Humsa*, this symbol remains a cross-cultural connection among many different peoples.

25. The *neshama* is the soul or spiritual past of a human being.

26. As the bookseller in Jorge Luis Borges' *El libro de arena* (The Book of Sand) tells Borges, "If space is infinite, we may be at any point in space. If time is infinite, we may be at any point in time" (Madrid: Emecé, 1975: 119). The book he sells him has Arabic page numbers, and is "called the Book of Sand because neither the book nor the sand has any beginning or end" (ibid.).

27. Whales are more similar to humans than they are to fish. As mammals, whales, and humans share the gift of nourishing our babies directly from our bodies. Humpbacks' babies, called calves, nurse from nipples hidden in the expansive folds of flesh that run from chin to bellybutton. The mother humpback squirts gobs of milk, as thick as heavy cream or even toothpaste, out of her nipples tucked away in her mammary slits. Like us, whales have umbilical cords. Humans, like whales, also have internal ecosystems called the microbiome—a kind of conviviality exchanged between the mother's body, her fetus, and later, her growing infant: "Recent studies suggest that infants incorporate an initial microbiome before birth and receive copious supplementation of maternal microbes through birth and breastfeeding. Moreover, evidence for microbial maternal transmission is increasingly widespread across animals. …It also engenders fresh views on the assembly of the microbiome, its role in animal evolution, and applications to human health and disease" (Lisa J. Funkhouser, Seth R. Bordenstein, "Mom Knows Best: The Universality of Maternal Microbial Transmission," PLOS Biology. August 2013, Volume 11, Issue 8, e1001631: 1 (www.plosbiology.org, Open Access).

28. The height of the brain's cognitive and linguistic development is between three years and five years old. The average five year old in the US has seen 6,000 hours of TV programming and eight times that when mobile devices are used. The development of a young person's limbic system—the brain's image-making center—is drastically diminished when half of his/her waking life is spent in front of screen technologies. The use of smartphones, TV, and other screen technologies stunt the neurological capacity of infants, babies, and children—including their development of imagination, literacy and social skills. For example, when children see people hugging in front of them in actual three-dimensional space—specific empathy developmental neurons are fired. In contrast, when they see hugging on a screen, empathy neurons are not fired. Critical research about the brain is a hot topic. Dr. Patricia Kuhl, a neuroscientist at University of Washington, researches the "social gating hypothesis: the idea that social experiences are a portal to linguistic, cognitive, and emotional development" (Yudhijit Bhattacharjee, "The First Year," *National Geographic*, January 2015: 39). See also: Barry Sanders' *A is for Ox: Violence, Electronic Media and the Silencing of the Written Word*).

Dr. Bruce Lipton, epigeneticist and author of "Conscious Parenting: Parents as Genetic Engineers," tells us that visual technologies are epigenetic: they override our genetic make-up and can disable intellectual and emotional development (*The Biology of Belief: Unleashing the Power of Consciousness, Matter & Miracles,* Carlsbad, CA: Hay House 2005). According to data from the Nielsen Company, the average preschooler in the US uses screen-media 4.6 hours every day. Common Sense Media released a study indicating that 39% of 2 to 4 year-olds and 10% of babies and 1 year-olds use a smartphone, MP3, or tablet (Vicki Glembocki, "How to Raise a People Person," *Parents Magazine,* Jan. 2015: 50). 13% of two-year-olds can order their own apps, including tooth-brushing and potty apps. The new iPotty used for potty-training includes a slot to hold an iPad that is attached to the portable toilet. "Because the adult mobile phone market is saturated, children are the next target" (Dr. Devra Davis, "The Truth about Mobile Phones and Wireless Radiation" (Dean's lecture, University of Melbourne, Australia, November 30, 2015). See also Davis' Environmental Health Trust: www.ehtrust.org.).

In contrast, in order to protect vulnerable bodies from the dangers of accumulated radiowave frequencies (Radio Frequency Exposure or RF), in 2009, France, Russia, Israel, Germany, UK, Belgium, India, Finland, and Toronto's Departments of Health outlawed or issued warnings against cell-phone usage by pregnant women and children under eighteen. According to this consumer protection research, the cumulative impact of cell phone exposure (including iPads and Tablets) is more toxic than asbestos and cigarettes. Predictably, in the US, Sprint recently signed a two billion dollar contract with Disney to market cell phones to children under twelve—unabashedly ignoring the dire health impact on neurological development. These findings are further corroborated by one of the top medical research journals, *The Lancet*. In 2012, they published a series of studies that found: "Physical inactivity results in 5.3 million deaths annually, which makes it almost exactly as deadly as smoking" (*Taproot Magazine.* 2013: 22). Hemorrhoids, the 'sitter's disease,' afflicts more than half of 50+ year-olds in the USA (Toscani 49).

Richard Louv, author of *The Nature Principle* (2011), argues that Nature Deficit Disorder is increasingly becoming a national crisis. He contends that limited time outside leads to vast social and emotional problems: "The more disengaged from nature, the lonelier we become."

Congruently, Harvard biologist, Edward O. Wilson, stresses the vitality of biophilia—the idea that humans are innately drawn to nature of all kinds.

29. For decades paleontologists believed that the first ancestor of the whale was a land-mammal that lived 65 million years ago. This canine-creature called a mesonychid (mes-o-NICK-id) existed on land while there was plenty to eat and gradually adapted to life in the abundant sea as land-food became scarce. They believed that the mesonychid's paws had almost parallel structures to the flippers of the humpback, and that both resembled the bone arrangement of human hands! Recently though paleontologists have discovered that the hippo, not the whale, is the missing evolutionary link. We include this historical re-examination to illustrate how thinking and knowledge are continually in flux. Hannah Arendt reminds us, "Thinking is never finished."

Congruently, the Talmud, like history, is alive; it has become an endless exegesis of multiple hypertexts—interpretations that never end: nothing is fixed; nothing is frozen. Knowledge itself is like the Jewish peoples—infinitely adapting and transforming.

In both whale and hippo paleontological interpretations, due to gradual climate and geographical changes, food became scarce so the land animals became sea-mammals, adapting to their aquatic environment where food was plentiful. Much of North Africa is an example of this radical topographical change. The Sahara Desert, one of the largest in the world, engulfing 3.6 million square miles (9.4 million square kilometers), was once lush, tropical land supporting millions of life forms that no longer exist. The era of the Green Sahara or African Humid Period occurred approximately 11,000-5,000 years ago. Once verdant and vast savannahs supported cerulean 'paleolakes' abundant with aquatic life and lush foliage. The Sahara was called the River of Giants, a huge swampland "teeming with giant fish and even bigger predators like Spinosaurus" (Brian E. Clark, *Saudi Aramo World*. Sept./Oct. 2015: 29). The Sahara was submerged under the ancient Tethys Sea. The dorudon, the ancestor of the modern whale may have come to birth their young where Egypt now lies in the Wadi Al-Hitan, وادي الحيتان "Whales Valley."

The lakes have now dried into the world's largest dust bowl—today's scorching Sahara Desert, an 'ocean of sand' (averaging 52 degrees C or 125 degrees F): Martian landscape of drifting dunes, massifs (sandstone table rocks), and yardangs (needle-like pyramids or Sphinx-shaped sand formations sculpted by the relentless harmattan trade winds). In his "Meterologica," Aristotle reminds us, "The same regions do not remain always sea or always land, but all change their condition *in the course of time*" (My italics to emphasize geologic time in contrast with contemporary anthropogenic time).

30. Humpbacks are adorned with warts (knobs or tubercles), ridges, and barnacles (one scientist found almost 1000 pounds of barnacles clinging to a single whale). Each wart supports a single hair. Like whiskers, these hairs are connected to clusters of nerves to help the whale detect vibrations in the water.

31. *Hilloula* is North African term designating a pilgrimage to the Jewish shrines of sainted rabbis (www.ericrossacademic.wordpress.com/2011/09/20/the-shrine-of-rabbi-amram-ben-diwane-in-azjen-morocco/). *Hilloula* takes place in the *midbar*, (the desert or wilderness) out of which come the words, *dabar* (thing) and *ledaber* (to talk). Literally and metaphorically, both the language of the Jews and their nation(s) emerge from the desert.

32. A *tzaddik* (*zaddiq*) is a Jewish Saint.

33. In 1628, Moses Cohen Henriques Eanes captured a Spanish fleet carrying a cargo of silver and gold. It is estimated that their booty was equivalent to 1 billion in today's dollars.

34. Sephardic Pirate Jean Lafitte was exiled from Spain as part of the expulsions of the 1700s. He later became an influential politician in North America, and helped the US win the War of 1812.

35. Similar to the Salem Witch Trials of the late 1600s in Massachusetts, thousands of Jews in the 1400s were charged with conjuring magic spells. They were forced to flee Iberia or to convert to Christianity. Thousands of Jews were publicly executed. Thousands of *conversos* (New Christians) practiced Judaism in secrecy. These Jews who had converted to Christianity were called *anusim* (forced ones), *marranos* (swine), *chuetas* (pig-eater)--all of which were officially sanctioned vilifying names. Additionally, many *conversos* who became zealot Christians were still denounced as *judios mamas*: "really a Jew." Crypto-Jews (hidden Jews) devised secret strategies to maintain their veneration for Jewish traditions. These include: touching a *mezuzah* hidden within the foot of a statue of the Madonna, pretending to light candles for Catholic saints, and doing so only on Fridays with a Shabbat prayer, and spreading sand over synagogue floors as symbolic of the Jews in Spain and Portugal who, during the Inquisition, had to cover their basement floors with sand in order to muffle the sounds of their chants and prayers. When denouncers discovered their secret, they were condemned as *Judaizers*—accused of practicing Judaism. Because mothers and grandmothers were responsible for maintaining Jewish beliefs and practices among converted Jews, more women than men were tried and convicted of heresy and burned at the stake.

36. The Spanish Inquisition of 1492 coincided with Spanish conquistadors' invasion of the Americas. It behooves present day activists who are fighting against historical and contemporary colonial oppression to recognize

the intermeshed histories between the expulsions of the Jews and the 'discovery'/ occupation of the Americas.

37. The Sephardim were not pirates in the sense of, for example, today's Somalis pirates; they were 'privateers' licensed by Spain's enemies. Official accounts have either intentionally ignored or conveniently forgotten the Jewish, Arab, African, and Islamic role in the 'construction' of the New World. A Chinese proverb offers: "The beginning of wisdom is calling things by their right name" (Krishtalka). (Arthur V. Evans and Charles L. Bellamy, Photographs by Lisa Charles Watson, *An Inordinate Fondness for Beetles*. Berkeley: University of California Press, 2000: 12). Stripping a people of their name is a classic colonial tool to erase identity and memory. Two recent 2014 /2015 PBS specials: Simon Schama's *The Story of the Jews* and David Grubin's *The Jewish Americans* made no reference whatsoever to Sephardic/ Mizrahi histories, let alone the pioneering contributions of Sephardim to colonial America as early as the 15th century. As Laila Lalami tells us in *The Moor's Account*, "a name is precious; it carries inside it a language, a history, a set of traditions, a particular way of looking at the world. Losing it meant losing my ties..." Even Christopher Columbus is said to have been Sephardic, negotiating his enforced departure with the Spanish monarchy (Edward Kritzler, *Jewish Pirates of the: How a Generation of Swashbuckling Jews Carved Out an Empire in the New World in Their Quest for Treasure, Religious Freedom—and Revenge*. New York: Random House, 2008**)**. Many sailors and navigators on board Columbus' ships were Sephardim escaping the Inquisition. Others escaped to Holland, Italy, and Anatolia. This history offers another example, of which there are unfortunately too many, where persecuted peoples justify their own survival by participating in inhumane systems of domination—like colonialism and slavery. The slave trade was a major contributor to colonial wealth—this perversely included some Arabs and Africans who sold their own people. The Spanish monarchy inflicted divide-and-conquer strategies among both Jews and indigenous peoples of the Americas. Because of this classic domination tactic, rather than collaborating for their collective freedom, some *conversos* participated in abusive systems. Clearly, we find abhorrent the history of genocide of indigenous peoples in the 'New World' that Columbus's legacy left in its wake; and, Columbus' ethnic-historical erasure should be mentioned. We must not ignore early Sephardi participation in the 'living death' that was the early African slave trade in the Americas. Ironically, both Jews and Moslems (*aljamas*) were complicitous in this heinous history. On the other hand, there are numerous examples of attempts to combat the slave trade. For example, Maimonides raised money to ransom Jewish prisoner slaves from other pirates.

38. As a child and into adulthood, Queen Isabella was under the guidance of the vile Tomás Torquemada, the Grand Inquisitor, who had served as her official confessor.

39. In ships bearing old-testament names such as the Prophet Samuel, Queen Esther, and Shield of Abraham, the Sephardi rebels looted the Spanish fleet while forming coalitions with European nations to safeguard Jews living in hiding.

40. Coral reef ecosystems are the carbonate landscapes that govern ocean communities (Michael Welland, *Sand: The Never Ending Story*. Berkeley: University of California Press, 2009: 139). Coral reefs are the rainforests of the ocean. There is almost no waste on a coral reef. Coral reefs are marine systems with one of the highest levels of biodiversity. They represent the perfect metaphor for symbiosis of, social permaculture, human ecology, and a social ecology of empathy. (For a detailed analysis of the distinction between social permaculture, human ecology, and social ecology (Murray Bookchin) see Alhadeff's "Challenging Petroleum-Parenting: Confessions of an Eco-Obsessed Mother (and Other Lies)," www.carajudea.com). Symbiosis (the Greek words for together—*syn*—and life—*bio*—lays the foundation for *mutualism*, in which each party helps one another. Coral reefs are the result of millions of years of teamwork between coral and algae co-existing across multiple lifecycles as they share food and shelter. The tiny algae, *zooanthellae*, live inside the coral and make food from sunlight that they share with the coral in return for a place to live. Each symbiont contributes a vital role in the interplay of mutualism: together they form coral reefs, including the largest living organism on the planet— Australia's Great Barrier Reef, visible from outer space. Patrick Whitefield defines permaculture as "the art of designing [mutually] beneficial relationships." In a coral reef, every organism, structure, and raw material, fulfills a job that benefits the entire community.

All twenty of the most abundant coral species throughout the Caribbean are threatened. There has been a 50% decline in coral reefs since the 1970s in almost all Caribbean locations. In 2005, the concentration of carbon dioxide exceeded the natural range that has existed over 650,000 years. Increased CO2 levels lead to trapped heat (thermal stress) in the atmosphere. Because the ocean has absorbed one quarter of atmospheric carbon emissions from burning fossil fuels, deforestation and other human activities (high-emission convenience-culture/ corporate practices), this excess CO2 alters ocean chemistry and has major corrosive effects on marine ecosystems such as ocean warming and ocean acidification ("Climate, Carbon and Coral Reefs," *World Meteorological Organization (WMO) DOCUMENT*. 2010: 22). As the ocean waters grow warmer due to climate change, salinity is accelerating. Maintaining homeostasis has become more challenging than ever before. Marine life that has survived for millions of years are now dying because of increased salt in our oceans.

Tropical coral reefs that provide habitats for thousands of

species are under siege; warmer sea temperatures disrupt the delicate symbiotic relationships among coral organisms, sea slugs, and algae. The sea slug (*Holothuroidea*) feeds on plankton and decaying matter on the ocean floor, along with grazing on the rocks and coral reefs for algae. Although sea slugs are relatively motionless, by eating the decomposing plant matter, they are essential to maintain algae levels within a homeostatic balance in all marine environments.. This is not a crisis only for sea-life, but an economic crisis: globally, coral reefs yield over $30 billion annually in products and services, such as coastline protection, tourism, and food. Because of global warming, coral reefs are on the brink of extinction—now identified as the ('graveyard of the Atlantic').

41. The Inquisition was forbidden by charter to enter Jamaican territory—the only safe haven throughout the Caribbean and the Americas. *Conversos* populated Jamaica—making it a rich trading island. The Sephardim arrived as refugees rather than colonialists. There is contradictory evidence about how their refugee status impacted indigenous populations—both through intermarriage or colonialist influences.

42. Invisible throughout US history, the oldest synagogues and Jewish cemeteries in the Western hemisphere are facing extinction in the Caribbean. Thousands of Sephardic Jews were called *La Nación*. They helped support the American Revolution. *La Nación* built the first synagogues in the colonies in New York City and Rhode Island. Jews from Curacao settled in Rhode Island. By the 1600s, the West Indies became a safe haven for Sephardic Jews who fled to Amsterdam and then Brazil. *La Nación* was fundamental to the foundation of the early Caribbean economy through their extensive experience of trade routes and their knowledge of agriculture, such as sugar cane cultivation. Only five synagogues remain and almost half of the original cemeteries are either in serious disrepair, or have been lost to time, vandalism, pollution, or natural disaster. The history of these Sephardim in the Americas is rapidly being erased. (Information culled from historian/ photographer Wyatt Gallery).

43. Caribs is the name Europeans called the indigenous Kalinago people.

44. *Querencia* refers to the safe place in the bullring that the bull retreats to regain his equilibrium to then continue the bullfight.

45. Even as they assimilated into indigenous communities, Sephardic Jews maintained both their religion and their unique culture and customs.

46. Since they had no access to fresh forms of vitamin C that prevents scurvy (they couldn't save fruit for months out at sea), pirates survived on fermented foods (like sauerkraut, pickles, olives). On their three-year exploration of the South Pacific, Captain James Cook kept each of his sailors alive (free from scurvy) by requiring they eat vitamin C-dense sauerkraut. In total they shared 30,000 pounds of sauerkraut.

47. Lusterware ceramic pottery was made through a complicated process that was gradually lost from Spain after 1492. Lusterware was a physical manifestation of dialogue with all the elements of the cosmos: oxygen, earth, water, fire, and time. The Arabic concept of *al-kimiya* (transmutation) combines earth material with the spirit, the *duende*, or intuition.

48. Historians have perhaps misjudged why the Sephardic pirates coveted these vessels. A common theory is that they were attempting to mimic the behavior of the upper classes. In contrast, we are suggested that perhaps the pirates were remembering and attempting to recreate how they lived before being expelled from their homeland: an attempt to enact *tikkun olam*; an attempt to repair their shattered worlds.

49. An 'old salt' is an experienced sailor.

50. Joha the Trickster scholar, Matilda Coen-Sarano, also collected the tale of *El Papagayo Djudió* ("The [Sephardic] Jewish Parrot") (Aude Samana and François Azar, *The Jewish parrot and other Judeo-Spanish tales*. Paris: Lior Press, 2014).

51. Judeo-Malayalam is a dialect of Malayalam, the official language of Kerala where the Cochin Jews have lived for thousands of years.

52. Refrain songs consist of non-sequitur strings of sounds or repeated lines arranged in fixed intervals. Among the refrain song varieties are songs that address a parrot. Refrain songs correspond with early Judeo-Malayalam folksongs called kiḷipāṭṭə, or parrot songs (Ophira Gamliel, "Judeo-Malayalam," ed. Lily Kahn and Aaron Rubin, *Handbook of Jewish Languages*. Leiden: Koninklijke Brill NV, 2016: 510).

53. Like today's Euro used throughout most of Europe, *reals* could be used anywhere the ships sailed. *Reals* were a hot commodity for pirates and merchants alike.

54. Similar to the exiled pirates who developed elaborate self-defense, beetles such as the highly destructive and instructive boll weevil (as we will see in footnote 66) have not only been targets of insecticide, they have their own diverse chemical arsenal for self-defense. Their cousin, the leaf beetle is not only poisonous, it excretes a sticky substance that glues its predator's jaws together when they try to take a bite; the iron cross beetle and violin beetle release acid that can burn and blister its predators (potentially killing large mammals, like a horse, who may accidentally swallow one); making a loud popping sound, the bombadier beetle squirts jets of blinding, boiling hot liquid into the face of its attacker; other beetle species simply discharge foul-tasting fluids (Steve Jenkins, *The Beetle Book*. New York: Harcourt Publishing Company, 2012: 22, 23).

55. Dung beetles' symbiotic, industrious activities demonstrate the meaning in these Ladino proverbs. (See also: www.whats-your-sign.com/symbolic-beetle-meaning.html). Similar to the scenario in which we are indebted to dust-mites for eating our dead skin (otherwise we would be suffocating in our own flesh debris), we are also indebted to dung beetles for clearing excrement off the world's grasslands. They clean up astounding quantities of organic waste produced by vertebrates. If dung beetles did not do their job, our earth would be piled high with manure. These poop-mountains would be infested with disease-carrying flies. A twist in the history of agribusiness is 'biological control' or Integrated Pest Management (IPM)—a critical alternative to the use of pesticides. Dung beetles have been a key player in this human-intervention version of symbiosis. Examples include: in 1778, dung beetles were used to stave off pestiferous horn flies. In 1887, 10,000 were imported and distributed throughout southern California to devour the infestation of the scales insect (thereby saving the fledging citrus industry). When cattle were introduced to Australia the native dung beetles that had adapted to marsupial manure didn't eat the cow poop. 30 million cattle were now grazing and pooping throughout Australia, producing over 10 million cow patties per hour. Poop was piling up in the fields, while disease-carrying worms and flies were piling up in the hot, smelly cow poop. Entomologist Dr. George Bornemissza organized The Australian Dung Beetle IPM project in which between 20-45 species of foreign dung beetles (primarily from Africa) were imported to clean up the mountains of manure. In the 1970s, the USDA introduced the brown dung beetle or gazelle scarab, a native of Africa and Asia, to the southeastern United States to suppress harmful dung-breeding flies such as horn flies. By burying this waste, they reduce possible contaminable disease as they fertilize the soil, making it rich for the growth of new life (Evans and Bellamy).

56. Like Al'Garnati, the young Andalusian boy [who was persecuted at the age of ten], Zazu and his companions go on a *yatra*, the Hindi term for a journey with a purpose—"a lifelong journey of expecting the unexpected" (Ingrid Bejarano Escanilla and Lousis Werner, "Travelers of Al-Andalus: Abu Hamid Al-Garnati's World of Wonders," *Saudi Aramco World*. March/Apr. 2015: 36-39, 36). The Little Prince reminds us: "*Les enfants seuls savent ce qu'ils cherchent*" (Only children know what they are looking for) (Chapter XXII).

The dung beetle is a potent model for such exquisite perseverance. Vic Strecher PhD, MPH, Professor and Director for Innovation and Social Entrepreneurship at the University of Michigan School of Public Health writes of the dung beetle as a symbol of profound magic and life-purpose (www.dungbeetle.org/behind-the-story/the-beetle/).

57. Male humpback whales are known for their complex series of sounds called songs—they are the noisiest of all whales. Even though no Western researchers have heard females singing, in our story Zazu's friend, the female humpback whale, does sing. Humpbacks share over 1,000 different songs. They consist of a series of continually changing repeated patterns. Scientists have not found a reason why, but all the whales in a specific population sing the same version of their song. Whales in the Pacific sing a different song from whales in the Atlantic. They share 'social sounds' when traveling, a 'feeding siren' to announce their arrival to group feeding grounds, love songs to attract a mate, and cooing sounds between mothers and calves. Hanging vertically upside down, their hypnotic songs, often extended and eerie melodies, can sound like rhythmic grunts, roars, chirps, whistles, groans, screams, thwops, snorts, barks, and trumpets. The songs have the largest range of frequencies used by whales, ranging from 20-9,000 Hertz. Whales often gather together in one area of the ocean to compose a single piece of music. This is another example (like co-nursing and pod feeding) of how they live cooperatively (see footnote 67). They sing the complex songs only in warm waters, perhaps used for mating purposes. In cold waters, they make rougher sounds, scrapes and groans, perhaps used for locating large masses of krill (the tiny crustaceans that they eat). Sound waves travel almost five times faster in the water than in the air. Because whale songs have a low frequency, their songs travel fast and far. Before noise pollution overwhelmed the underwater world, their mighty songs once traveled across thousands of miles of ocean.

58. Thousands of whales, dolphins and other marine mammals are in grave danger. In their Five-Year Plan (2012-2017), the Obama Administration opened up the US East coast to oil and gas exploration. Deafening noise from seismic airguns for this exploration not only injures thousands of sea creatures, it also ravages fishermen and coastal communities up and down the US Eastern seaboard. Similarly, on the US West coast, deadly and reckless Navy exercises (such as underwater explosions, surface-to-air gunnery, missiles, and mid-frequency sonar) maim and kill marine life—including endangered whales. In a landmark settlement on September 14, 2015 after over a decade in court, finally acknowledging the dramatic negative impact on whale migration patterns, the US Navy finally agreed to limit the use of their sonar and high explosives during training and testing operations: "The Navy's own environmental review conceded that sonar use across all range could kill nearly 1,000 marine mammals over the next five years and cause more than 13,000 serious injuries" (National Resource Defense Council

(NRDC) newsletter, 2015).

59.   Hydroacoustics, the study and application of sound in water, allows engineers and scientists to make ocean technology safer for marine mammals. Hydroacoustics is how these mammals communicate. Because whales cannot see well under water, they make clicking sounds—sound waves that travel, bounce off objects, and return to the whales' ears. Noise pollution severely interrupts this sonar or echolocation process. Acoustic onslaught from military exercises, commercial shipping, energy exploration, and private boats is doubling (if not more) with each decade. This lethal sound pollution reduces the range at which whales can hear one another. Extreme noise frequently causes internal bleeding and ruptured eardrums. Activists fear that this explosive mid-frequency sonar not only potentially deafens the animals, but also disorients them to the point of not being able to find a mate—reproduction is rapidly dropping. Deadly oil explorations disrupt whale breeding, nursing, feeding, breathing and migration. I.P. Johnson Director of the Bioacoustics Research Program (BRP) Christopher Clark has developed listening buoys that help ships avoid deadly collisions with endangered whales. These buoys indicate where and when ships need to slow down in order to prevent injury or killing a whale (www.listenforwhales.org/Page.aspx?pid=430). Until recently it was thought that only toothed whales (which includes dolphins), not baleens, use echolocation. New studies find that humpbacks and other baleens may indeed use this form of communication, too. The new term, Megapclicks, refers to the clicking sound and the scientific genus of humpbacks, Megaptera (Royal Society journal *Biology Letters*; www.dolphincommunicationproject.org/index.php/2014-10-21-00-13-26/dolphin-science-factoids/item/94362-do-humpback-whales-echolocate).

60.   (Noah Gordon, *The Last Jew*. New York: Thomas Dunne Books, 1992: 46).

61.   In 2014, an estimated 300 tons a day of marine plastic debris ended up on the shores on India's coast.

62.   Their nostrils have evolved into two blowholes on the top of the humpbacks' heads. These two blowholes function like human lips.

63.   Kinship terms in Judeo-Malayalam differ depending on which paternal/ maternal side is being addressed and on each person's specific age.

64.   Kerala is the home of two separate communities: Malabari Jews (known as the Black Jews, arriving in India as traders in the time of King Solomon) and Paradesi Jews (known as White Jews, from a community of Sephardim, arriving in Cochin after the Edict of Expulsion from Iberia). The two communities are not connected. Ironically, Sephardim in Israel are called Black Jews. Additionally, most Sephardim in Israel are identified as Mizrahi.

65.   There is almost a 100% literacy rate, a women-run economic infrastructure (the Grameen Bank—worthy of capitalist critique), and institutionalized ecological consciousness, to name a few of Kerala's remarkable political successes.

66.   The critical importance of diversity spans every aspect of life—whether cultural (multiple ethnicities co-existing in contrast with ethnocentrism), agricultural (crop diversification in contrast with monocultures), cosmological (multiple non-hierarchical galaxies in contrast with geocentrism). For example, instead of understanding the crucial necessity of difference and multiplicity for survival, let alone a thriving, sustainable world, the history of cotton plantations and slavery has been mired in ethnocentric, racist, monoculturalist ideologies. When agriculture shifted from family-needs to business-demands, diversity was sacrificed. Before the advent of industrialized agriculture farmers produced approximately 80,000 different species of plants. Today they rely on about 150. Beetles have taught farmers and industry unintended lessons. When the boll weevil demolished Alabama's cotton crop (60% loss In yield), farmers were forced to shift from the cotton monoculture and diversify their crops (including peanuts, corn, and potatoes). Unexpectedly (to the farmers), they reaped radically higher profits than from strict cotton production—diversifying their economy allowed it to begin to thrive. The citizens of Enterprise, Alabama erected a monument of gratitude to the boll weevil. Today, both boll weevils and cotton thrive (Evans and Bellamy 151). But, because people are often resistant to learn from our mistakes, cotton is once again a pesticide-saturated crop. Beetles are not only the most diverse population of insects, they also are teaching us how critical diversity is to a balanced ecosystem.

Not only can we learn the importance of diversity from beetles, we can also learn how valuable *unanticipated* symbiosis is. Beetles (the assumed reason for economic disaster) actually often help humans, as seen in the above example of 'biological control.' Our relationship can be a model for how humans relate to all kinds of seemingly unwanted aspects of our lives. These could range from feces to algae to the root causes of drought and famine. One foundation of this relationship is to examine *how* we present the problem. (See footnote 293 on the Green Revolution and monoculture tyranny).

Monocultures dominate not only our food systems, but also our brains (Vandana Shiva, see footnote 232) and our guts. Tragically, there are too many examples of shrinking microbial diversity: "In *The Good Cut: Taking Control of Your Weight, Your Mood, and Your Long-Term Health*, The Stanford University gut microbiome researchers Justin Sonnenburg and Erica Sonnenburg describe how the Western lifestyle methodically diminishes the diversity of the gut microbiome. Easily digestible processed foods starve gut microbes of nutrients, highly sanitized environments deprive them of microbial visitors, antibiotics knock them down and Caesarian sections distort their populations" (Sonia Shah, "Inside Job," review of *The Diet Myth, The Good Gut* and *The Hidden Half of Nature, New York Times Sunday Book Review*. Jan. 3, 2016). See also: Michael Graziano's 2015 documentary film, "Resistance."

In contrast, the conviviality model of the Commons represents a kind of microbiome—the complex web of all microbes in the body—in which dynamic ecosystems of thousands of different bacterial species co-habitate. A handful of terrestrial dirt contains more information than all the other planets combined. Dirt's microbial diversity is vital to the earth's biosphere. Resilience is established with root diversity below the ground and green diversity above. This diversity can be translated into convivial energy consumption. One such translation is the practice of micro-husbandry: the harnessing of the power of microscopic organisms. Harvard biologist Peter Girguis is investigating microbial fuel cells as devices to harness energy from naturally occurring cycles that take place in soils (Common Ground Media's 2009 documentary "Dirt! The Movie"). Rather than dumping and ignoring vital potential forms of energy/ electricity, Girguis compels us to use food scraps from homes and businesses, organic rich waste that comes from many industries, soils, sediments, and waste-water. Although Girguis does not mention the vitality of human excrement, poop is one of our most critical organic rich waste resources. In his *The Humanure Handbook: A Guide to Composting Human Manure*, Joseph Jenkins shares four general ways of dealing with human excrement. These include first: *dispose of it* as a waste material (such as defecating in drinking water supplies), second: *apply it raw to agricultural land*—such as Chinese 'night soil' (creating a vector for disease organisms), third: *slowly compost it over an extended period of time*, and fourth: use *thermophilic* composting (cultivate heat-loving microorganisms in the composting process) (all italics are Jenkins, Joseph Jenkins, *The Humanure Handbook: A Guide to Composting Human Manure*. Grove City: Jenkins Publishing, 1999: 45-6). Thermophilic composting of humanure is key to harnessing energy of microscopic organisms. In contrast, each time we flush a toilet, we not only waste soil nutrients, increasing our dependency on quick fix synthetic chemical fertilizers, we add to the sewage monstrosity growing each day in the US: "Everyday, America must find a place to park 5 billion gallons of human waste, and our country appears increasingly unable to find the space. …A civilization that cannot escape its own fecal matter is a civilization in trouble—unless, of course, the uneasy relationship between man and his effluents can evolve. Perhaps we could bridge the chasm, heal the rift, transform the untouchable into something rich and strange and marketable" (Frederick Kaufman,"Wasteland," ed. Elizabeth Kolbert, *The Best American Science and Nature Writing*. New York: Houghton Mifflin Harcourt, 135-155: 135, 136). The average person's excrement weighs about eight tons—this is eight tons of 'waste' that could produce 20 kg of organic fertilizer (Toscani 37). Scientifically, we know the final product is pathogen-free: no traces of meningitis, hepatitis, malignant protozoa, no tapeworms, no whipworms, no oocysts, no streptococci (Kaufman149). Poop is not the problem! (Ibid., 151); effluvial consequences are. These include: dioxins, furans, coplanar plychlorinated biphenyls, pneumonia germs, encephalitis, arsenic, lead, and mercury. Hospital waste is some of the most dangerous and irreparable. But, a lot of toxins can and are removed from our cities' sludge: "Now that biochemists could scour the particles on the atomic level, the plant could recover ibuprofen acetaminophen, endocrine disrupters, DEET, Prozac, and Chanel No. 5. Even caffeine could be extracted from the mix" (Ibid., 140).

We must collectively and actively question the range of implications of agribusiness, pharmaceutical businesses, or power-grid businesses using such bacteriological processes as thermophilic composting of humanure. In the 1980s the Environmental Protection Agency (EPA) "began a campaign to acclimate U.S. consumers to the commercial use of human waste…superior to cow manure and commercial fertilizers….ton after ton of EPA-subsidized sludge and cake arrived in low-income rural areas, distributed free of charge to cash-strapped farmers" (Ibid.,147). But, poop (ranging from the sewage mafia to official sludge processors) is big business. Investors and companies (including Dow, Honeywell, Monsanto, Siemens, Toshiba) sell products such as Granulite, Milorganite, Soil Rich, and Vital Cycle—all "Wonder Soils"—sold at Agway, Home Depot, Kmart, Target, and Wal-Mart. In 2009, Synagro Technologies, a Residual Management Company, was the largest recycler of biosolids in US—making over $8 billion annually (Ibid.). Organic fertilizer companies sell US waste to "the Arabs. It works in the desert" (Ibid.,146; See also: Sludgewatch email listserv and the National Resource Council's *Biosolids Applied to Land*).

The mainstream reality, like the 'Western lifestyle' mentioned above, is that the majority of our behavior leads to desertification, and desertification kills dirt. Clearly there is no quick fix for impoverished soils—especially when we are dealing with complex ecosystems that have established an equilibrium over millions of years. In addition to wasting precious poop resources, studies show that the majority of chemical fertilizers (nitrogen, phosphorous, and potassium) do not stay in the soil, but are lost to leaching and then pollute groundwater (J. Jenkins 40-41). This is another example of the magic of contradictions: "These materials are pollutants when discarded into the environment. When responsibly recycled, however, they can be beneficial nutrients" (Ibid., 223).

67. Whales gather to socialize and feed. More than any other whale, humpbacks use a wide range of ingenious feeding techniques. Sometimes up to 20 whales share cooperative feeding practices that include herding or disorienting their prey. For the extraordinary cooperative technique called bubble-netting, these feeding groups gather together in their pods (groups of humpbacks), shoot up into the air, together splash back to the water creating a flurry of bubbles that disorient their fish prey as they pack together in their schools, making them easy to gulp in mass. Or, hanging vertically in the water, three or more humpbacks form a circle and release huge lungs full of bubbles—ranging from the size of pebbles to basketballs that form a circle or spiral. The bubbles rise to the surface, and as the fish prey tries to avoid the bubbles, they bunch together—caught in the circle of whales. With wide, open jaws, the humpbacks surge toward the surface of the water and as their massive throats expand, gulp down the fish. Mouths agape for lunge feeding the trapped fish, the water strains through the horsehair-like teeth made of keratin called baleen. Baleen whales (also known as Mysticeti: mi-sti-SEE-tee) have long, tightly grouped hairy fringes that hang from their upper jaw allowing the water to pass through while holding in the plankton (plants) and krill (shrimplike creatures). A remarkable food chain or food web, the world's largest animal (whales) eats the world's smallest animal (krill)—up to a ton a day! Once again, the macro and the micro beautifully co-exist. Like human hair and fingernails, baleen, also known as whalebone, continuously grows.

Another co-operative whale behavior is how they feed their babies, called calves. Nursing whale mothers trade off so other mothers can hunt for food. (Rare among other primates, this form of 'baby-sitting' is also practiced among Barbary Macaques. The entire troop engages in alloparenting—every adult monkey is responsible for all the young ones). Co-nursing was (and still is among various indigenous peoples) a common practice before the advent of the nuclear family and its accompanying privacy and entitlement behaviors. Ironically, "A Cooperative Game for Little Kids!" (for three-to-six year–olds) made by the Peaceable Kingdom company defines cooperation as playing "together against a common obstacle." Rather than exploring cooperation simply as working together toward a common goal, this typical pedagogical approach chooses to distinguish between a winner and a loser. Similarly, 'tolerance' is often defined as 'co-existence.' We choose to define cooperation and co-existence as empathetic practices, mutually benefitting experiences in which no one suffers. Symbiotic relationships demonstrate this capacity for *convivencia*. Nature offers limitless examples: pilot fish swim near migrating humpbacks' faces, eating their parasites while being protected from potential predators; remoras, also called suckerfish, cling to her skin and eat her whale droppings. Other delightful and beautifully illustrated examples can be found in Steve Jenkins' and Robin Page's *How to Clean a Hippopotamus: A Look at Unusual Animal Partnerships*. Boston: Houghton Mifflin, 2010.

68. Their flukes and skin are marked with scars from being tangled in fishing lines, nets, ropes, both small and huge boats, and conflict with other males and orcas.

69. In the late 1800s, Wilson 'Snowflake' Bentley discovered that each snowflake has its own individual crystalline structure—no two are alike.

70. Our title, *Zazu Dreams: Between the Scarab and the Dung Beetle*, comes from this awareness of simultaneous sameness and difference that we hope will inspire transdisciplinary and transgenerational collaborations.

71. Antonio Negri writes that Spinoza's work was about the function of the imagination—leaping across boundaries while making unanticipated connections. (See also: Ivan Illich's *Tools for Conviviality*. New York: Calder & Boyars, 1990). Visible changes might include more communities of Jews, Arabs, and Arab-Jews working and living together. Similarly, the realization of a two-state solution, less friction in Israel, and modern manifestations of conviviality are all reminiscent of Spinoza's 'declaration of cooperation.' For example, *ummah* refers to the co-existence of Jews and Muslims as a community of believers. Under Medieval Islam, over 90% of Jews flourished throughout the Islamic world—a *convivencia*. In 2005, prompted by the efforts of a Jewish Ugandan farmer named J.J. Kei, Jewish, Christian, and Muslim Ugandan coffee farmers formed a fair-trade cooperative to build peace and economic prosperity—a form of modern economic *convivencia*. Their cooperative that they called *Mirembe Kawomera* translates as 'delicious peace' (See also: the documentary film "Delicious Peace Grows: In a Ugandan Coffee Bean," www.deliciouspeacethemovie.com and www.mirembekawomera.com/farmers?farmer=1). This remarkable collaboration in Uganda is a contemporary example of Spain's 14th century *Convivencia* during which the Jews, Moors, and Christians lived and worked together in relative harmony. Other convivial fair trade examples include: *Salam Shalom*, a mix of Jewish and Palestinian olive oil; *Sindyanna of Galilee*, combining olive oil from Galilee Arab and Jewish farmers for use in *Peace Oil* and providing Arab and Jewish women an opportunity to work together to promote land preservation, environmental quality, and women's and labor rights. Additionally, Green Action Israel encourages

socio-ecological change through youth empowerment and community programs. In 2015 at a community health fair, the first of its kind in the United States, the New York-based Foundation for Ethnic Understanding participated in a collaboration between Muslim and Jewish doctors to provide free medical screenings to low-income and uninsured residents of Houston, Texas (www.jpupdates.com/2014/11/16/vision-utopia-muslim-jewish-doctors-join-forces-treat-houston-residents/). Although the Jews and Arabs in these programs may not be Arab Jews, we include these coalitions as examples of pro-activism that achieves sustainable reconciliation. Most recently, Amato's art exhibition at The Palestine Center, Jerusalem Fund Gallery Al-Quds in Washington D.C. tread this both precarious and fertile territory for the purpose of *cante jondo* for *tikkun olam*—a deep song to repair what has been broken between the Islamic and Jewish peoples.

72. Orangutans, Sumatran orangutans (*Pongo abelii*) and the Bornean orangutan (*Pongo pygmaeus*) share almost 97% of the same DNA of humans; they are our closest relatives and are born with the ability to reason and think. Indigenous peoples of Indonesia and Malaysia call them 'orang hutan' which translates as 'person of the forest.' The only apes found in Asia, these largest tree-living mammals in the world are critically endangered. Nestlé, Inc. is one of the corporations responsible for destroying the rainforest—the home of orangutans. Tragically, they are killed because they are seen as 'pests.' In our story, orangutans live in Cochin as refugees. In fact because they are endangered, they now only exist in the wild in Sumatra and Borneo. (See also: www.orangutans-sos.org).

73. Palm oil (*Elaeis guineensis*) comes from the fruit of the oil palm tree native to West Africa. Because it is the cheapest vegetable oil to produce due to its high yield, and because it is unusually versatile (ranging from snack food and shampoo to biofuel—over 50% of *all* consumer goods contain palm oil—including soaps, detergents, deodorants, toothpastes, cosmetics, foods), its global production has doubled in the last 10 years. Palm oil production and harvesting is disastrous for wildlife, ecological relationships, and human rights. Once again, social justice, environmental regulations, and animal protection are inextricably bound.

Since palm oil is now getting bad press among concerned consumers, euphemisms abound. Possible Palm Oil derivatives include:

- Elaeis guineensis
- Etyl palmitate
- Glyceryl
- Hydrogenated palm glycerides
- Octyl palmitate
- Palm fruit oil
- Palm kernel
- Palm kernel oil
- Palm stearine
- Palmate
- Palmitate
- Palmitic acid
- Palmitoyl oxostearamide
- Palmitoyl tetrapeptide-3
- Palmityl alcohol
- Palmolein
- Sodium kernelate
- Sodium laureth sulfate
- Sodium lauryl lactylate/ sulphate
- Sodium lauryl sulfate
- Sodium palm kernelate
- Stearate
- Stearic acid
- Vegetable fat
- Vegetable oil

(www.treehugger.com/sustainable-agriculture/25-sneaky-names-palm-oil.html).

'Palmitate' is a palm oil derivative that can be found in baby's milk formula. Another gruesome Nestlé specialty.

74. Animal habitat loss has historically been the result of human preoccupations: advanced capitalism, rampant consumerism, war, neo-colonialism, humanitarian imperialism, international development, free-market driven infrastructures. Now because of global warming (the results of these convenience culture practices), we are establishing a new language for those who are suffering most directly and immediately. The term 'environmental refugee' is a new demarcation for how climate change is now generating floods of refugees—both animals and people. The United Nation projects that by 2020 more than 50 million people will be environmental refugees—landless, homeless—without food or country. The Climate Institute defines people who flee from environmental crises (droughts, rising sea levels, deforestation, desertification, floods, corporate-induced disasters) as environmental refugees. Disaster-induced displacement is becoming the norm across the entire globe, including the US. The Academy Award nominated film, "Sun Come Up," documents the direct impact of climate change on human beings. "Sun Come Up" follows the transmigration of the Carteret Islanders, a community who for thousands of years have lived on a remote island chain in the South Pacific Ocean, and because of rising sea levels and hyper-salinization of their crop soil, they must relocate or starve and drown. Disaster-induced displacement worldwide is becoming commonplace. The imposed transmigration of the Carteret Islanders, now environmental refugees, parallels that of the Marsh Arabs—those who lived for thousands of years between the Tigris and Euphrates Rivers. (Zazu visits the Marsh Arabs in Chapter Five).

Lester Brown first used the term 'environmental refugee' in 1976. Since then, 'environmental migrant,' 'forced environmental migrant,' 'environmentally motivated migrant,' 'climate refugee,' 'climate change refugee,' 'environmentally displaced person (EDP),' 'disaster refugee,' 'environmental displacee,' 'eco-refugee,' 'ecologically displaced person' and 'environmental-refugee-to-be (ERTB)' have become part of our language. Due to agribusiness tyrannies throughout the global south, for the first time in history, more people live in cities than in rural envionments; 80% of these city-dwellers live in slums. 200,000 farmers in India have committed suicide in the past decade, many by drinking the very pesticide they could no longer afford on their crops (Vandana Shiva cited in "Dirt! The Movie").

We may need to establish a new acronym for those of us who have fled American states because of mandatory vaccination laws—perhaps Parents Refusing Fascism (PRF) is an appropriate designation. In 2015, I took my four year-old son, Zazu, and left the state of California (where he was born) because of the newly instituted bill SB277. Regardless of Constitutional rights (such as the Nuremburg Code or the 2005 UNESCO Universal Declaration on Bioethics and Human Rights) and religious, medical, or philosophical exemption options, the new law states that parents who intend to send their children to public or private school are *required* to vaccinate. We moved to Pennsylvania where a similar bill is currently being debated. Will we have to move again? This may become a refugee crisis for parents and children across the United States.

75. As technology renders our global community more immediately interconnected, the impact we have on one another is becoming more direct and profound. In 2008, Abdurrahman Wahid, the Iraqi-born, former Indonesian president, received the Simon Wiesenthal Center's Medal of Valor. Just as environmental devastation has many faces, so does potential coalitional justice. Former President Wahid offers an example of a convivial, social ecology of empathy. He shares his memory in 1968 when nine Jews were hung in Baghdad's Tahrir Square after being wrongly convicted of spying for Israel. Wahid's friend mourned and wept for the impending loss of Iraq's ancient Jewish community. Wahid recalls: "'This is not only your fate, it is my fate,' He then decided that 'the Islamic people should learn' about the Jews and their faith, and it has been a central part of his mission to this day" (www.jewishvirtuallibrary.org/jsource/anti-semitism/iraqijews.html).

76. Although strictly forbidden in the Bible, medico-magic was liberally practiced among Jews. As seen in some Hispano-Moresque Haggadah's, in Medieval Judaism there was little distinction between medicine and magic.

77. Transnational corporations, not governments, control the flow of economies and people.

78. In 2007, PepsiCo. and Nestlé explored a potential merger. According to the *Wall Street Journal,* no deal was reached because Nestlé hypocritically feared PepsiCo.'s snack-food/ soft-drink market "could weaken its aim of building a more health conscious business" (July 19, 2007, CNNMoney.com). Once again the perverse ironies of Nestlé's Health-Science Division reign (see footnote 21 addressing vivisection).

79. Consumers need to navigate advertisements' misleading messages. Numerous companies that manufacture obviously unhealthy products like Nabisco's Oreos, claim to be 'Certified Vegan'—yet, they too are responsible for the destruction of human and animal habitats where palm oil is harvested. Overt ethically-questionable corporations like Cargill are not the only culprits; many 'health-conscious,' 'sustainable-production' companies are also responsible. Earth Balance, the company that makes a popular plant-based butter spread claims sustainability is its number one production standard. It also claims that its products are 'animal-free.' Yet, Earth Balance's primary ingredient is palm oil (www.onegreenplanet.org/news/earth-balance-vegan-butter-commits-to-sustainable-palm-oil-but-is-it-enough/). Even though Earth Balance states that its products are part of an 'environmentally friendly food chain chain,' it proves to be yet another greenwashing company using 'sustainable' and 'healthy' as manipulative marketing tools. 'Green' business maintains some of the most insidious economic practices today (Jeff Conant, "Going Against the Green," *Yes! Magazine.* Fall 2012: 62-64).

In contrast, there are companies discovering ethical alternatives. While researching biodiesel, the algae company Solazyme came up with a product, called 'algalin' that may be a sustainable alternative to palm oil.

80. Similarly, Nestlé purchases cocoa from cocoa plantations that use child slavery in the Ivory Coast and Mali. In 2005, three former child slaves from Mali filed a suit against Nestlé. They claim they were exposed to dangerous working conditions, forced to carry 100-pound bags of cocoa, forced to work between 12 and 14 hour days—often six days a week without pay and little food. As recently as 2013, the Fair Labor Association found evidence of Nestlé's continued forced child labor (on at least 7% of their farms). Nestlé's own code of conduct condemns such practices yet because they are not held accountable, they continue to hurt children for the big business of 'slave chocolate.' One of the world's largest companies, their earnings exceeded $15 billion in 2015.

81. Palm oil plantations are the leading cause of rainforest destruction in Malaysia and Indonesia; at this rate, 98% of their natural rainforests will be destroyed by 2022. Not only does the $44 billion palm oil industry

maintain gruesome practices towards animals who are considered pests (such as orangutans who are clubbed to death by plantation workers, while others are buried alive during massive clear-cutting that also burns elephants), it displaces thousands of people, involves hundreds as slave-laborers, and on a broader scale, *has the greatest impact on greenhouse gases—the most significant global warming culprit.* In 2009, transportation (planes, cars, trains) globally accounted for 15%, while industry accounted for another 15%. "Deforestation and [industrial] agriculture account for almost a quarter of global emissions" (Barbara Bramble, National Wildlife Federation). Deforestation in Indonesia and Brazil accounted for approximately 70% of greenhouse gases. Because of deforestation, Indonesia is the third largest carbon emitter; it is stripped more than any other land on earth. The burning of both Indonesia's and Brazil's forests can be seen from outer space (see www3.epa.gov/climatechange/ghgemissions/global.html for more details).

"After he saw the devastating environmental effects of colonial plantations [let alone the human atrocities] at Lake Valencia in Venezuela in 1800, Humboldt became the first scientist to talk about harmful human-induced climate change. Deforestation there had made the land barren, water levels of the lake were falling and with the disappearance of brushwood torrential rains had washed away the soils on the surrounding mountain slopes. Humboldt was the first to explain the forest's ability to enrich the atmosphere with moisture and its cooling effect, as well as its importance to water retention and protection against soil erosion. He warned that humans were meddling with the climate and that this could have an unforeseeable impact on 'future generations'" (Andrea Wulf, *The Invention of Nature: The Adventures of ALEXANDER VON HUMBOLDT, The Lost Hero of Science*. London: John Murray, 2015: 5).

American mycologist, author, and advocate of bio-remediation and medicinal mushrooms, Paul Stamets, calls deforestation (that includes genetically modified single-crops) an 'ecological armagedon.' Consumers are as guilty as agribusiness: "Each year 100 million trees are turned into 20 billion mail order catalogues" ("Dirt! The Movie"); (articles.mercola.com/sites/articles/archive/2015/06/13/healthy-soil.aspx#_edn1).

Tropical rainforests and oceans are our two primary global carbon sponges—another manifestation of biological control (homeostasis). Soon, neither will be left to absorb relentless corporate and consumer arrogance.

82. Incidentally, Nestlé has been identified as one of the "10 Global Businesses that Worked With the Nazis" (www.businesspundit.com/10-global-businesses-that-worked-with-the-nazis/). In 1939, Nestlé helped finance a Nazi party in Switzerland. Additionally, it won a lucrative contract to supply all the chocolate demands of the German army during World War II. In 2000, Nestlé paid over $14.5 million into a fund, attempting to deny claims of slave labor by Holocaust survivors (www.whale.to/b/nestle.html). In Mark Achbar, Jennifer Abbott, and Joel Bakan's 2004 documentary film, "The Corporation," Michael Moore urges us to review history: "I believe one of the greatest untold stories of the 20th century is the collusion between corporations, especially in America, and Nazi Germany."

83. "While we're all distracted by Monsanto's GMO corruption of the food supply, Nestlé is taking steps to profit off of the natural world with patents on breast milk and medicinal plants, and the privatization of water, and giving the seed company a run for the title of The Most Evil Corporation in the World" (Daisy Luther, www.theorganicprepper.ca/nestles-wet-dream-they-mark-up-water-53-million-%-06052013). Nestlé has contributed $1 million to the 'Say No to 37' campaign. This campaign fought the California proposal to label GMOs.

84. Sometimes orangutans get so sore from swinging on vines they can barely move. Rubbing this dracaena leaf-paste to help soothe muscle soreness is a common practice among orangutans. Their first-aid kit is also preventative—their wide range of nourishment (at least 300 different foods, including fruit, leaves, flowers, honey, bark, insects and clay) ensures healthy bodies.

85. Indian South Western Ghats Purple Frogs (*Nasikabatrachus sahyadrensis*) were only discovered in 2003. Considered, 'a find of the century' (discoveries such as the purple frog are extremely rare—the last one was in 1926) has an unusual facial structure and behavior (which is why it was only recently seen and recorded by scientists): it has pig-shaped snout and lives underground—coming out only to mate during particularly heavy monsoons. It, too, is endangered because of dams and deforestation that are integral to transnational corporate agendas. The project, EDGE of Existence, run by the Zoological Society of London, attempts to protect rare discoveries—wildlife, such as the tiny bumblebee bat and the golden-rumped elephant shrew that is almost completely unknown.

86. The male orangutan throat sac is used to make a distinct call that can echo through the forest. This 'Long Call' that can be heard over a mile away, is used to tell females where they are or warn other males to stay away from them.

87. A *shofar* is made from a ram's horn; its horn is made of keratin—like the whale's baleen teeth. Sephardi *shofars* often have a carved mouthpiece, while Ashkenazi *shofars* do not.

88. According to Jewish law, freedom doesn't include a slave who will "become free in the next month."

89. Humpbacks had been hunted to the brink of

extinction for economic profit—killing whales to produce lamp oil, soap, candles, cosmetics, buggy whips, umbrellas, corsets, and clothes' stiffener. Whaling almost decimated the humpback whale population—plummeting by 90%. In 1985 there were approximately 7,000 humpbacks. Three years later the International Whaling Commission established laws to protect humpbacks. Their population has regenerated to about 50,000. This prodigious increase demonstrates how people can work together to mend what has been broken, *tikkun olam*. It took almost 40 years of cooperation to help the humpback whale population rebound. All that work could be undone if the National Oceanic and Atmospheric Administration (NOAA) succeeds in removing the humpback whale from the endangered species list. The endangered species list requires the US government to address multiple threats including climate change, ocean acidification, noise pollution, and habitat disruption—none of which are covered under the international whaling ban and Marine Mammal Protection Act (MMPA).

90. In order to communicate to possible predators that they feel threatened, orangutans blow into folded leaves—the first known animal-instruments. The leaf produces deep frequencies that give the impression of great size. Researchers conclude that these 'kiss squeaks' are socially-learned behavior. Other orangutan tools include using big leaves as umbrellas and sticks to dig honey out of beehives.

91. Ecofeminists such as Janet Biehl and Chaia Heller critique the conservation/ preservation language of mainstream environmentalists. They argue how the goal of 'saving' the planet originates from and maintains hierarchical forms of patriarchy. Similarly, Alice Walker chooses a non-mainstream perspective on her role as environmentalist; rather than 'saving the earth,' she states: "activism is my rent for living on the planet" ("Go to the Places That Scare You," *It's Your Body, Yes! Magazine*. Fall 2012, interview with Valerie Schloredt).

92. Conglomerate fishing consortiums over-fish the oceans and seas. All over the world, small fishing villages are losing access to their livelihood. Destructive bottom-trawl fishing gear destroys reef ecosystems and kills marine mammals. Our hunting and fishing habits are so out of balance that scientists are now referring to humans as 'superpredators' (The Thom Hartmann Program, "Are We Humans Destroying Our Own Nest?" www.truth-out.org/opinion/item/33413-are-humans-destroying-our-own-nest). One hopeful change is that the Mid-Atlantic Fishery Management Council has proposed a plan to proactively protect life-giving coral ecosystems.

93. Varanasi is also called the 'City of Death'—a city of ritual endings and beginnings; living and dying that is infinitely interwoven into the cycles of the water, the Great Ganges.

94. Clearly, the ubiquitous presence of human and animal fecal matter throughout the streets of Varanasi is an indication of poor sanitation that potentially leads to infectious disease. But, it is also an indication of India's extraordinary 10,000 year-old history of efficacious use of biomaterials. The properties of cement fail in comparison to dirt. Mud plaster (dung/ manure—an antiseptic to fight infestations and functions as a natural glue) keeps buildings cool in the summer and warm in the winter. On the other hand, cement radiates heat in the summer and locks in cold in the winter. Yet, aside from water, concrete is the most consumed material on Earth (Welland 59), while poop is vilified. We must examine the usefulness of poop—and the fact that not all poop is created equal. This examination includes the toxins that the fecal-maker is exposed to and has consumed/ absorbed and whether he/she/it is a vegetarian or carnivore.

95. Tagore believed in the concept of continuous adaptability to change. He never saw himself as belonging exclusively to India. Nevertheless, in 1950 his poem "Jana Gana Mana" (written in 1911) was adapted as India's National Anthem. Tagore and his family were Pirali Brahmins. Found throughout Bengal, which is split between India and Bangladesh, these Brahmins were stigmatized because their families had converted to Islam. The pejorative term 'Pirali' came from Pir Ali, a Brahmin Hindu who had converted to Islam.

96. Tagore parallels human blood and water moving throughout nature. This metaphor is both beautiful and painful in the Sephardic context of the tyranny of *limpieza de sangre*. As with all racial purity and ethnocentrism, **t**he edict of purity of blood (*limpieza de sangre*) is horrific—it meant that Jews were systematically eradicated from the human global family because of the so-called impurity of our blood.

97. Estuaries are a dynamic stage of contradiction and balance; they demonstrate continual interaction between river and sea, freshwater and salt water (Ibid., 104).

98. (Jourdan Keith, "Your Body is A Body of Water," *Yes! Magazine*. Fall 2012).

In 2000 at the World Water Forum, Nestlé successfully lobbied to stop water from being declared a universal human right. Nestlé maneuvers both clandestine operations and overtly bullies communities and governments around the world into giving up control of their public water sources. It steals the water, resells it to citizens in toxic petroleum plastic bottles (who pay an increase of up to 2,000% more) and gains billions of dollars in profits. It operates in 36 countries and owns dozens of bottled water brands. Globally, as with their baby formula campaigns, Nestlé propagandizes water in plastic bottles as a status symbol. Access to clean, drinkable water is a public civil right, not a privilege for only the wealthy. Multinational corporations such as Nestlé drain local aquifers for profit—ravaging the public watersheds. Water tables are drastically reduced, degrading local wells, when water is pumped at such a high volume (Annie Leonard's collaborative educational project, *The Story of Stuff*). Even in drought-stricken areas such as California, Nestlé refuses to stop its water bottling operations. The Story of Stuff, Courage Campaign, and the Center for Biological Diversity are defending public lands by filing a federal lawsuit against Nestlé's illegal occupation of public lands. Consumers must confront privatization and bottling of a shared resource by choosing tap water instead of Nestlé products (see The Story of Stuff and Courage Campaign emails). Internationally, factories burn 18 million barrels of oil while they consume 41 billion gallons of fresh water every day—just for the production of bottled water sold to the United States.

99. Our bodies consist of two-thirds salt water, the earth consists of two-thirds water (oceans, lakes, and rivers—97% of the earth's water is in the oceans-salt water), and life (the forms that we are familiar with) can only exist in relationship with liquid water. Because climate change is radically changing weather and rainfall patterns, we cannot continue to mistakenly believe water is infinite (see Beatrice Hollyer, *Our World of Water: Children and Water Around the World,* Foreword by Zadie Smith, New York: Oxfam and Henry Holt and Company, 2008). If we persist, "two-thirds of the world's population will have no access to fresh drinking water by 2025." ("The Corporation." 2004. Directed by Mark Achbar, Jennifer Abbott, and Joel Bakan, based on Bakan's book, *THE CORPORATION: The Pathological Pursuit of Profit and Power*).

100. Tagore's famous conversation with Einstein titled, "We Think That We Think Clearly, but That's Only Because We Don't Think Clearly," refuted the faulty assumption characteristic of industrialized humans "that the world we see is all there is" (Maria Popova, "Force of Impact," review of Lisa Randall's *Dark Matter and the Dinosaurs: The Astounding Interconnectedness of the Universe, New York Times Sunday Book Review.* Nov. 29, 2015).

101. Kabbalah scholar, Daniel Matt tells us: "Israel's spiritual task is to unite these halves [the *Shekinah*] through living a holy life" ("Zohar and Kabbalah," The Allen and Joan Bildner Center for the Study of Jewish Life, Lecture, 2013). Like the Zohar (the foundation of Kabbalistic thought), the Islamic-Arabic concept of *adab* and the *yamas* and *niyamas* of Patanjali's *Yoga Sutras* in the Hindu tradition offer both individual and social behavioral ideals for which to strive to live an ethical life. The word yoga translates as 'to yoke,' to unite. Similarly, Matt explains that the Zohar crosses binaries, interweaves our differences. *Beriah, Yetzirah,* and *Assiyah,* the aggregation of the three faculties of thought, speech, and action, form *mazalot* (constellations). "To those without spiritual attainment, The Zohar reads like a collection of allegories and legends that can be interpreted and perceived differently by each individual. But to those with spiritual attainment, i.e. Kabbalists, The Zohar is a practical guide to inner actions that one performs in order to discover deeper, higher states of perception and sensation" (www.kabbalah.info/engkab/mystzohar.htm#.V0sVL9c7Efo).

The *yamas* and *niyamas* parallel Jews' commitment to read the Bible (The Talmud, Midrash) exegetically—through a contemporary context magnifying glass—learning about how to live in the Now. In *The Story of the Jews,* Simon Schama defines Judaism as living in "the here and now." He explores the *Mishnah* as a text which presents "how to be and stay Jewish in a non-Jewish world" through repetition, oral interpretation, and laws of daily life (PBS 2014). Like the *yamas* and the *niyamas,* the synagogue's mosaic floor in the ancient Israeli village of Sepphoris (a major cultural crossroads) depicts life itself as a place of worship. Examples of the affinity among Judaism, Hinduism, and Buddhism are *hakarat hatov* (gratitude), recognizing the good things in our lives that we might take for granted if we don't pause to acknowledge them, *l'dor v'dor* (from one generation to the next), reminds us of our responsibility to lovingly share our values, history, sense of interconnectedness, and ethics/ ideals, *chesed* (lovingkindness)—it is written in the Talmud: "Torah begins with kindness and ends with kindness." Small acts offered in the everyday create a world of love and respect and foster *tikkun olam.* Additionally, the essence of the Torah, according to Hillel, advises that we treat all people as we wish to be treated. The connection between Judaism and Buddhism has been a subject of much interest. *The Jew and the Lotus* is one of the most popular books addressing the relationship between the two and the recognition of God in all things. Once again in the context of Hinduism: Spinoza's theory can be classified as a version of 'qualified Advaita Vedânta,' the beginning of Jewish Modernity, where everything that we ordinarily think of as existing, *does exist* as a *part* of God. Spinoza's pantheism has also played a role in environmental theory. Along with Rachel Carson's 1962 book *Silent Spring,* Spinoza was an important inspiration for the founder of the deep ecology movement, Norwegian philosopher Arne Næss. Einstein, like Spinoza, did not believe in a personal God who cares about what humans do. Instead, Einstein marveled at the majesty and complexity of the universe, which he believed could be attributed only to some higher power. "The most beautiful emotion we can experience is the mysterious," Einstein wrote in 1930.

102. See D.W. Winnicott, *Playing and Reality.* Abingdon, Oxen, UK: Routledge, 1997: 95, Chapter 7, "The Location

of Cultural Experience," begins with this quotation from Tagore (cited in Aviva Zorenberg, *The Murmuring Deep: Reflections on the Biblical Unconscious.* New York: Schocken Books, 2009: 224). Zazu and his friends travel shore to shore, enlivening 'the interplay of edges,' where new things are born" (D.H. Winnicott cited in Ibid.).

103. 20th century nets were constructed much more commercially effective and ethically ineffective. No longer getting shredded along the rocky terrain of the ocean bottom, the new plastic, monofilament nets now drag everything in their scope—irreparably changing ocean habitat. A bottom-dragger is a type of ship that totally depletes fish populations; bottom-dragging nets have begun to destroy the ocean floor—once extraordinarily diverse, thriving ecosystems are becoming deserts (Mark Kurlansky, *World Without Fish.* New York: Workman Publishing, 2011).

104. *People will become more like animals:* As humans continue our trend of over-consumption, wars over basic 'resources' such as water will become increasingly scarce; people will become even more aggressively territorial. *Animals will become more like people:* As humans continue to perform genetic modification experiments on animals in which animal bodies are surrogates for humans, the line between animal and human blurs. Big Pharma routinely uses newborn human babies as subjects for their medical experiments. Because of their unique physiology, neonate humans are too often victims of such 'research.' The entire vaccination industry, along with the collusion of the Center for Disease Control (CDC), World Health Organization (WHO), and The American Academy of Pediatrics (AAP), is an example of such virulent disdain for life of any kind (www.naturalnews.com/037728_Big_Pharma_medical_experiments_infants.html and my article, "Decolonizing Our Wombs: Gender Justice and Petro-PharmaCulture," ed. Hager Ben Driss, *Women, Violence, and Resistance.* Tunis: University of Tunis, Tunisia, 2016). Tragically, the most prevalent socially accepted symbiotic relationships are between the agrichemical lobby and the Food and Drug Administration (FDA), the FDA and Big Pharma, the CDC and the AAP. These corporations are synergistically aligned. "GMO foods and vaccines jam genetic traits across species into each other, in combinations not possible in nature. Because of disturbing data on how GMO foods disrupt beneficial human gut microbes, trigger allergies or cancers, and injure organs, other countries refuse American GMO crops, ban GMO foods, or require GMO labeling. Not us. The government's symbiotic relationship with Big Food ensures that we have no idea what we're eating. No action is taken on a federal level since the FDA dubbed GMO foods 'generally regarded as safe' (GRAS), a designation that requires *no safety testing*" (my italics) (www.fearlessparent.org/americas-new-normal-chronically-ill-kids/). Such gross abuse is the 1992 result of a Monsanto attorney who ordered the FDA to bypass its own regulatory process. Claiming that the industry of genetically-modified crops could increase US exports, then Vice President Dan Quayle led the Council on Competitiveness to "speed up and simplify the process of bringing" GM products to market without "being hampered by unnecessary regulation." Three days following Quayle's reform proposal, the FDA committed to a non-regulation policy: no safety testing (www.responsibletechnology.org/allfraud/an-fda-created-health-crisis-circles-the-globe/; Dan Quayle, "Speech in the Indian Treaty Room of the Old Executive Office Building," May 26, 1992). Perversely, the same year, the United Nations held their first major climate summit. A quarter century later, consumers are becoming more food-safety literate—attempting to implement state-mandated labeling laws. Yet, as uninformed consumers continue to buy GMO products, staggeringly high pay-offs continue to pour into politicians' pockets from corporate interests. See also: Jeremy Seifert's 2013 documentary film, "GMO OMG."

105. Writer Linda Sechrist further explains this "mythological sense of water's endlessness. ...Virtually all water, atmospheric water vapor and soil moisture presently gracing the Earth has been perpetually recycled through billions of years of evaporation, condensation and precipitation" (See also: Meredith Hooper and Chris Coady, *The Drop in My Drink: The Story of Water on Our Planet.* London: Penguin Books, 1998).

106. In 1930, Mohandas Karamchand Gandhi, known as "the great soul," chose to fight for independence from British colonialism using salt. Salt represented both British economic domination and the potential to free the Indian people from their tyranny. Because the British has prohibited local production of salt, even those Indians living in salt-producing regions were economically bound to their oppressor who forced them to buy imported salt. Gandhi chose to defy British law in his infamous Salt March. Walking 240 miles to Dandi on the Arabian Sea, Gandhi led initially 78 followers. 25 days later when he reached the Arabian Sea to symbolically make salt, thousands of people had joined him—including photojournalists from all over the world.

107. India gained independence from Britain in 1947, the year before Israel became its own nation-state.

108. While Jewish communities in Syria, Iraq, Yemen, Egypt, Morocco, and Algeria have almost vanished, Iran still has almost 35,000 Jews—the largest Jewish population of any Muslim country. Jewish communities have lived in Iran for over 1400 years. Judeo-Iranian Languages include Judeo-Persian, Bukhari (Judeo-Tajik), Judeo-Tat (Juhuri), Judeo-Ishfahani, Judeo-Shirazi, Judeo-Median, Judeo-Gurgani, Judeo-Hamandani, Judeo-Yazdi, and Judeo-Kashani. This thriving Jewish presence includes a Jewish representative in the Iranian parliament. Many of the

synagogues in Iran have Hebrew schools. In an attempt to protect Iran's Jewish and Christian minorities, Khomeini decreed a *fatwa*, distinguishing Israeli Jews as different from Iranian Jews, integral to the Islamic republic. However, since the 1979 Islamic revolution, less than half the original Jewish population now lives in Iran.

109.   Whales, sea lions, seabirds, and other ocean creatures may get caught in or choke on ocean trash—plastic trash is only one kind, there are other forms of pollution across the seas (noise—from sound cannons, boats and chemicals—paints, household cleaners, medicines, pesticides, fertilizers, and other hazardous materials). These toxins travel into the gills of the fish; when the whales eat the fish over a period of time, they too are poisoned. This lethal food chain is equally disastrous for human nursing mothers, whose breast milk might become contaminated from toxic fish. Because toxins are stored in fatty tissues, breast milk can be dangerous depending on mother's consumption choices and where she works and lives. Babies, of course, are the most vulnerable victims affected by our toxic soup.

110.   Ghost nets, usually made of non-biodegradable materials, are lost or discarded fishing gear that float through the ocean waters strangling marine life. Ghost nets make up 10% of all marine litter.

111.   The Great Pacific Garbage Patch (GPGP) is a swirling vortex of plastic debris that has gathered where ocean currents meet. It covers at least 270,000 square miles of ocean, twice the size of France. There are five major plastic gyres around the world. Marine plastic pollution expert, Captain Charles Moore stated, "the ocean has turned into a plastic soup."

More than one million single-use non-biodegradable bags are used every 60 seconds. The average US consumer uses between 500-700 plastic bags per year. In the US (let alone the rest of the world), 50 billion petroleum plastic water bottles are discarded each year—most of which are produced by Nestlé and its affiliates. Their production consumes 20 billion barrels of oil and releases 25 million tons of greenhouse gases into the atmosphere. Eight million tons of plastic ends up in the ocean every year; the equivalent of five grocery bags per every foot of coastline across the planet. Ocean plastic can be found everywhere, from deep in the sea to frozen in remote Arctic ice.

According to National Geographic, a staggering 700 species of marine wildlife have reportedly ingested plastic. Plastic will be found in 99% of seabirds by the year 2050. There will be more plastic in our oceans than fish by 2050. Ocean plastic has a life expectancy of thousands of years.

Floating plastic waste serves as transportation for invasive species like barnacles, tubeworms and algae, causing all kinds of ecological havoc. In one example on an island west of the Antarctic Peninsula, ten species of foreign invertebrates were found clinging to plastic trash on the ice.

Eight out of every ten babies in the U.S. have measurable levels of phthalates in their bodies. Phthalates are used as plasticizers in a number of product categories. The U.S. Centers for Disease Control and Prevention did a study that found 93% of people had detectable levels of Bisphenol A (BPA) in their urine. BPA is used in polycarbonate bottles and the linings of food and beverage cans.

299 million tons of plastics were produced in 2013, a 4% increase from 2012.

As mentioned earlier, breastfeeding saves an annual $13 billion. Using glass instead of plastic would have similar economic benefits—saving US taxpayers billions of dollars. An example of refusal to participate in single-use plastic pollution is the $70,000 saved by Le Petit Vincent, the private resort island in the Caribbean.

112.   Jellyfish are considered the cockroaches of the ocean—not just surviving global warming, but thriving because warm waters enable further jellyfish reproduction. As coral reefs die, sea slugs (predators of jellyfish) lose their habitat and die, resulting in a mass proliferation of jellyfish. Jellyfish are the canaries in the coalmine—they are the harbingers of global disaster. Additionally, as global warming escalates jellyfish will compete with whales for plankton food sources. The jellyfish 'epidemic' has multiple origins, including increased salinization, acidification, and the result of industrial agriculture's mobile nitrogen fertilizer pumped into soil hundreds of miles away from coastlines. The excess nitrogen flows into streams and eventually ends up in ocean waters; it feeds algae blooms that suffocate all marine-life—all except for jellyfish. While jellyfish thrive, the oceans will increasingly consist of dead-zones that spread like plagues. As above, so below: Mobile nitrogen fertilizer is also responsible for climate change. When nitrogen combines with oxygen, it creates nitrous oxide that floats into the atmosphere—contributing to the greenhouse effect.

113.   Many fisherman fear giant jellyfish invasions. In 2007, the coast of the Fukui Prefecture of Japan was inundated with swarms of Nomura jellyfish that clogged fishing nets. Their toxic stings poisoned potential catches, costing the local fishing industry billions of yen.

114.   Cousteau's entire life was focused on education about sea life. He became its most creative and productive defender, inventing a vast array of exploration equipment. The Cousteau Society is committed to protecting the underwater world from pollution and corporate tyrannies (www.cousteau.org www.cousteaukids.org).

115.   Many marine biologists are emphatic in their declaration that the worst plastic pollution, microplastic, is spread throughout the ocean's water in fragments smaller

than a grain of rice (www.io9.com/5911969/lies-youve-been-told-about-the-pacific-garbage-patch). Microbeads have replaced various types of sand such as fine silica (a non-toxic ingredient, unlike its microbead replacement), and are most commonly found in whitening toothpastes and facial scrubs. These tiny plastic particles absorb motor oil, pesticides, flame-retardants, and other toxic agents. These carcinogens migrate through the food chain—poisoning fish and then humans. In 2015, The Story of Stuff Project successfully banned plastic microbeads, and won their lawsuit against Johnson & Johnson in California. Their success impacts global markets (*The Microbeads Movie*, the newest educational project from *The Story of Stuff*: www.storyofstuff.org/blog/microbeads-movie-press-release/).

116. Ibn Sina (980-1037), also known as Avicenna or the Hebrew version Aven Sina, was the world-renowned physician called the 'Prince of Physicians.' Historically identified as Muslim-Arab, Ibn Sina was in fact Persian-Jewish (his mother was Jewish). Because the Shah, the sultan of Bukhara, supported the arts and sciences, ibn Sina was appointed court physician. The sultan's protection of the Jewish community of Shiraz was paradoxical—as with all government 'protection.' Ibn Sina was first and foremost a *hakim*, a healer who did not treat disease; rather, he treated people who had diseases. His philosophy was rooted in harmony and resonance. A forerunner of preventative medicine, ibn Sina, advocated good sleep habits, exercise, and even music to maintain healthy bodies. He also focused on pre- and post-natal medical care for mothers and babies. Through a combination of philosophy and the natural sciences, he intended to heal the 'disease of ignorance.' Maimonides studied ibn Sina's medical theories and Aristotelian philosophies. Ibn Sina was a pioneer also in psychology—exploring the connections between emotional and physical states. Recognizing how our environments directly impact our well-being, he may have been the first scientist/ physician to understand the contagious nature of certain diseases and how disease may spread through contaminated water and soil. Although he did not know about 'germs' (the microscope had yet to be invented), Ibn Sina understood how people could catch measles, smallpox, and tuberculosis from other people and he introduced quarantine as a means of containing infectious diseases. If Western societies had effectively learned from ibn Sina 800 years ago, possibly better sanitation and nutrition would have developed, instead of pharmaceutical tyranny and Big-Brother vaccination giants. Furthermore, he strongly disagreed with medical testing on animals: "The experimentation must be done with the human body, for testing a drug on a lion or a horse might not prove anything about its effect on man" (Ibn Sina's Rules of Clinical Trials, cited in David W. Tschanz, "The Islamic Roots of Modern Pharmacy," *Saudi Aramco World*. May, June 2016: 21).

117. Because of their commitment as guardians of their communities, Ghashghai women are known as maternal warriors. Ghashghai (also spelled Qashqai, Qeshqayı, Ghashghai, Ghashghay, Gashgai, Gashgay, Kashkai, Qashqay, Qashqa'i) pastoral nomads primarily live near Shiraz, Iran—migrating with their flocks, about seven million head, twice a year between the Persian Gulf and the Zagros mountains. Their annual migration is the largest of any Persian tribe. The majority of Ghasghai tribe are Shi'ite Muslims and speak a Turkish dialect.

118. Khalil Gibran wrote: "There must be something sacred in salt. It is in our tears and in the ocean."

Salt offers a vivid model of Tagore's philosophical insight that the same stream that flows through your veins, flows through the universe in rhythmic measure. Blood, sweat, and tears all contain salt; both the skin and the eyes are protected from infectious germs by the antibacterial effect of salt. Salt has astonishing detoxification healing powers--from within our own bodies, as well as salt from the earth. Salt water (manufactured as saline solution) has the same fluid quality as blood plasma.

Various types of salts in underground caves emit electromagnetic charges that can be healing; these caves are popular therapeutic environments. This air is rich in natural salt microns and ions, which, in addition to soothing irritated skin and restoring ionic balance within the body, have been found to alleviate asthma, allergies, and breathing problems. Speleotherapy is the medical use of salt that focuses on the treatment of respiratory diseases. Halotherapy (Salt Therapy) uses the anti-bacterial, anti-inflammatory, anti-viral, and anti-fungal properties of salt for the following health conditions:

- Asthma
- Allergies
- Bronchitis
- Sinusitis
- Cystic Fibrosis
- Skin Conditions such as Eczema and Psoriasis, Acne
- Chronic Respiratory Illnesses
- Cardiovascular Illnesses
- Thyroid disorders
- Cold and Flu prevention or reduction in severity
- Weakened Immune System

Examples of salt's healing properties abound across history and geography. For instance, the Khewre Salt Mine in Punjab is a medical centre attached to the salt mine known for therapeutic healing for those with respiratory problems (en.wikipedia.org/wiki/Khewra_Salt_Mine#Mosque).

Both ibn Sina and Maimonides declared the importance of salt in daily health.

In the fourteenth century an epidemic of the bubonic plague swept through Europe killing 75 million people; 50% of Europe's population was decimated. The residents of a small French fishing village were untouched—immune to the contaminating disease because of mountains of salt stock-piled for preserving anchovies, their primary economy. Salt has repeatedly proven to be a protective/immune-enhancing antibacterial.

Additionally, if someone is 'salted,' they are said to have developed resistance to a disease by surviving it. The argument for "salted' natural immunity (through vaginal births, breastfeeding, eating non-GMO unprocessed, chemically contaminated food, for example) is key to our investigation of vaccinosis (illness produced in an individual after receiving a vaccine) and the exponentially increasing pharmaceutical industry's annual income. Since 1986 pharmaceutical company revenues have risen over 300%. Merck, Connaught Laboratories, and Wyeth-Lederle, producers of mandated vaccines, grotesquely profit from their officially sanctioned infringement of freedom. Manufacturers' profits exceeded $1 billion in 1996, an increase from $500 million in 1990. Today, Big Pharma makes over $711 billion annual net profit, an increase from $33 billion a little over a decade earlier. The global vaccine market total revenue reached $10 billion in 2005; 10 years later it exceeded $41 billion.

119. Unlike 99% of other species, brine shrimp thrive in hyper-salinated water. Because they eat fish poop, they are ideal symbiotic animals. Brine shrimp's waste-consumption behavior parallels jellyfish and algae-eating sea slugs and mammal poop-eating dung beetles: brine shrimp clean coral reefs by eating dead sea animals. Like pink algae that live in ice and create what is called, watermelon snow, the pink color pigmentation helps brine shrimp microbes survive sun, salt, and oxidation damage. These halophiles (salt-lovers) are organisms used as models to explore adaptation to extreme environments and toxic chemical levels. Such microbes have the ability to stay alive during total desiccation due to high UV exposure and high salt content. Part of their life cycle includes totally drying up and living inside salt crystals. Scientists are researching these microorganisms' survival strategies—potentially for detoxifying areas contaminated with mercury (one toxic example), and for biofuel production.

120. An element of Bedouin philosophy includes the Spirit in every living thing—every living thing emits its own electromagnetic field and interacts with other electromagnetic fields. Not necessarily integral to Bedouin thought, but scientifically proven, bioelectric magnetics are radically disturbed by radiowave frequencies.

121. In astronomy, a halo is a sphere of hot gas combined with old stars that surround a spiral galaxy.

122. Phytoplankton (the beginning of the sea's food chain) are made up of diatoms (*Bacillariophyceae*). Like millions of microscopic snowflakes, they drift through the ocean and provide the single most important food source for marine life—ranging from tiny microanimals (like brine shrimp) to the largest mammal in the world—the blue whale—their food source, krill, feeds on diatoms, the 'grass of the sea'). Through photosynthesis, diatoms provide one third of the world's oxygen supply.

123. The Ghashghai women are known for their geometric-patterned Kelim carpets made from sheep wool, goat, and horsehair.

124. Gazelles are symbols of the beloved in both Hebraic and Arabic love-poetry. The traveler/ trickster of 11th century Al-Andalus, Yahya ibn Hakam Al-Ghazal, was known as 'the Gazelle.' Like Joha, he was a knowing fool who practiced his satire in royal courts and "knew how to cross [through] all doors" (Translated from Ibn Dihya who wrote about *Al-Majus,* from which English gets the word magician) (Jesús Cano and Louis Werner, Art by Belén Esturla, "Al-Ghazal: From Constantinople to the Land of the Vikings," *Saudi Aramco World*. July/Aug. 2015). In Urdu, a form of Hindustani written in Persian script, *ghazal* means poem. The gazelle (*ghazaal* in Arabic and Persian) is an integral part of *ghazal* symbolism—the gazelle's temperament overflows with contradictions. Because it is elusive, it foils its beloved and at the same time represents a human soul's mystical quest for union with God (Mehr Afshan Farooqi, www.dawn.com/news/1190816/column-ghazal-ghazaal-and-gazelle).

The Saudi Gazelle from the Arabian peninsula is now an extinct species. Our story observes God as the interconnectedness between humans and nature.

125. *Gazella subgutturosa* means 'full below the throat.' The name refers to the male gazelle's enlarged neck and throat during mating season. Many animal species that have this ability to swell their necks to attract mates are becoming endangered. For example, the Great Prairie Chicken's (*Tympanuchus cupido*) with its Goitered-Gazelle-like inflatable neck sac exhibits courtship dances (they strut, shuffle, and make booming noises). These rituals inspired the many dances of the Great Plains Native Americans. The Great Prairie Chicken is threatened with extinction. Since 1492, colonialism (and now industrial agriculture) has condemned their habitat for developed farmland (Sarah Lovett, *Extremely Weird Birds Book*. Sante Fe: John Muir Publications, 1992: 26). Another model of such behavior is the male hooded-seal who attempts to attract a female mate and marks his territory "by inflating a sac of looke skin that hangs from its left nostril, blowing it up like a big red balloon. …They make a pinging sound by shaking their inflated nasal sac back and forth" (Steve Jenkins, *Living Color*. Boston: Houghton Mifflin Company, 2007).

126. Following Tanzania's Serengeti National Park, this

diverse ecosystem offers a complete ecological pyramid. The Khar Turan National Wildlife Refuge is home to the critically endangered Asiatic cheetah, known in Iran as *yuz*. Iran is the final country where the *yuz* still survives—where they had once lived, they are now extinct. The Iran-Iraq war of the 1980s marked extensive slaughter of the *yuz*'s primary food source—the gazelle. Due to gradual governmental protection, both the gazelle and cheetah population are gradually recovering (www.wildlifeextra.com/go/news/cheetah-iran.html#cr). Their decline and restoration are inextricably linked. We are drawing a parallel between the near extinction of the *yuz*/ Asiatic cheetah and the psychological, historical, and physical extinction of the Asiatic (Oriental, Mizrahi, Sephardic) Jew.

127. Increasing breastfeeding can save taxpayers up to $13 billion annually. Breastfeeding leads to better health for baby, fewer (if any) doctor's visits, which means less days off work, while avoiding long-term conditions for both baby and mother—such as diabetes, respiratory illnesses, and breast cancer. These are benefits that save money for individual families, employers, and even for the federal government.

128. Traditional Jewish superstitious practices with amulets include: kissing the mezuzah, wearing the *hamsa* and evil eye, painting five dots above a door, eating garlic, hanging a red ribbon above a baby's bed, depicting spirals, and knocking on wood. Some of the 'perils of motherhood' in ancient Mesopotamia were addressed through medio-magical means. "Jewish amulets usually name the mother of the person to be protected unlike Jewish legal documents which usually name the father" (Rebecca Lesses, "Amulets to Protect Mother and Child against Demons," *Jewish Museum of Berlin Journal*. Nr. 13, 2015: 23).

129. In many cultures salt is used to drive away evil spirits. For example, in Japan before beginning his wrestling match each Sumo opponent throws salt into the ring. Throughout the Middle East, salt was used to ceremonially seal an agreement. The ancient Hebrews made a covenant of salt with God—sprinkling their offerings as a demonstration of their trust in God. In Judaism, salt seals a bargain, while in both Judaism and Islam, practitioners bless bread by dipping it in salt. In Judaism and Islam, and Mahayana Buddhism, salt is believed to ward off evil spirits. When returning home from a funeral, Mahayana Buddhist's throw a pinch of salt over the left shoulder to prevent evil spirits from entering their house. In Shinto, salt is used for to ritual purification and small piles of salt are placed in dishes by the entrance to ward off evil patrons (Robert Camara, "Can you pass the salt, please?", www.japanesereligions.blogspot.com/2009/03/can-you-pass-salt-please.html).

130. Using powder, rock, and compact layers of salt along with natural tree resins and gums, Emitaz Designing Group built the Gaudiesque Salt Restaurant in Shiraz, Iran in 2011. The local Marharloo salt lake and the beauty of natural salt mines inspired the architects who used locally sourced, affordable salt. The salt tables are supported by legs made from recycled aluminum cans gathered from nearby restaurants. (Recycling was also integral to Antonio Gaudi's creative architectural process—although rather than cans, he incorporated discarded ceramic shards—in our tale, reminiscent of the broken vessel of *tikkun olam*). Melting aluminum requires lower temperatures than other metals, so the energy consumption during the process of casting is much less, thereby taking another step to reduce carbon footprint. Again, we must question whether recycling trends may increase consumption because they alleviate conscious-consumer guilt.

Salt is one of the strongest and safest natural elements. When salt isn't refined and ground down, it is an extremely hard substance and has a natural gum covering; it is a perfect energy efficient building material. The chemical reaction between salt and natural gums creates a strong building material that does not dissolve.

Salt is a natural air purifier that removes irritants and bacterial or fungal pathogens. It disinfects allergens like pollen and smoke from the air. By diffusing Cl_2 and oxygen ions, natural salt filters and purifies the urban polluted air. Salt can filter kitchen odors and carcinogenic oven air-born residue out of the air (www.ecofriend.com/the-eco-friendly-iranian-salt-restaurant.html).

131. Anti-infectious and anti-microbial agents can be extracted from beetles' bodies (see the work of entomologist, Roland Lupoli: (www.christophelepetit.com/entomed/monsite/BUGS/source/08.htm).

132. The most ancient stone used for personal adornment, amber also has many medicinal properties. It is used for general cell regeneration, detoxification, and overall health protection/ illness prevention. It potentially heals the central nervous system, including brain trauma and memory loss, and protects against radiation. It is helpful in ailments of the endocrine system, spleen, and heart. Wearing amber can help ease short-term problems such as sore throat, earache, headache, and digestive troubles; and, long-term ones such as asthma, arthritis, and rheumatism. Holding a piece of amber helps overcome heat exhaustion.

133. "Throughout its long history of denial, waste has lurked behind countless appellations: egesta, dejecta, sharn, stale, skite, dynga, ordure, oriental sulfur, occidental sulfur, and carbon humanum, to name but a few. Witches' potions called for *eiths*; alchemists' elixirs required *botryon, aureum, oletum,* or *zibethum*. ...What could be more magical, more *godlike,* than the metamorphosis of that which we abhor and expel into that which we desire, embrace, and

ingest?" (Kaufman 140, 144). The sun's ultra-violet radiation releases bacterial gases from fecal matter, transforming potentially noxious material into exactly the opposite. Dung becomes an antiseptic therapy. Folk remedies for tuberculosis, dysentery, deafness, or sore beasts came from badger dung, crocodile dung, the droppings of milk-fed lambs, and human feces. The Chinese have been using composted waste for thousands of years for medicine, agriculture, and construction (Oliviero Toscani, *The Encyclopedia of Poo: Cacas*, Cologne: Taschen, 2000: 46). (See also: footnotes 66 and 325 for Joseph Jenkins' critique of Chinese 'night soil'). Bedouins of Qatar use dried camel dung to wipe babies' butts; rural Indians and Pakistanis coat their floors with dung, inviting its antiseptic properties to heal or prevent athlete's foot and bacterial infections (Ibid., 20). Homes of dried dung have been built for thousands of years. Afghans use camel dung mixed with mud and straw to build walls, Maasai Kenyans build their huts out of ash and cow dung. It is easy to form and adhere. The houses stay cool in the heat and warm in the cold weather, and supposedly they have a pleasant smell. Japanese dry it at high temperatures and use it in road construction (Ibid., 74). The Creative Paper Company in Tasmania makes paper out of wombat scat. It is marketed as having a 'nice organic smell' (Michael Hearst, *Unusual Creatures: A Mostly Accurate Account of Some of Earth's Strangest Animals*. San Francisco: Chronicle Books, 2012: 98).

134. When it comes to poop, we have many models of conviviality from which to learn. The luwak, a tropical weasel who lives in Indonesia, eats coffee berries, and once excreted, people gather the poop, separate it, and roast it. This highly specialized fermenting process makes this coffee the most expensive in the world: US $660 per kg (Ibid., 42).

135. This phrase comes from Bill Logan (author of *Dirt: The Ecstatic Skin of the Earth*) and Wangari Maathai (Kenyan environmental and political activist; the first African woman to receive the Nobel Peace Prize) of the Greenbelt Movement and The Wangari Maathai Institute for Peace & Environmental Studies (cited in "Dirt! The Movie").

136. In Jewish, Muslim, and Christian traditions God blew breath/*ruach* or *ruh* into dirt to create humans. In Hebrew, *Adam* means dirt or clay.

137. Dr. Vandana Shiva, physicist, ecologist, seed activist, and founder of Navdanya, a biodiversity farm connected with Earth University in India, works with the web of life in relation to seeds and soil as dynamic and living things (cited in "Dirt!"; see also: "Everything I need to know I learned in the forest," *Yes! Magazine*. Winter 2013: 47-50). See footnotes 66, 74, 232, 270. Her Earth Democracy project teaches the significance of human responsibility.

138. Isfahan is an international heritage site protected by UNESCO. The Jewish population was supported during Shah Abba's 'tolerant rule.'

139. Conspire means to breathe together. We seek the possibility of breathing together as a form of *convivencia*. Adrienne Rich reminds us: "The breath is also *Ruach,* the spirit, the human connection to the universe" (Adrienne Rich, *What is Found There: Notebooks on Poetry and Politics,* New York: W.W. Norton & Company, 1993: 82). Breath also produces song, the whales' song, the voice of the shofar.

140. Quantum entanglement, one theory to come out of quantum mechanics and string theory, proposes that two entangled quarks (the building blocks of matter) give rise to a wormhole that connects the pair. This entangled pair occupies multiple states—simultaneous opposites (for example, spinning clockwise and counterclockwise). "According to Einstein's laws, gravity "acts to 'bend' and shape space-time. …Gravity itself may be a consequence of entanglement—pairs of particles strung together by tunneling wormholes" (Jennifer Chu, review of Julian Sonner's research published in the journal *Physical Review Letters* (senior postdoc in MIT's Laboratory for Nuclear Science and Center for Theoretical Physics). *MIT Technology Review*. Vol. 117, No. 2, 2014).

141. Einstein's *Gedanken* experiments, thought-experiments, remind us that creativity evolves from imagination. At the age of 16, Einstein attended a school based on the educational philosophy of Johann Heinrich Pestalozzi who encouraged students to *visualize* concepts. "That ability to visualize the unseen has always been the key to creative genius" (Walter Isaaacson, CEO of Aspen Institute, "The Light-Beam Rider," *New York Times*. Sunday, Oct. 30, 2015).

142. This statement is derived from Einstein's famous: "Imagination is more important than knowledge."

143. Algerian-born Pierre Rabhi is the founder of agroecology, the field of organic biodynamic agriculture that combines scientific knowledge with traditional wisdom (cited in "Dirt!"). His invention of the concept *oasis en tous lieux* (oasis in any place) is becoming increasingly critical as a form of resistance not only to the desertification of our planet, but the desertification of our minds.

144. In Muslim villages surrounding Esfahan (or Isfahan), a distinctive Jewish dialect of Farsi is spoken. Judeo-Ishfahani, like Judeo-Shirazi, is spoken in their respective cities.

145. "When the Jews emigrated from Jerusalem, fleeing from Nebuchadnezzar, they carried with them a sample of the water and soil of Jerusalem. They did not settle down anywhere or in any city without examining the water and the soil of each place. This they did all along until they reached the city of Isfahan. There they rested, examined the water and soil and found that both resembled Jerusalem. Upon they settled there, cultivated

the soil, raised children and grandchildren, and today the name of this settlement is Yahudia" ("Sacred Precincts: The Religious Architecture of Non-Muslim Communities Across the Islamic World, Gharipour Mohammad," BRILL. Nov 14, 2014: 179).

146. *Dar-Al-Yahud* is also known as the *mellah*.

147. Daniel's coffin is buried in a river. In order to bring rain in times of drought, his coffin is brought out for veneration.

148. Ummah can refer to the co-existence of Jews and Muslims as an integrated community. David Shasha, scholar of Sephardic cultural erasure and director of The Center for Sephardic Heritage in New York, like his many colleagues, such as Maria Rosa Menocal, insist upon the positive historicity of convivial relationships between Jews and Muslims in Medieval Islam. See also: Meir Mazuz's article www.jpost.com/Experts/Rabbi-Meir-Mazuz-and-the-battle-for-Orthodox-Judaism-341771.

In contrast, perhaps a result of internalized anti-Semitism and internalized anti-Sephardi racism, there are Sephardim who deny *convivencia* in Muslim Spain (groups.google.com/forum/#%21topic/davidshasha/_nrcdGWekO0Shasha) argues that this denial is indicative of the relationship between Ashkenazi anti-Sephardi sentiment and Totalitarianism. See also Shasha's groups.www.google.com/forum/#!topic/davidshasha/zwaRDoJ0IRo and David Ramirez's follow-up www.groups.google.com/forum/#!topic/davidshasha/g1NBZuT1i-M.

149. The Roman catacombs were exempt from relegating class status: rich and poor, old and young were buried together.

150. *Qanats* (ghan-AHTS) are domestic and agricultural irrigation technologies that was developed over two thousand years ago. Today, Iran relies on 50,000 *qanats*. Unlike massive modern electrical-powered water pumps, pipelines, and dams that deplete stores of underground water and dry out oases, the ingenious, practical, and sustainable *qanat*-method of harnessing limited water supplies is perfectly adapted to its arid environment. The use of *qanats* included farmers rationing and conserving their water consumption. As for a similar environmentally-conscious infrastructure, non-polluting architecture (without air-conditioning units) is used to mitigate the desert heat. Buildings include tall wind towers with angles that catch the air currents and circulate them inside.

151. The extensive water distribution systems of *qanats* are still in use throughout the Middle East. For example, in the city of Turpan, which lies below sea level, *qanats* channel water from the foothills of the Tien Mountains to Shan to flood the fields. *Qanats* have different names depending on the region: *karez* in Persia, *falaj* in Oman and the United Arab Emerites, *foggara* in North Africa, *khettara* in Morocco (Robert W. Lebling, "The Water Below," *Saudi Aramco World*. Sept./Oct. 2014: 39).

152. The *mushhushshu* is a Neo-Assyrian (Iraqi) dragon mosaic found at the Gate of Ishtar in Babylon.

153. Carl Jung wrote of the dragon as part serpent and part bird, the elements of earth and air—opposites in balance, a combination of both fear and attraction.

154. Biblical pāṭṭǝ are traditional Sephardic rhyming songs. Rhyming songs were adaptations of biblical stories, particularly from the midrash (Gamliel 509). Similarly, African-American slaves communicated among themselves in riddles that the white slave owners could not understand.

155. Surrounded by desert, the ecoregion of the Tigris-Euphrates included shallow lakes, swamps, and vast marshes. An extraordinarily rich agricultural area, this part of the Fertile Crescent was once known as the 'Cradle of Civilization.' Until recently, the wetlands of Iraq had almost completely dried out due to human interference. The drastic decline in the Tigris-Euphrates groundwater followed thousands of years of monoculture overproduction agribusiness, the Iran-Iraq War of the 1980s, mass-development of canals, dykes and dams that routed the rivers' water around the marshes (instead of allowing it to slowly flow through the marshland), and multiple nations fighting over ownership of water rights. Many nations and mega-corporations seem to follow the same path of attempting to control water as if they own it. The United States Forest Service, Department of Agriculture (USFS) has allowed Nestlé to illegally pump 25 million gallons a year using a permit that expired over 28 years ago. When companies like Nestlé bottle municipal tap water (bought for pennies on the dollar) and resell it back to the local citizens, they are making grotesque profit. Turkey's Great Anatolia Project (G.A.P.) to some degree parallels Nestlé's global attempts to privatize water, i.e., stealing water. In the illegal case of California's San Bernardino Valley 2014-16, Nestlé illegally takes the water, then sells it back in plastic bottles at vertiginous prices to those who own the land from which the water originated. They profit from a 53,908,255% mark up. See Urs Schnells' 2012 documentary film, "Bottled Life: Nestlé's Business with Water," Sam Bozzo's 2008,"Blue Gold: World Water Wars," Stephanie Soechtig and Jason Lindsey's 2009, "Tapped." Turkey's actions are legal, while Nestlé's are illegal. Both are laden with human and environmental rights' violations. Nestlé's global CEO denies that water is a human right—insisting instead that water is a corporate product. Similarly, Turkey is entrenched in a power play of water domination. G.A.P.'s irrigation strategies that dam the Tigris-Euphrates are benefiting Turkish residents, while reducing Syrians'

access by 40% and Iraqis' access by 90%. Iraq has suffered significant water shortage and reduced crop yields because of the drought. Their water infrastructure, like in Flint, Michigan and much of the US, must also recover from years of neglect and conflict. The result of these water battles is deepening violent conflicts over water rights, *not water shortage*—there is plenty of water for all. As with our international epidemic of malnutrition—there is more than enough food in the world, the problem is not quantity, bur rather distribution, infrastructure, and quality.

The Sustainable Water Infrastructure Investment Act (currently debated in the US Congress) would address the debacle of corrosive lead pipes that run through many parts of this country. This Act offers amazing potential to bolster the US economy: every $1 billion invested in water infrastructure generates up to $3.46 billion of total national output and $82.4 million in state and local tax revenue, while supporting 28,500 jobs. There are many 'solutions' that would benefit both the economy and the environment. Similarly, Turkey has undertaken a plan known as the 'Peace Pipeline.' Unfortunately the plan remains only a plan (Peter Swanson, *Water: The Drop of Life,* Public Television Series, Foreword by Mikhail Gorbachev, Woodstock, ON: Northwood Press, 2001: 120-1).

Irrigation waters that accumulated salts in the soil also contributed to the gradual degradation of the once-fertile valley. Not only did desertification and soil salination obliterate numerous species of fish, amphibians, reptiles, migrating birds, and wild animals, but the Marsh Arabs, known as the Ma'dan people, have suffered tremendous losses.

156. Sand grains are both porous and permeable. There are spaces between sand grains and connections between those spaces. Water, air, bacteria, oil, and gas live in between grains of sand. "The world's largest accumulations of oil and gas are found in the spaces between sand grains" (Welland 264). Like Spinoza as a lens-maker for the microscope and telescope, Rachel Carson was in awe of the simultaneity of macrocosms and microcosms—worlds literally between grains of sand: "… our human senses cannot grasp its scale, a world in which the micro-droplet of water separating one grain of sand from another is like a vast, dark sea" (Ibid., 60).

The history of the Tigris-Euphrates Valley river system is one of multiple in-between worlds, including freshwater habitats in which salt-tolerant vegetation was plentiful. *Salicornia bigelovii* is one such example—every part of this annual salt-marsh leafless succulent is usable (Edward P. Glenn, J. Jed Brown and James W. O'Leary, "Irrigating Crops with Seawater," *Scientific American.* 1998: 6).

The Middle East is a perfect environment for adaptable plant habitats: coastal deserts and inland salt deserts. These 'green areas' could be used for seawater agriculture (or agriculture using irrigation from salty underground aquifers) to grow a variety of salt tolerant crops for food or animal forage. Another in-between agricultural zone is the plankton-rich waters that fertilize adjacent desert soils. The wandering, nomadic nature of plankton (*planktos from the Greek*) requires adaptability.

157. Babylon's Ishtar Gate, on which bulls and dragons are depicted, was built between 604 and 562 BCE.

158. Three times during the 6th century BCE, Nebuchadnezzar forced almost fifty thousand Jews from Jerusalem into captivity in Babylon.

159. Schools of fish illustrate the crucial importance of working collaboratively. In order to protect themselves from their predators, they swim together in a tight group making eating any one of them much more difficult than if they were on their own. Collectively, they increase their chances of living.

The Trembling Giant (also called Pando), an 80,000 year-old clonal colony of Quaking Aspen trees in Fishlake National Forest in Utah, is tied together by a single root system. As a unified being, the individual trunks, branches and leaves of these genetically identical trees weigh about 6,615 tons--the heaviest known organism on earth.

160. "It takes a whole village to raise a child" is an Igbo and Yoruba (Nigeria) proverb. In 2016, presidential candidate Hillary Rodham Clinton published *It Takes a Village: And Other Lessons Children Teach Us* (New York: Simon & Schuster, 1996).

161. "There is no such thing as society. There are individual men and women and there are families." Margaret Thatcher's infamous declaration belies our integrity as a global interdependent whole. In contrast with Thatcher's tendentious individualism, in which the public as a collective body is stripped of any relational context, Tibetan Shambhala Buddhism asserts that in order to experience the depths of one's spiritual potentials, one cannot go on a journey alone; one must practice within a community (even if that community consists of simply one other person). In 1981 Toni Morrison declared, "We don't need any more writers as solitary heroes. We need a heroic writers' movement: assertive, militant, pugnacious." Biologist Scott Gilbert asserts the criticality of teamwork, the radical impact of symbiotic relationships.

162. In the eighth century, Zubayda, the niece of Queen Khayzuran (Arabic for 'reed'—reminiscent of adaptability), took power over the region now know as Baghdad, and beyond—an empire that extended from Morocco to Persia. Known for her tremendous financial support for the greatest public-works of the era, Zubayda spent millions of *dinars* (the annual cost of living for the average family in Baghdad was 240 *dinars*) to improve the water supply during a drought that had drained the sacred

well of Zazam. These public-works included an aqueduct and the famous 'Spring of Zubayda.' She also endorsed her step-son, al-Ma'mun, who founded Baghdad's famed think-tank, *bayt al-hikma* (house of wisdom)—not only the center for translating Greek, Roman, and other classical texts into Arabic, but also became the foundations of the European Renaissance. Zubayda was also the basis for the fictional character Scheherzade. Her husband, Harun al-Rashid, was the protagonist caliph in *alf layla wa layla* (*1001 Nights*)—one of the oldest literary manuscripts in Arabic.

163. Incantation or magic bowls of Mesopotamia are imprinted with spiral forms to render the demons impotent. Jewish Babylonian Aramaic was also used in magic bowls to exorcise evil spirits and in magic booklets that contain love spells or recipes to garner someone's love.

164. The dehistoricized assumption is that the Middle East has always and continues to be primarily populated by Arabs; the Middle East is generally perceived as the 'Arab World.' This is inaccurate. For instance, Loolwa Khazoom, editor of the *The Flying Camel: Essays on Identity by Women of North African and Middle Eastern Heritage* (see footnotes 4 and 13), points to the too often overlooked fact that: "Jews are indigenous to the Middle East and North Africa, and that we predated the Arab Muslim invasion and conquest of the region, by well over 1,000 years. We are not Arabs, and neither are the Berbers, Persians, Copts, or other indigenous Middle Eastern peoples. …Arab Muslims launched a brutal campaign of invasion and conquest, taking over lands across the Middle East and North Africa. Throughout the region, Kurds, Persians, Berbers, Copts and Jews were forced to convert to Islam under the threat of death and in the name of Allah. Jews were one of the few indigenous Middle Eastern peoples to resist conversion to Islam, the result being they were given the status of *dhimmi*—legally second-class, inferior people. In the best of circumstances, Jews were spared death but forced to endure an onslaught of humiliating legal restrictions—forced into ghettos, prohibited from owning land, prevented from entering numerous professions and forbidden from doing anything to physically or symbolically demonstrate equality with Arab Muslims" (www.jewishjournal.com/opinion/article/whos_to_blame_for_palestinian_despair_20031226).

It is significant to note that in mainstream North American press (such as *The New York Times*) dhimmi translates as non-Muslim citizens of an Islamic community, but the reality was *dhimmi* implies outcaste.

Berbers, Copts, Jews, Persians, and Kurds were polyglots—speaking and conducting business in multiple languages. Historians consider French the language of the colonialists, but ironically, Arabic was also a colonial language, a language of privilege that was imposed on minorities who inhabited lands centuries prior to Arabic-speakers settling. Everything, including colonialism is replete with gray zones—in between spaces that remind us how dynamic history is.

165. In 1948 there were 150,000 Jews living in Iraq, many of whom were part of the one of the world's oldest Jewish communities there. Following years of persecution and alienation, Israel absorbed about 132,000 Iraqi Jews. Many Iraqi Jews endured similar bigotries in Israel. Currently, there are about eight Jews who still live in Iraq; only four of these are under the age of eighty.

Iraqi Jewish population statistics are as follows: 1948: 150,000/ 2004: ~35/ 2008: <10. In the entire country of Iraq, one synagogue remains (www.jewishvirtuallibrary.org/jsource/anti-semitism/iraqijews.html).

166. Ladino absorbs the idiosyncracies of its host languages. For example, *leshos de aki ma serka de korason* (far from here, close at heart) is the Istanbul dialect, *londje de aki ma serkanos de korason* is the Salonika dialect, and *leshus di aki ama sirka de korason* is the Rhodesli dialect (conversation with Dr. Devin E. Naar, Stroum Center for Jewish Studies, University of Washington).

167. Since the 1970s, almost 90% of the marshes had been on the brink of irrevocable damage. But, due to tremendous efforts to restore the marshes, the devastation is being reversed; the ecosystem is undergoing a slow, but remarkable recovery.

168. In 1994, Hussein's regime decimated 60% of the Tigris-Euphrates wetlands. His armies drained the wetlands for military access and to ensure political control of the indigenous Marsh Arabs.

169. In 2003, in search of weapons of mass destruction (WMDs) U.S. soldiers searched through the flooded detritus of Saddam's notorious intelligence ministry (the Mukhabarat). Instead they found 2,700 books and tens of thousands of holy and secular documents in Hebrew, Arabic and Judeo-Arabic. These 'Iraqi Jewish Archives' include Hebrew artifacts including: scholarly manuscripts, materials of halachic (Jewish religious law) religious significance (Torah scrolls fragments, Mezuzot), and privately owned documents (family pictures, graduation diplomas)—the last heirlooms of an ancient community on the cusp of extinction (www.jewishvirtuallibrary.org/jsource/anti-semitism/iraqijews.html; www.inminds.com/jews-of-iraq.html).

170. We not only can learn tremendous structural and behavioral lessons from the sea slug (see following footnote), but also from its cousin, the brainless and eyeless brittlestar. "[T]he brittlestar's survival depends on its capacity to discern the reality of its changing and relational nature. …*Embodiment is a matter…of being in the world in its dynamic specificity*" (Authors italics, Karen Barad, *Meeting the Universe Halfway: quantum physics and the*

entanglement of matter and meaning. Durham & London, Duke University Press, 2007: 369-384, 376, 377). Physicist Karen Barad explores the ethical social implications of its entire body functioning as an optical structure without actually seeing. Barad's initial brittlestar research stemmed from the *New York Times* article, "Eyeless Creatures Turns Out to Be All Eyes" (based on the study in the scientific journal, *Nature*). "The brittlestar architecture is giving ideas to scientists who want to build tiny lenses for things like optical computing" (John Whitfeld, "Eyes in their Stars," *Nature*. August 23, 2001). What the ingenious brittlestar can teach us extends far beyond technology mimicking nature (such as opening new terrain for fabricating 'smart' materials). Sephardic histories echo the functionality of the brittlestar. "The brittlestar is a visualizing system that is constantly changing its geometry and its topology—autonomizing and regenerating its optics in an ongoing reworking of its bodily boundaries" (Barad 375). See footnotes 178, 256, and 314 for further discussion of the performative biodynamic lessons of the brittlestar.

171. Like a flamboyant snail that has no shell, sea slugs opisthobranches ('rear gills') or nudibranchs (literally, 'naked gills') (*Holothuroidea*) are 500 million years old shell-less mollusks. There are over 4000 species throughout the world, and 175 in the Red Sea that have been isolated for 5 million years. 400 new species of mollusks are discovered each year. These gastropods (their foot is their stomach) with their two-feathery sensory horns for defense, represent both total vulnerability and extraordinarily diversity. Individuals can travel up to 20 meters a day.
Sea slugs, considered 'potential life-saving pharmacies,' produce acids and chemical compounds that scientists are now using as maps for new pharmaceuticals. Like the monarch butterfly, whose diet of the milkweed plant poisons its predators, sea slugs "toxify chemicals they 'capture' from their prey, and some even make their own pharmacies of complex toxins to fend off predators or communicate alarm or reproductive readiness. …They eat anemones, jellyfish [tentacles] and stinging hydroids and–in an amazing feat—collect their stinging cells without setting them off, and swallow and digest them. They then store these for their own defense in sacs" (Nathalie Yonow, "Sea Slugs of the Red Sea," *Saudi Aramco World*. July/Aug. 2012: 9). The blue sea slug's main diet is the treacherous and equally beautiful Portuguese man-of-war whose tentacle length can be up to 165 feet. The Portuguese man-of-war is not technically a jellyfish, not even a signle creature, but a composite of four kinds of polyps (thousands of tiny animals that live together—an expression of conviviality). Each colony of polyp "does a different job: floating, stinging, digesting, or reproducing" (S. Jenkins 2007). Perhaps it is a peculiar twist in our story that jellyfish (or at least Portuguese man-of-war), the very symbol of global warming effects arising from our free-market consumer, biophobic frenzy, actually demonstrates a model of collaborative behavior to which the authors aspire.

Like the survival of the dung beetle whose job it is to keep the savannas and prairies 'clean,' because nudibranches eat most dead matter (almost every marine creature except fish), their survival is critical to keep the seas 'clean.' Coral reef ecosystems, the most diverse habitats in the world, are the home of sea slugs. Warming sea temperatures threaten their existence. The result is that the earth's salt waters will not only fill with human trash, but with marine waste.

172. Amber, from the Arabic 'anbar [عنبر], is a fossilized resin, and can be more than 50 million years old. For practical purposes, we can define hardened resin, or amber, as a 'plastic.' Like a plastic milk jug or fiberglass boat, amber is an unstable organic polymer. Through a natural polymerization process that transforms the original organic compounds, the buried resin fossilizes. Resin is also produced when a tree releases excess acetate. In his *The Natural History,* Pliny the Elder wrote: " …amber is thrown up by the waves in spring, it being an excretion of the sea in a concrete form; as, also, that the inhabitants use this amber by way of fuel, and sell it to their neighbors…" (*The Natural History*. John Bostock, M.D., F.R.S. H.T. Riley, Esq., B.A. London. Taylor and Francis, Red Lion Court, Fleet Street. 1855: 37.11). *Electrum,* meaning Sun, is another name for amber. It has been described as 'hardened rays of the sun.' Iranians use the Pahlavi word *kah-ruba* for amber—referring to its electrical properties; in Arabic the word for electricity is كهرباء *kahrab*□ '. Some amber that is between 125 to 135 million years old demonstrates complex ecosystems. The Greeks named it *elektron*, from which the word 'electricity' is derived. Saltating, or moving, sand grains create electricity: "As soon as the sand grains start moving, their collisions generate static electrical charges" (Welland 156). Like saltating sand, amber generates and holds static electricity when rubbed.

173. The sperm whale produces ambergris (*ambre gris* or 'grey amber') a solid waxy substance that was once integral to the whaling (whale poaching) economy.

174. One out of every three animal species is a type of beetle (Order *Coleoptera* meaning sheathed wing).

"Beetles, the largest groups of insects, representing a fifth of all living organisms and a fourth of all animals, epitomize diversity" (Evans and Bellamy 11). Using behavior, defense, reproduction, and adaptation survival strategies, beetles are the most successful group of insects and animals on earth. Their survival success comes from their astounding diversity of body forms/ shapes, colors, sizes, patterns, their symbiotic relationships with plants, and their ability to adapt. They eat nearly every type of food (plants, insects, fish, dead animals, leaves, bark, wood, and dung), and live in every terrestrial habitat on Earth (forests, deserts, mountains, ponds), except polar ice caps and salt water. Considering they have lived on earth for over 265 million years and are the largest single order of animals, their inability to survive in salt water is an ironic twist in a beetle's fate given that climate change will exponentially increase salt water on the planet. Until global warming completely takes over, we are likening beetles' adaptability to the Jewish Diaspora. The Iranian-Jewish community is an illuminating example of this paradoxical adaptability: the Islamic Republic of Iran is both one of the most virulent anti-Israeli countries and at the same time is home to between 25,000- 35,000 Iranian-Jews—far exceeding Jewish populations of any Muslim country.

175. Beetle fossils can retain their extraordinary bright colors, such as a blue metallic hue, for millions of years because their chitinous armor preserves their exoskeleton.

176. Fossilized beetles can sometimes be sheltered in prehistoric mammalian dung heaps and sometimes in amber. Paleoclimatology examines fossil beetles as indicators of climate change. "Fossil beetles also reveal the age of their symbiotic relationships with other organisms, particularly other animals" (Evans and Bellamy 75, 92; and, news.nationalgeographic.com/news/2003/08/0818_030818_beetlefossil.html).

177. Because spittle was seen to be the most powerful fluid (a similar belief with traditional Chinese healing), spitting three times is a good luck gesture.

178. The firefly beetle (Family, *Lampyridae/Phausis splendidula*) creates its cold, mysterious light, its bioluminescence, by mixing luciferin and luciferinase chemicals in a chamber located in its abdomen. Named after Lucifer, meaning light-bearer, the son of the morning, or the Angel of Light, these substances exchange oxygen and carbon dioxide in a complex enzymatic-driven system. (Like the firefly, brittlestars use bioluminescence as a survival tactic). "This process—the use of (adenosine triphosphate) ATP and oxygen to produce light—is the exact opposite of the process by which plants capture the energy of the sun: photosynthesis. This form of bioluminesce is nearly 100% efficient: almost all the energy that goes into the system is given off as light. By comparison, an incandescent light bulb is only about 10% efficient; the remainder of the energy is lost as heat. The light-producing organs of one firefly have been said to produce 1/80,000 of the heat produced by a candle flame of comparable brightness. We know now that adult fireflies control their flash patterns by regulating the oxygen supply to the light organs" (Evans and Bellamy 98, 101). Their 'breath-pattern' is reflected by their light flashing sequence.

"Since ATP powers many biological reactions, systems sensitive to ATP levels can be a useful biochemical tool. NASA is using the bioluminescence system…to determine if there are life forms on other planets. A mixture of luciferin and luciferinase is included aboard exploratory spacecraft" (Ibid., 101).

As with the whale songs sent on space-probes, NASA frequently uses animals (including microbial communities), spiders, and insects as models for their space experiments or extraterrestrial communication. NASA water research includes the Advanced Life Support Systems lab at the Johnson Space Flight Center in Texas. They are learning how to recycle water from laundry, showers, and urine while preventing bacterial build-up in the recycling water systems. "The space shuttle's fuel cells combine hydrogen and oxygen to make electricity. This also produces water" (Swanson 133).

179. "Bioluminescence in fireflies is nearly 100 percent efficient, meaning that little energy is wasted to produce their light. By contrast, an incandescent light bulb is only 10 percent efficient—90 percent of the energy is lost as heat" (www.nwf.org/Wildlife/Wildlife-Library/Invertebrates/Firefly.aspx).

180. The way fireflies use their light to communicate with one another is an example of the fertility of contradictions—the firefly's light is used for both creation (for males to attract females for reproduction) and destruction (for females to trick males with various light signals to attract them, and then the predaceous female eats the male) (S. Jenkins, 2012: 21; Evans and Bellamy 101).

Institutional predatory deception is integral to cross-cultural Jewish histories. Because they were not allowed to enter any professions except as economic middleman, Jews' host nations have historically betrayed them. See also: footnote 211. The Turkish Sultan of the Ottoman Empire encouraged Sephardic exiles to settle in his domain. He mocked the Inquisitional Spanish monarchy for impoverishing Spain while bolstering his empire with Jews' experience in finance, trade, and administration. Unlike other governments, the Turks never turned on the Jews (at least according to my grandmother from Izmir). Turkey was the one country where she felt safe. We do, however, question Children's Day, during which children run the government in Turkey. M. Kemal Atatürk believed the "root of social change was in the hands of children." He established Children's Day to be celebrated on April 23rd, the same day as Turkey's National Sovereignty/Independence Day. UNICEF recognizes April 23 as the International Children's Day (www.turkishnews.com/DiscoverTurkey/culture/april23/). Because Atatürk had a history of anti-Semitism, we are questioning a possible connection between Hitler Youth and Atta Turk's focus on children.

181. The shofar has many purposes: to call people together for Jewish celebrations or commemorations,

it is blown to signal the High Holy Days and to rouse the Divine within each listener. As when the Jewish people received the Ten Commandments, the call of the shofar herald's God's presence. The shofar may not be constructed using artificial material; it must be a natural form that is naturally hollow (preferably with a bend). Its organic sound represents the humane lives it calls Jews to lead—reminiscent of the ethical practice of *adab* (see footnote 101). Some scholars identify the bend as our willingness to bend or conform to God's will (www.breakingisraelnews.com/21693/praising-god-sound-shofar/#ZPUCgOGZ8g8DO7M5.99).

Those following Rudolf Steiner's biodynamic farming practices identify the energy that moves around the bend or spiral in a cow's horn in relation to predators and biological control. See also: Barry Lia and Maria Linder's "Radiation and the Prosperity of Agriculture," Biodynamics, Spring 2014: 35-54; www.pfeiffercenter.org/index.aspx.

182. How are we describing the problems we are faced with? There are multiple faces of environmental devastation. When we are examining who is responsible for sustainable collective justice, we of course need to take a multi-pronged approach. But in climate change discussion, too much attention is on governmental band-aids and not enough on how we can educate—how we can shift people's relationship to their own empowerment. The expanded discussion we are suggesting is *not* about "50 Things You Can Do To Save The Planet." It is about engaging a social permaculture approach that undergirds our relationship with use-waste dynamics. Social permaculture includes the practice of self-regulation, observation, establishing feedback structures, responding creatively to change, designing from pattern to detail, amplifying diversity, using the fertile edge, integrating rather than segregating, focusing on slow and small solutions, flexibility, adaptation. This approach does not offer a 'solution,' but rather an alternative. In a letter to Alexis Surron, Anton Chekov wrote: "….you confuse two things: *solving a problem* and *stating a problem correctly*… In *Anna Karenina* and *Evgeny Onyegin* not a single problem is solved, but they satisfy you completely because all the problems are correctly stated in them" (October 27, 1888). The question is *how* are we describing the structural, legal, and ethical problems we are confronted with? Only then can we begin to decipher the perverse reality that 54% of children in the US are chronically ill (suffering from autoimmune disease or neuro-developmental disability), 1 in 4 are malnourished, and 12 million are obese—the majority of whom are *also* malnourished. When we acknowledge that misrepresentation of the problem massively acerbates it, we can begin to experiment with ever-expanding possibilities of change, not fixed 'solutions.' As Chekov tells us: there are no solutions in life, there are only alternatives. In our story, Zazu looks for alternatives for a better world in the least expected places, the places you would think the opposite would be the case. He investigates different paths away from our current destructive vortex: microbials, poop, sand, salt, and amber as alternatives to coal, oil, and plastic. By understanding the connections between our malnourished bodies and our impoverished soils, we can collaboratively witness, create, and act on alternatives in our everyday lives.

183. The 'green economy' backfires when it is purely profit-driven, when clean energy is hiding its dirty agenda inside bank accounts of pocket-politicians.

How we measure our ecological footprint and global biocapacity is often riddled with paradox. For instance, the green push to 'buy local' may not account for "water use, cultivation and harvesting methods, quantity and type of fertilizer, even the type of fuel used to make the package. Sea-freight emissions are less than a sixtieth of those associated with airplanes, and you don't have to build highways to berth a ship" (Michael Specter, "BigFoot," ed. Elizabeth Kolbert, *The Best American Science and Nature Writing*. New York: Houghton, Mifflin, Harcourt, 2009: 280).

Many alternatives to fossil fuels, such as fracking, were once thought to be 'clean'—leaving little carbon footprint. We now know how incredibly dangerous fracking is to the earth's stability and to our bodies' health.

The first 'modern' oil well was drilled in Pennsylvania in1860, 20 years after peak whale oil (in which the whale population had been decimated for oil economy). In 1861, *Vanity Fair* published a drawing of whales celebrating the new oil wells. Little did *Vanity Fair* or the surviving whales know that the replacement fossil fuels would nearly equal the devastation to whales and their ecosystems. Fortunately for the ecosystems of our cosmos, as Ralph Nader states: "The use of solar energy has not been opened up because the oil industry does not own the sun."

Naomi Klein's 2014 *This Changes Everything: Capitalism vs. The Climate,* a book that has short-sightedly been identified as the contemporary *Silent Spring,* misses many key paradoxes in various environmental movements. Such undeserved association with Rachel Carson obfuscates the hypocrisies within western environmental movements. In her documentary film of the same title, she tells the audience that repeatedly, when she asks people what they think about climate change, they answer with "one word: China." She then goes into a brief exploration of the solar/ smog dichotomy in China. She fails to do two things: 1) Examine the fact that one primary reason there are so many factories in China is because of Western consumer-demand for both high-tech gadgets and cheap, disposable single-use products; 2) Examine parallel contradictions in Western countries' economies.

Both China (whose renewable electricity growth between 2010 to 2012 was double that of the U.S.) and Germany (who is lauded as implementing the primary green economy globally and who runs its country on 30% renewables) are still building coal plants. Simultaneously, China's coal-pile-use households, even more than their corporations, may be contributing to their pollution dome. "China is in a process of dismantling some of its oldest coal plants that have low-efficiencies. Germany is building plants that can burn lignite coal—this is a very low-energy density substance and can have lots of sulfurous chemicals from combustion. In both cases, the idea of 'energy transition' must be interrogated in relationship to energy use and demand (meaning cultural as well as infrastructural dynamics), and within the context of transnational processes and political economies" (conversation with Jia-Ching Chen, Professor of Geography, Penn State University; see also: www.climatecentral.org/blogs/chinas-growing-coal-use-is-worlds-growing-problem-16999).

Again what we see is always, only partial; we can never see the whole picture, and if we think we can see the entire picture, we are cheating ourselves and our children. Klein's film neglects to address one of the *primary underlying* causes of global warming: CONSUMERISM. It took Klein an hour and 18 minutes to only briefly mention consumption-habits, let alone corporate-driven consumer society. It is obviously gratifying to see a film that demonstrates global grassroots victories that cut across class, gender, and nationhood. However, Klein's entire film was anchored in an us vs. them division. Even within the 99%, *consumers are capitalism*. A Greek activist Klein interviews is reluctant to identify her belief that capitalism is the 'core of the problem.' But, what is this core without consumers? Without convenience-culture/ mass consumer-demand, the machine of the free-market would have to shift gears. We can't blame the oil companies without simultaneously implicating ourselves, holding our consumption-habits equally responsible. How can we insist the government and transnational corporations change, when we refuse to curb our buying and disposal habits? As a single mother committed to barter-economies and zero-waste, I offer my practice as one strategy to begin to undermine US parent's/culture's extraordinary addiction to consumption-disposal. We can make change if we are willing to change.

A 'green economy' may include infrastructural practices of biomimickry. Biomimesis and bioengineering offer technology a chance to borrow designs from nature, 'multifunctional biomaterial' (Barad) whose thousands of years perfecting particular processes, can serve as models for 'smart' materials, nanotechnologies, and telecommunication networks.

184. Government regulation is fought in the name of 'freedom.'

185. In our contemporary world of 'disaster capitalism' (Klein), in addition to accelerating time, scale is blown out of proportion. Corporate giants stalk the planet: Nestlé=food giant, Nestlé=water giant, Shell=oil giant, Apple=technology giant, Merck=pharmaceutical giant, Monsanto=biotechnology/ agribusiness giant, Goldman Sachs=bank giant, Comcast/Mega Cable=telecom giant, the Agrichemical Lobby=political giant, CDC=health giant, World Bank and International Monetary Fund=international aid giant. We must analyze the cultural and ecological impacts of small dams compared to big dams, small palm oil production compared to miles of plantations. We must ask: how do we shift convenience-culture's profligate gluttony and high-demand as a rationale to create large-scale productions? How can we align our deepest needs with a collective dignity to make small-scale, sustainable systems rooted in moderate consumption and energy-use that depend on community relationships (such as infrastructural bartering)? Examples of the criticality of small scale include: Peter Rosset, "Small Is Bountiful," E.F. Schumacher, Small Is Beautiful: Economics as if People Mattered, Frances Moore Lappé's, *Diet for a Small Planet,* and her co-authorship with her daughter, Anna Lappé, *Hope's Edge: The Next Diet for a Small Planet,* and Arundhati Roy's *The God of Small Things.* In contrast, China's city-sized solar valleys offer another example of precarious 'green' territory.

186. These desert bighorn sheep are caught in a double-bind in which the green economy, that which is supposed to help them, has a devastating impact on their existence. 2,500 acres of solar fields, a substation, access roads and other buildings would undermine years of efforts by the National Park Service, the California Department of Fish and Wildlife, and others who are attempting to restore movement of desert bighorn sheep populations. In 1994 there were only about 50 desert bighorn sheep left. Today, due to tremendous collaborative efforts, the ram population has increased to more than 300. Keeping the herds connected to one another is also critical to ensure genetic diversity and disease resistance. This means roads, buildings, and dam-construction must be appropriately located and limited. Stuart L. Pimm is professor of conservation at Duke University and director of SavingSpecies, a non-profit that, by procuring land to be reforested, reconnects fragmented environments for many migratory animals. Pimm's, like many activists, is a practice of *tikkun olam*. In contrast with industrial-sized solar energy projects, solar panels installed on people's homes and businesses 'turn consumers into producers.' This decentralized power generation undermines Big Energy impacts (Rebecca Solnit, "Power in Paris," *Harper's Magazine.* December 2015: 6). Fortunately,

many researchers are developing devices that mitigate, rather than adapt to the exorbitant pressures of energy consumption. For instance, such acoustic engineers in Ithaca, New York have designed bat recorders that ecologists use to monitor their populations at potential large scale wind farm sites to assure that wind turbines are not installed in places where they might kill endangered bats. Jay Whitacre, professor of materials science at Carnegie Mellon University and founder of Aquion Energy, focuses on practical and economical renewable energy for poor non-industrialized communities. "By 2030, one billion people are expected to get electricity for the first time. That will mean a lot more use of fossil fuels unless renewable power options are as cheap, safe, and reliable as possible." Aquion Energy's batteries for future solar-powered villages are constructed using "inexpensive manufacturing equipment repurposed from the food and pharmaceutical industries. Hydraulic presses originally designed to make aspirin pills stamp out wafers of positive and negative electrode materials and robot arms built to wrap chocolates are used to package electrode wafers with foils that act as current collectors" (Kevin Bullis, "Storing the Sun," *MIT Technology Review*. Vol. 117, No. 2, 2014: 84-86, 86). It is imperative that engineers, activists, and researchers, such as Whitacre, embrace the social scientific concept of embodied energy that designates both the local and global cycles of extraction/ production/ representation/distribution/consumption/ disposal/ containment/permeation.

187. Organizations that are supposed to be helping often create even worse problems. Examples on both water and land abound. The current National Oceanic and Atmospheric Administration (NOAA) attempt to remove humpbacks from the Endangered Species list has reset their vulnerability: humpbacks are endangered once again (see footnote 89). One land example involves the mass planting of *tamarix ramosis-sima*—originally intended to fight soil erosion during the Dust Bowl. Described in both the Bible and the Koran, the tamarisk or saltcedar was planted by the millions in the US. But because native plants could not compete with this new species, it swarmed unhindered across the Western United States. These invasive saltcedar thickets now infest more than 3 million acres (Rowan Jacobsen, *Down by the River,* ed. Rebecca Skloot, *The Best American Science and Nature Writing*. New York: Houghton, Mifflin, Harcourt, 2015: 93).

188. As we transition to carbon-free electricity and renewable energy project development (waste to energy facilities, anaerobic digestors, biomass, biofuel, solar panels, wind turbines, geothermal energy), we must ensure protection of all peoples' livelihoods and their environments (that includes wildlife in all forms—from the microbial to the largest mammals). Glaciologist Richard B. Alley enthusiastically tells us that we are the first generation that can farm renewable energy in ways that are economically sustainable.

In 1860, the same year oil was 'discovered,' Abraham Lincoln extolled the possibilities of wind power: "As yet, the wind is an *untamed* and *unharnessed* force, and quite possibly one of the greatest discoveries hereafter to be made, will be the taming and harnessing of it" ("Discoveries and Invention: A Lecture by Abraham Lincoln Delivered in 1860," John Howell, San Francisco, 1915). Now used by many Texas Ranchers who even deny the reality of climate change, wind turbine energy offers such an enormous abundance of energy, TXU Energy offers free electricity at night. Again, even though appropriately located wind farms would supply far more energy than humanity uses (Richard B. Alley, "Powering Sustainability: The Good News on Energy, the Environment, and the Future," Penn State University, Lecture, 2016), we must investigate possible detrimental impacts of this emerging 'mailbox money' economy.

'Creative' alternatives may unintentionally perpetuate the violence of wasteful behavior; they may actually *conserve* the original problem. Greenwashing is a key example, along with numerous trash-based art projects, and much of the recycling industry. In 1991 when I initiated Sarah Lawrence College's recycling program, the head of Student Affairs was delighted: "Now we can use more!" That comment has haunted me for twenty-five years. On Pennsylvania State University's campus only 8% of the content in the recycling bins actually gets recycled; 92% ends up as landfill. One example of engineering ingenuity's precarious implication (and its too frequent insidious consequences) is Melinda Hale's startup, Loci Controls. Her company 'vacuums' landfill gas (LFG), a greenhouse gas consisting of methane and carbon dioxide, and tranforms "it into a fuel that can be used to produce electricity" (Rob Matheson, "Talking Trash," *MIT Technology Review*. Vol. 117, No. 2, 2014: 20-21). Aside from the potential toxic gas leaks (resulting in fines from the EPA), underground fires, and killing bacteria necessary for decomposition, these landfill-gas-to-energy (LFGTE) landfills may 'encourage' consumers and corporations to waste more (i.e., consume more) because they are being taught that trash accumulation enables them to use more electricity. Hale's Descartian proclamation sums up the dangers of the Anthropocene Era: "Once you understand how a process works, you can control it" (Ibid.).

'Socially responsible investing' is another insidious green illusion. 'Socially responsible' Calvert Mutual Funds include investments in such companies as Merck, Apple, Nike, Bank of America, and PepsiCo. because they are not (directly) involved with the tobacco, alcohol, or arms industries.

189. The original quote comes from Kobo Abé's *The*

Woman in the Dunes: "You can't really judge a mosaic if you don't look at it from a distance. If you really get close to it you get lost in detail. You get away from one detail only to get caught in another. Perhaps what he had been seeing until now was not the sand but grains of sand" (New York: Vintange International, 1991: 235). Again we revisit another angle of our theme that things are not necessarily what they appear to be. One example of this may be the literal and metaphoric use of sand itself: "The global demand for concrete is massive: after water, concrete is the most consumed material on Earth" (Welland 59). The concrete construction companies use 75% sand and gravel, 15% water, and 10% cement (a combination of limestone and clay that forms a chemical glue—hardening is due to chemical reactions). Rather than injecting toxic substances into sandy soil in order to form solid rock, scientists are now exploring how to enhance sands' innate bacteria that glue its own grains together: "Inject sand with cultures of these bacteria, feed them well, and provide them with oxygen, and they will turn loose sand into solid rock" (Ibid., 59). Given global catastrophic consequences, we must discuss the usefulness of sand: "Sand not only absorbs liquids, but also absorbs energy" (Ibid., 237). Motor-racers, runners, golf etc. uses "energy-absorbing character of sand." Sand can be used as a filter to capture chemical pollutants and as a water-treatment process: "the spaces between the grains capture solid materials but allow the clean water to flow through" (Ibid., 245). Shallow domestic water wells in Nepal, Bangladesh, and throughout Asia use slow sand to filter the lethal levels of natural arsenic (Ibid., 246). Nanotechnology (Ibid., 263) works with carbon nanotubes—an application of fluidized beds of sand in incineration. "Materials burn more easily and efficiently in a fluidized bed. Not only do coal and other conventional fuels burn more efficiently, but so does garbage—'refuse-derived fuel' or RDF. Power generation that uses the technology creates fewer emissions and can be far more easily controlled than in traditional power stations. Fluidized-bed technology is also a way of generation hydrogen from methane for energy" (Ibid., 263) In contrast with sawdust that holds much higher levels of fecal bacteria, "[t]here are machines specifically designed to process the sand and remove the manure" from cow bedding (Ibid., 237). Sand eliminates weeds and fungal growth, and can transform into soil when soil-disintegrating enzymes are applied (Abé 220).

When activists, scientists, parents, artists, etc. examine our impending crisis of global desertification (during times when flooding is not wreaking havoc), we can begin to investigate what to do with over-abundant new 'resources' such as sand, salt, or feces. We must explore organic properties that already exist rather than spending phenomenal quantities of money and time on technology and chemicals to make resources 'better,' 'stronger,' 'more useful/ productive.' We are suggesting that in order to maintain inclusive radical sustainable global change, we must simultaneously redefine our compulsive habits of consumption and production—curtailing consumer-desire as we deploy creative alternatives.

190. *Nusah Sephardi* are different traditional melodies and modes of prayer among Mizrahi/ Sephardi compared to that of Ashkenazi Jews. We include Uum Kalthoum (also spelled Oum Kalsoum) in our story to emphasize our Jewish communities' affinity with Arabic music and popular culture. Her legacy spans three generations. In the 1920s, Uum Kalthom's father dressed her as a boy so she could sing in public. Four million mourning fans lined the streets of Cairo at her funeral.

191. Sephardi/ Mizrahi Jews' history with Uum Kalthoum is another example of the significant cultural differences with Ashkenazim. Egyptian Jewish, Eyal Sagui Bizawe's documentary, "Arab Film," vividly demonstrates Jews' profound alliance with Arabic cultures. In contrast with Ashkenazi Israeli detached viewer response, Sephardi/ Mizrahi Israeli viewers responded in tears as they watched Uum Kalthoum perform.

192. Moises ben Maimon, Musa ibn Maimun, was known both as Maimonides and as Rambam (1135–1204) (not to be confused with his contemporary Ramban, a prominent medieval Jewish scholar, Catalan Sephardic rabbi, philosopher, physician, kabbalist, and biblical commentator also known as Nahmanides, Rabbi Moses ben Naḥman Girondi, and Bonastruc ça Porta. Ramban was born in Spain and died in Palestine in the 13th century). Inspiring poets, philosophers, theologians, painters and architects, the 12th century Maimonides (Rambam) was a Torah luminary; he reanimated contemporized Talmudic custom in a tremendous legal tome known as The Mishneh Torah. Maimonides' code of Jewish law set the standard for future Jewish legal codes. For his Muslim readers, he wrote in classical Arabic (his medical works); throughout the Jewish Diaspora, he wrote in Judeo-Arabic (Arabic dialect with Hebrew letters)—for example, *The Guide to the Perplexed,* one of the most famous philosophical works ever written.
David Shasha tells us: "Over the past century Sephardic rabbis have been demoted from the larger Jewish discussion. The interpretive methods and conceptual values of Ashkenazi rabbinical culture have overtaken religious Jewish discourse. The Maimonidean tradition which fuses ancient Biblical and Talmudic values with the Greco-Arab synthesis of science and philosophy has been simultaneously rejected and sharply transformed by the Ashkenazi rabbinical authorities" (Shasha e-newsletter 2015).

193. Maimonides's body was transferred to Tiberius, on the coast of Israel.

194. In 2015, the Oriental Institute at the University of

Chicago held the exhibition: *A Cosmopolitan City: Muslims, Christians and Jews in Old Cairo*. Because of its *convivencia*, the thriving co-existence of mosques, churches, and synagogues; Arabic, Hebrew, and Old Coptic languages, the medieval city of Fustat, or 'Old Cairo,' became the cultural capital of Egypt. One example of the residents of Fustat's shared way of life that crossed differences can be found in ancient manuscripts of the Hebrew Bible written in Hebrew using Arabic letters with Arabic commentary.

195. Unfortunately, Israel's history does not offer such conviviality. Israel's Jewish social body is utterly disjointed, suffering from acute autoimmune disorders. In her article, "Blow-Ups in the Borderzones: Third World Israeli Authors' Gropings for Home," Smadar Lavie, as well as Victor Perera, author of *The Cross and the Pear Tree: A Sephardic Journey*, refers to Sephardim and Oriental/Asiatic Jews as "the Other Israel" (Berkeley: University of California Press, 1996: 168). Dr. Eliyahu Eliachar speaks of "the cultural abyss:" Eastern European Jews—Ashkenazi leaders such as Ben-Gurion, Moshe Dayan, Golda Meir, Abba Eban feared Sephardi and Oriental/Asiatic Jews would "undermine his plans for a European Zionist state. And so they began creating myths about the 'primitive' and 'backward' North African Jews. …They not only were denied educational opportunities, but had to submerge their cultural distinctiveness in humiliating and menial pursuits. Only in recent years are young leaders emerging who have the pride and determination to cast off shackles and assert their Sephardic identity" **(**Ibid.). Dr. Eliachar counseled Perera "to meet with Iraqi and Moroccan political leaders, including Black Panther activists [Saadia Marciano and Charlie Britton, Kochavi Shemesh] **(**Ibid.). This "oppressed *majority*" in Israel consisting of Asian North African, and Middle Eastern Jews lose privileges to new immigrants from the Soviet Union, and are kept "at the bottom of Israeli society…to provide cheap manpower for their wars and their industry without contaminating the European image they wish to project to the world. ….In the prisons, whose population is 98% Sephardic and Arab…[they turn] us against one another" **(**Ibid., 169-170). "What is needed now is a profound change in our conception of ourselves as Jews. Our enslavement to history and to biblical precedent is so insidious that it prevents us from undertaking initiatives that could break our impasse with the Arabs. …The only way to shed our fatalism is to break our preoccupation with the past and learn to improvise. We must create a new Jew" (Ibid., 174).

196. Kabbalah is an esoteric theosophy from 13th century Spain and France. Kabbalists' believe that the Tree of Life is modeled on human anatomy. Each of the ten attributes corresponds to a part of the body. The combination of these ten (plus three) *sefirot* (divine emanations) result in 'truth.' The microbiome, conviviality *within* all organic living bodies (and exchanged between the mother's body, her fetus, and later, her growing infant), represents and functions as another version of The Tree of Life. See Also: Seth R. Bordenstein, Kevin R. Theis, "Host Biology in Light of the Microbiome: Ten Principles of Holobionts and Hologenomes," PLOS Biology. August 18, 2015, DOI:10.1371/journal.pbio.1002226 (www.plosbiology.org, Open Access), and Lisa J. Funkhouser, Seth R. Bordenstein, "Mom Knows Best: The Universality of Maternal Microbial Transmission," PLOS Biology. August 2013, Volume 11, Issue 8, e1001631 (www.plosbiology.org Open Access).

197. "Much of Turkey's coal is low-grade lignite, which burns even dirtier than the hard coal commonly mined in Appalachia" (Jennifer Hattam, "The Olive and the Power Plant," *Sierra Club*. Sept./Oct. 2015: 54).

198. "Turkey is the world's second-largest producer of table olives and fourth-largest producer of olive oil" (Ibid., 55).

199. The Kolin Group coal company is suing Yirca villagers "who stood guard over the groves last fall, on charges of property damage for their attempt to block the power plant's construction" (Ibid., 54).

200. Turkey could supply power to the entire country using renewable resources. "[It] could have the highest potential for solar [power] in Europe in terms of the sun hours it gets, over quite a big landmass" (Itamar Orlandi, analyst with Bloomberg New Energy Finance cited in Ibid., 55).

201. Across the globe, unprecedented deluging rains and flash floods accompany relentless drought and fire. Due to byproducts from the fossil fuel industry, the World Health Organization estimates 150,000 people die each year. Ironically (given its politics of imperialism that have directly exacerbated global warming), the World Bank estimates that by 2030, 100 million will suffer from the effects of climate change. Clearly, climate change does not affect all people or environments equally. The world's marginalized and vulnerable groups are disproportionately affected by the impacts of global warming. But, as conditions worsen, no one will be able to choose ignorance and arrogance.

202. Homer wrote *The Iliad* and *The Odyssey* in 700 B.C.

203. In Judaism, the number thirteen is associated with good luck: Bar and Bat Mitzvah are held at the age of thirteen; the Hebrew Bible enumerates thirteen divine attributes; the Hebrew words for 'one' and 'love' contain the numerical value of thirteen. The Kabbalah offers thirteen *sefirot*. (See also: Yehuda Berg, *The Power of the Kabbalah: Thirteen Principles to Overcome Challenges and Achieve Fulfillment*). In the introduction to the Zohar, it is said that "Just as a rose has thirteen petals, so Assemlbly of Israel

has thirteen qualities of compassion surrounding Her on every side. Similarly, from the moment *'elohim, God,* is mentioned, it generates thirteen words to surround Assembly of Israel and protect Her" (www.sup.org/zohar for the Aramaic text; Matt 2004:1.1-2 for the English translation).

204. *Zaghlouta* is the Egyptian word for the joyful clucking of tongues.

205. Rhodes is one of the Greek Dodecanese islands off the coast of Turkey.

206. There are few moments throughout history and geography where Jews have lived as the majority population. Leading up to the catastrophic fire of 1917 in Salonika, Northern Greece, Jews were the majority population. The blaze decimated the 450 year-old Jewish quarter—wiping out its inhabitants. The Nazis killed the rest—98% perished in Auschwitz-Birkenau concentration camp in Poland.

We are dedicating our story to forgotten Sephardim who died during the Holocaust.

207. A common Ladino proverb shared when grandmothers hug their grandchildren.

208. In 1883, the Statue of Liberty arrived at New York Harbor. According to the press, it was reminiscent of the Colossus of Rhodes—both massive and powerful—except the Colossus of Rhodes was built to intimidate enemy intruders, while the Statue of Liberty was an invitation to those who had suffered to find refuge. Emma Lazarus, a Sephardic young poet of Portuguese descent and a student of environmentalist-poet Ralph Waldo Emerson, was asked to write about the statue. Highly acclaimed for her writing denouncing the pogroms in Russia and her persistent activism for Ashkenazi immigrants, Lazarus named the Statue of Liberty the Mother of Exiles, and wrote "The New Colossus:" "… *Give me your tired, your poor, / Your huddled masses yearning to breathe free, / The wretched refuse of your teeming shore. / Send these, the homeless, tempest-tost to me, / I lift my lamp beside the golden door!"* We are reminded of the statement the Vatican released in June of 2015. In his Encyclical on Climate Change and Inequality, Pope Francis wrote, "Today we have to realize that a true ecological approach *always* becomes a social approach; it must integrate questions of justice in debates on the environment, so as to hear *both the cry of the earth and the cry of the poor" ("Encyclical Letter Laudator si':* On Care for Our Common Home," Pope Francis.The Vatican Press, May 2015). Two months after Pope Francis' statement, Islamic leaders issued a statement about the connections between capitalism and climate change.

209. In 1876, Lazarus wrote "Don Pedrillo" and "Fra Pedro," two poems that have been characterized as virulently anti-Sephardic. Given the humanitarian context in which Lazarus originally operated, we choose instead to interpret her poems as illustrations of the Inquisition's horrific vilification of Spanish Jews throughout the centuries and across the globe.

210. This street was also called *el espejo* (mirror) in memory of those who were abducted to concentration camps during WWII.

211. Throughout Europe, the Middle East, and North Africa, districts that are called 'The Old City' are also often 'The Jewish Quarter.' Jews were relegated to enforced settlements such as the *mellah* in Morocco, *hara* in Tunisia, *mahaleh* in Iran, or *qa`at al-yahud* in Yemen. Suspended between lands of the cross and the crescent, regions that had been their original homelands, Jews had to negotiate subjugation, vilification, and being used as an economic 'necessity' by local governments. The enclosed quarters in which they were restricted were supposedly established to protect Jews from increasing hostility of both the local inhabitants and outside invaders. The reverse often occurred: the Jewish ghettos became targets. Systematic isolation (including sealing the gates of the *mellah* at night) was overtly discriminatory but also served as a method of protecting Jews from extremist Muslim violence. The meaning of *mellah* changed to the 'place where the Jews lived' (occupying their protected, yet precarious ghetto within the strict confines of the Islamic republic). See also: footnote 180.

212. Minarets are tall, thin towers, often attached to a mosque with a balcony from which a muezzin calls Muslims to prayer.

213. The Jersey Tiger Moth or monarch butterfly (*Euplagia quadripunctaria rhodosensis*) is a spectacular example of migration phenomena, traveling up to 1,000 miles in groups of millions. But, monarchs are in grave danger: "since the 1990s the migrating population of monarchs has plummeted 85%, due largely to the skyrocketing use of the herbicide glyphosate, marketed as Roundup by Monsanto." Among other critical elements of our food chain and integrated ecosystems, "the herbicide kills milkweed, the butterfly's main food supply in its breeding habitat in the US and Canada" (National Resources Defense Council Newsletter (NRDC) Fall 2015). Also, monarch butterflies have no stomach, so they get tired easily when their environment is disturbed, which because of agribusiness and tourism, is happening more and more frequently.

Pollination is one of the most beautiful models of symbiosis—the plants have an opportunity to repopulate while the insects, birds, bats, and bees have an opportunity to eat and feed their families. "Pollinators are keystone species that provide the foundation of our ecosystems" (National Wildlife Federation president, Collin O'Mara). Pollination keeps the cycle of life in motion. Like the migrating monarch butterfly, many beetles (such lady bugs, the hairy-jewel from Africa, and the tumbling flower beetle) are pollinators of flowering plants. Without these pollinators who offer an invaluable ecosystem service, people would have no food. More than three-quarter's of the world's food production depends on pollinators (primarily bees).

Krill are the bees of the seas—essential for our marine food chain. As with greenwashing, "health-conscious" marketing, production, and consumption frequently sabotage nature's ecosystems. The mass populations of krill that are killed in the harvesting process for fish oil supplements could lead to another fishery collapse. The most biologically-productive region of the Southern Ocean has seen an 80% drop in krill. "CHILL THE KRILL KILL" is a grassroots attempt to divert consumer and corporate habits away from krill and forage fish-based (herring and anchovies) supplements. (SierraRise e-newsletter, Monday, June 6, 2016).

Similar to pollen and seed distribution, poop is an integral part of the food chain, both on land and in the water; animals' feces can function as a 'distribution pump' (The Thom Hartmann Program, "Are We Humans Destroying Our Own Nest?" www.truth-out.org/opinion/item/33413-are-humans-destroying-our-own-nest). Fecal matter is not only essential to nourish the soil, but also essential to the health and ecosystems of many insects, birds, and mammals. "Coprophagus insects like butterflies, beetles and maggots live entirely off nutrients in feces. ….Excrement is rich in trace minerals and yeast, is 15% protein, and quenches thirst (it's 65% water). Most animals that eat shit, however, do it for the bacteria. By ingesting feces, elephants, dogs, beavers, rabbits and iguanas coat their digestive tract with flora that help break down food and fight infections. Feces-deficient diets can cause health problems. Laboratory rats deprived of their own feces become malnourished, and turkeys and chickens raised in cages (and unable to eat their mother's droppings) develop more infections than free-range fowl. To curb salmonella outbreaks, battery [industrial cage-based] farmers now pour commercially produced fecal bacteria into chicken's drinking troughs" (Toscani 50).

Additionally, a new study on whale feces shows that protecting endangered baleen whales, including humpbacks, could boost the carbon storage capacity of the Southern Ocean. Because of the mass decline in whale populations the ocean is now literally anemic—deprived of baleen whales' iron-rich feces.

Because of the high quantities of iron in their feces, protecting Antarctic whales could increase mass populations of carbon-sequestering phytoplankton, which *absorb carbon dioxide*. Antarctic krill (*Euphausia superba* (*www.newscientist.com/article/dn13374-amazing-discovery-finds-krill-in-antarctic-abyss*)) feed on the phytoplankton, concentrating the iron in their tissue; in turn, baleen whales eat the krill, and poop. The phytoplankton eats their poop and the cycle continues. Helping the whales to recover allows the ocean ecosystem to slowly reset itself. "This will ultimately increase the amount of CO2 that the Southern Ocean can sequester" (www.newscientist.com/article/dn18807-whale-poop-is-vital-to-oceans-carbon-cycle/).

214. Reminiscent of amber, Oriental Sweetgum (Liquidanbar orientalis) can be used medicinally to heal emotional disorders, flesh wounds, and skin conditions. The gooey trees are also used industrially to produce polystrene plastics, such as styrofoam. Because the trees have both medicinal and industrial purposes, they have been overharvested. The trees are also in danger because of dam construction and its accompanying deforestation.

215. Papoo had learned Swahili when he lived in Jenkinstownship, Zimbabwe, where he had a trading post. As a rite-of-passage, like most coming-of-age Sephardic young men from Rhodes, both of my great-abuelos traded tools, food, and cloth with the local people.

216. Fear of the evil eye is deeply ingrained in the Sephardic consciousness. Kabbalist rabbis have special therapeutic formula (mezuzahs, *hamsa*s and turquoise beads) that they place on doorjambs, diapers of newborns, clothing of pregnant women, and the sick. Sacred amulets such as crystals, worry dolls, and protective symbols are often used during healing rituals and ceremonies. These objects are tucked inside medicine pouches, crafted as jewelry to be worn as guards, incorporated in healing sessions, and displayed in sacred spaces and home altars.

217. The following details can give the reader a sense of Moroccan Jews' complex history:
- Jews lived in Morocco prior to Arabs and Islam by at least 1000 years.

-The Moroccan Jewish Museum in Casablanca is the only Jewish museum in any Arab country.

-Essaouira once was a model of an Arab town where Muslims and Jews co-existed in both rich and poor districts. In every other Moroccan town and city, and throughout the Arab World, the term 'minority' was applied to Jews. In Essaouira, Jews were not considered minorities because almost as many Jews as Muslims lived there.

-*Megorashim* was the word for Jews expelled from Spain; *al azma* were 'those who ran away' from Spain; *toshabim* were the Jews who had lived in Morocco before the Inquisition.
- During their years of persecution, many Moroccan Jews fled to remote mountain Berber villages. They spoke Judeo-Berber and lived symbiotically for over 700 years.
- Maimonides fled Fez and the forced conversions of the intolerant Al Moravid Dynasty (1056-1147) (encouraging other Jews to do the same). In Egypt, he became the

Chief Rabbi of Cairo and the physician to Saladin.

-"Morocco: Jews and Art in a Muslim Land," the 2000 exhibition at The Jewish Museum of New York, explores "the concepts of difference and sameness" and the history of "two intermingled cultures without a single, distinct voice." During the Mimouna festival, Jews dress as Muslims, frequently borrowing clothes from their Muslim neighbors. Harvey E. Goldberg suggests that the Mimouna festival was an attempt for Jews to re-integrate into Muslim society following their religious seclusion during the eight days of Passover. In this way, they could maintain their religious differences (and stave off anti-Jewish phobias, such as "Where are the Jews?" and perhaps, "Are they plotting against us?" while staying connected to their Muslim neighbors. In the context of the exhibition, Oumama Aouad Lahrech states: "Tell me what you remember and I will tell you what you will become." The show serves as an important bridge among dispersed family members who may have had lost contact for hundreds of years (www.aljadid.com/content/different-kind-diaspora-moroccan-jews-looking-back#sthash.3JvLxLRg.dpuf).

218. Cross-cultural collaborating scholars in arts and sciences explore abstract, mystical thought in the study of *girih* (knot) designs that "inspire contemplation and make a statement about the imponderable harmonies of a divinely ordered universe" (Robert Irwin, Islamic Art in Context cited in *Saudi Aramco World*. Sept./Oct. 2014: 31). *Girih* patterns are tessellations—embodying "spiritual cogitation and emotion through geometry. …Mathematics is the only universal language, and has shown itself consistently capable of connecting people through time and space" (Peter Lu cited in Ibid., 31). In *Zazu Dreams*, we are witnessing mathematics in the context of cosmology and include love in that universal language.

219. Istanbul is the only city in the world that publishes a newspaper in Ladino: *Los Muestros, La Voix des Sefarades*.

220. *Zellig* are mosaics decorating Moroccan buildings.

221. *Haketi*a is a Judeo-Spanish language spoken mostly in Northern Morocco.

222. We are interpreting *Lag B'Omer*, the 33rd Day of the Counting of the Omer, between Pesach and Shavuot, The Bonfire Night as an opportunity to acknowledge one's personal strength. Following "the biblical account of Joseph instructing Pharoah to store grain in years of plenty, for the years of drought that lay ahead; Rabbi Nachman tells us that this is a hint that we should do the same in our own spiritual journey" Yehudit Levy, www.breslev.co.il/articles/holidays_and_fast_days/lag_bomer/building_bonfires.aspx?id=24317&language=english). We must gather all of our positive thoughts and deeds as reminders of our collective and individual wholeness.

223. Every town in Morocco has its own *tzaddik*. Muslim *marabouts* are like the Jewish *tzaddiks*.

224. According to legend, Amran ben Diwan entered the Cave of the Patriachs in Hebron which was forbidden for Jews at the time. He was disguised as a Muslim. When he was recognized as a Jew, he was reported to the Ottoman Pasha who ordered his arrest. Ben Diwan was finally able to flee and return to Morocco. Rabbi ben Diwan, the most revered tzaddik, is buried under a tree that never burns despite the fire and multitude of candles that have been lit there for centuries.

225. Strangers who enter the tents are welcomed and fed. The Talmud tells us the mitzvah of hospitality is one way to honor God, and is as important as Torah study. Hospitality teaches us the habit of thinking about other people's feelings—what they might be experiencing. Hospitality teaches us compassion and empathy—both are integral to ritualistic prayer.

226. Daniel Matt states the Zohar, taken from the Book of Daniel, is the "third holiest book in all of Judaism, after the Bible and the Talmud" (Bildner Center, Lecture, 2013).

227. The phrase, "A reconciliation with the earth," comes from the documentary "Dirt!"

228. Bar-Yohai was affectionately known as Rasbhi in the year 2nd century. Composed in Aramic supposedly by Kabbalist Rav Shimon bar Yochai, the Zohar (the foundational text of the Kabbalah), which translates as זֹהַר, splendor, or radiance, offers possibilities of healing, miracles, prosperity, and protection. "The Zohar [known as The Book of Enlightenment] is the internal soul of the Bible…it reveals the secrets of the Bible" (Matt, Bildner Center, Lecture, 2013). Rashbi's Hilloula may be the most popular among Sephardim in North Africa. Some contemporary rabbis question whether or not Rashbi did in fact write the Zohar. Kabbalah scholar Daniel Matt claims that the Sephardic Rabbi Moshe (Moses) de Leon of 13th century Spain actually wrote the Zohar and hid his identity behind the famous Rashbi in order to gain credence so that his words would be read and spread. By claiming the Zohar was "written under the influence of a holy spirit," under the guise of an authority alive 1,000 years before the Kabbalah, Moses de Leon was able to profit financially. We include this debate as an example of the fluidity of interpreting history and Judaic commentary always in flux.

229. We focus on the 'Zoar' (Ladino translation for Book of Jewish Mysticism) as integral to the climax of *Zazu Dreams* because it both reinterprets the *lekha* (to yourself): "Travel in order to transform yourself, create yourself anew" (Zorenberg 139), paying deep attention to what already exists. The Zohar embodies the "delectable delight diverging" (Matt, Bildner Center, Lecture, 2013) from the essence. In other words, the Zohar, which emerged from within the context of 13th century Spain,

still offers an invitation to receive the ongoing choice of being fully alive, fully present, fully connected to one's communities. The Zohar reminds us: "Love comes *from affinity*" (author's italicis, Zorenberg 251), no matter how unpredictable it may be. (See footnote 242 for a discussion of unpredictable affinities.)

230.   Quantum theorists discuss our multiverse as an ensemble of universes.

231.   (Arundhati Roy, *The Cost of Living*. New York: The Modern Library, 1999: 123).

232.   In her 2016 lecture with the Institute for Arts and Humanities at Pennsylvania State University, Rosi Braidotti cited Vandana Shiva, who advocates for "an end to the monoculture of the mind " In Mark Achbar, Jennifer Abbott, and Joel Bakan's 2004 documentary film, *The Corporation,* Shiva discusses the implications of 'terminator technology' and 'terminator seeds.' Sterilizing seeds means that "farmers are not able to save their seeds, seeds that will destroy themselves through a suicide gene, seeds that are designed to only produce crop in one season. You really need to have a brutal mind. It's a war against evolution to even think in those [profit-driven] terms." See also: Dr. Shiva's *Monocultures of the Mind: Perspectives on Biodiversity and Biotechnology*, London: Zed Books, 1993.

233.   The possibilities of ethically shared seeds are becoming radically dimished as intellectual property rights and utility patents monopolize US agriculture. In resistance, the Open Source Seed Initiative (OSSI), inspired by the conviviality of open source software, has attempted to protect the Commons and its 'ethic of sharing.' Rather than treating seeds as software (codes that can be rewritten and patented), a shared distribution of germplasm (seeds) establishes a shared distribution of power. More than ever because of climate disruption, we need a diverse, publicly accessible seed supply. 'Open-pollinated' ('The O.P.') seeds undermine ownership implied in the intellectual-property system. This commitment to the Commons ensures food security, thus national security (Lisa H. Hamilton, *Linux for Lettuce,* ed. Rebecca Skloot, *The Best American Science and Nature Writing*. New York: Houghton, Mifflin, Harcourt, 2015: 75-89). "Knowledge, Humboldt believed, had to be shared, exchanged and made available to everybody" (Wulf 2). In comparison with the Commons in which people belonged to the land (the land did not belong to the people), our modern industrial lifestyle demands diminished public regulation: Privatization "means you take a public institution and give it to an unaccountable tyranny" (Noam Chomsky cited in "The Corporation").

234.   Proper poop-use includes thermophilic composting of humanure (see Joseph Jenkins' reference in footnote 65).

235.   Marine-life, many of which are endangered, gets entangled in Illegally set nylon rope fishing nets called gillnets. "[S]ometimes [gillnets] break away from their moorings and roam the ocean, continuing to catch fish until the net is so fish-laden it sinks to the bottom of the ocean to become food for predators" (Kurlansky, 2011: 100).

236.   Currently, there is a battle going on in Morocco over a major ban on destructive and unselective drift gillnets. The activists from Oceana fought hard to officially phase them out in 2010. A recent undercover Oceana investigation discovered that illegal driftnet gillnets are being used again in Tangier. Even though the US and the European Union provided financial aid to Morocco to phase out the killer nets, critical enforcement of the ban is failing. "The nets not only torture sea life, slowly drowning dolphins, whales, and sea turtles, but they also hurt honest fisherman who catch swordfish locally and legally. Illegally obtained swordfish are imported into Spain and are then to Italy, cheating fisherman and conscientious buyers in these other countries" (Oceana e-newsletter, 2015). Ignoring the ban encourages other illegal fisherman to break the law and destroy more life.

237.   Marine activists, such as Oceanna or Greenpeace, are attempting to stop the US construction of a military airstrip in Japan that would destroy the last habitat for endangered Okinawa dugongs (a cousin of the manatee).

238.   The SeaVax can suck up to 22 million kgs of plastic a year.

239.   Again, we revisit the concept of *adab*: lived values for personal and social conduct that social permaculture supports. This ritual praxis of ethics can be found in the Zohar. We are suggesting that *tikkun olam* can be a result of *bal tashchit*.

Congruently, Mahatma Gandhi's "Experiments in Truth" included eleven vows of ashram living. He taught that the vow not to waste is integral to Satyagraha, passive non-violence. See the children's book written by Gandhi's grandson: Arun Gandhi and Bethany Hegedus, illustrated by Evan Turk, *Be the Change, A Grandfather Gandhi Story,* New York: Atheneum Books, 2016.

240.   Within a five-year period, the Falasha population of Ethiopia, also known as Beta Israel (House of Israel), was almost annihilated. In the late 1970s to early 80s, by the time Israel decided to allow them to escape ethnic cleansing in Ethiopia and migrate over the border into the state of Israel as legitimate Jews, the Falasha population had decreased from 500,000 to 30,000.

241.   Crypto-Jews who have maintained Sabbath and other traditions in secrecy for 500 or more years often are required to *convert* back to Judaism, rather than their faith being accepted as legitimate! The children's book, *Hush Harbor: Praying in Secret* (written by Freddi Williams Evans and illustrated by Erin Bennett Banks) tells a similar story of how enslaved Africans in the nineteenth century in

the US collectively worshiped—maintaining their spiritual traditions in secrecy.

242. Abra= אברה translates as 'to create' and cadabra= כדברא translates as 'as I say.' Zazu's dreams invite magic to manifest from stories—woven words. Salman Rushdie describes one origin of Abracadabra as a kabbalistic formula from which spirits emanate from the G-d Abraxas (547). Like the *hamsa*, it is found engraved on Abraxas stones that were worn as amulets. Abracadabra was a mystical word, an incantation used to ward off disease and bad luck. Its magical power emerges from its border-crossing capacity, a crossing over like Abraham who "is urged to unseal himself...to create love connections in the world..." (Zornberg 156). The origin of the word *Abracadabra!* is an evocation of how we are all intermeshed—a crossing-over of boundaries, an integrating of unpredictable affinities (such as fair treatment of workers is a food issue or lead poisoning inner city children is a water issue—case in point: Flint, Michigan, USA 2016). This social permaculture offers "[t]he playful discovery of our interdependence, of emergence, of coevolution. ...That is the principle: that we should allow the translation [reciprocally carry across] to transform this world through an invitation to participate in the discovery of what already is" (Cecilia Vicuña with Camila Marambio, *The Miami Rail*. Summer 2015: miamirail.org/visual-arts/cecilia-vicuna-with-camila-marambio). For sustainable change to take root, we much remember that to educate means 'to draw out,' (not to impose, as in the case of standardized education in the US, and not to erase, as in the case of the way too many of our histories are conventionally taught).

The legacy of Alexander von Humboldt offers a prime example of social permaculture—theory in action as a lived understanding of the intricate relationships that support nature in conjunction with a profound respect for human life. For example, Humboldt invented and ensured the use of respiratory masks and lamps that would work in oxygen deprived shafts to protect coal miners—an attempt to ease their horrendous working conditions (Wulf 21).

243. Moslems who live in the Sahara refer to the desert as "The Snow of Sand." Due to climate change and environmental degradation, the Sahara Desert is expanding one mile each year while rainfall has declined 30% in the last 40 years. The UN Environmental Program predicts there could be a 70% drop in crop yields in the region if violent conflict persists.

244. Dunes are said to boom, roar, thunder, shine, squeak, and sing.

245. The diversity of bacteria is a prime example of the media telling us one thing, while biological facts are actually quite the opposite. For centuries, rice has been grown in the same fields throughout Asia without depleting the soil and without adding fertilizer. The key is that cyanobacteria live in the ground and fertilize the fields. Decay bacteria, like the shenanigans of Joha the Trickster, can work for us and against us—they provide fertile soil, but they also can spoil food. Again, we suggest that contradictions can keep us curious and alert, instead of entrenching our societal behaviors in 'sanitary ideologies'—Paul Virilio's term for fear-based, reactionary bacteria-phobic cultural practices. Donna Haraway shares that "the world is a coding trickster with whom we must learn to converse" (*Simians, Cyborgs, and Women: The Reinvention of Nature*. New York: Routledge, 1991: 201).

Bacteria break down waste into chemicals that can be re-used. Models include using oil-gobbling bacteria to clean oil spills in both water and soil, cyanide-gobbling bacteria used near gold mines, or bacteria that break down trichloroethylene (TCE) in industrial solvents such as creosote (a wood preservative on railroad ties and telephone poles to prevent wood from rotting). In their search for "microbes that naturally feed on toxic substances...[and] microbes with useful appetites," (Howard Sacklam, *Bacteria*. New York: 21st Century Books, 1994: 44) scientists are experimenting with 'rapid-action' dioxin, DDT, and PCB-eating bacteria. Instead of relying on our downward spiraling addiction to pesticides, many activists/farmers deploy biological control; for instance, employing a bacterium called *Bacillus thuringiensis* (Bt) containing a protein that eats through the gut of a caterpillar that potentially could destroy thousands of crops and farmland.

Engineers are relying on similar biological control methods to use algae-eating carp (like poop-eating dung beetles or brine shrimp and marine debris-eating sea slugs) to eat/ clean natural build-up of algae in canals that divert billions **of** gallons water from Lake Havasu to Phoenix. The Central Arizona Project (C.A.P.) is the largest and most costly aqueduct system ever constructed in the US—except for the cost-effective algae-eating carp. And sometimes, engineers do the opposite and specifically employ algae, rather than try to get rid of it. MIT researcher, Issac Berzin, planted an algae-farm next to a power plant, another example of biological control. Algae become a super photosynthetic machine that sucks up the carbon dioxide like a sponge. The algae can then be gathered, dried, and used as a biofuel for renewable energy. This process removes 50 million tons of carbon dioxide from the earth's atmosphere.

The Village of Living Water in Japan's Shiga prefecture uses carp as a natural vacuum to consume food scraps. Their ingenious zero-waste method provides people and their crops with fresh, clean water. In contrast, in addition to the current epidemic of water contamination due to corroding lead pipes, 40% of food in the US is thrown away each year; this amounts to throwing away $165 billion of food each year. At least in the "Star Wars" series, George Lucas demonstrated an awareness of the cycle of life by including a dianogas, a garbage squid who feeds on scraps of decaying organic matter in sewers, trash compactors, and garbage pits across the galaxy. Maybe US politicians and entrepreneurs could follow suit?

246. The dung-rolling beetle is a type of scarab belonging to the beetle family *Scarabaeidae*, the scarab beetles; and, is one of the most remarkable of all the 350,000 different beetle species. A small (1.5 Kg) pile of Elephant dung on the African savannah can attract about 16,000 dung beetles of various shapes and sizes, who among their flurry, will completely eat or bury that dung in only two hours. One dung beetle can bury 250 times its own weight in one night.

They use "their serrated foreleg and broad hoe-like head to carve out chunks of fecal material to use as food. They ingest huge quantities of dung, using their membranous mandibles to strain out remnants of undigested food, bacteria, yeasts, and molds" (Evans and Bellamy 115). Carefully cutting, shaping, rolling, and burying chunks of animal excrement into perfectly round spheres for food and nesting, their parental care is exceptional in the insect world. Few six-legged creatures demonstrate "the industriousness of dung beetles carving up the spoils of juicy bovine leavings, carting them away to provide for their young" (Ibid., 170). Poop is prime living material and the dung beetle has found a way to bypass the competition of flies, wasps, and other beetles: they break off a chunk and roll it away from their competitors. Later they eat it or lay their eggs in it; once born, the larva will have a feast as it eats its way out of its snuggly home!

We are making a false division between the scarab and the dung beetle to emphasize how something historically revered has simultaneously been historically reviled. For instance, in Medieval Christianity, the dung beetle symbolized the sinner and was associated with "foulness and wickedness" (Ibid., 141)— quite the opposite of its actual role in our ecosystem. In contrast with the holy rollers, the ancient Egyptians deified the dung beetle, their most significant religious symbol. It's persistence and repetition represented both highly rational behavior, and was thought to be governed by the supernatural, symbolizing "the invisible forces that move the sun across the sky in a geocentric universe" (Ibid., 9).

Symbolizing the Sun's rays and Moon's cycle, the shape of its head and body reinforced the scarab's intimate relationship with the heavenly bodies. Simultaneously, its daily actions—the rolling of the poop, paralleled Ra, the Sun God, rolling the sun across the sky.

Thriving in waste, while worshipped by all ancient civilizations, the dung scarab beetle represents the *both/and*, the *la'am* (simultaneously yes and no in Hebrew and Arabic), the balance of contradictions. It represents life itself: hieroglyphic inscriptions from ancient Egypt designate the scarab with the syllable *kheperi*, 'to be,' 'to exist.' It is also associated with birth: In some South America Indian tribes a dung beetle called *Aksak* is said to have modeled the first man and woman from clay. Interfacing biology with anthropology, our story offers possibilities of cultivating life from death, birth from waste (www.earthlife.net/insects/dung.html).

247. *Onthophagus gazella*, gazelle scarab or gazelle dung scarab beetle, is the species identification for the common named, brown dung beetle. Their lamellate antennae (branched like antlers) are characteristic of the scarab beetles (6legs2many.wordpress.com/tag/gazelle-scarab). In Turkey, the extraordinary horns projecting from the head or thorax of the stag scarab beetle (a cousin of the dung beetle) are associated with the evil eye (Evans and Bellamy 142).

248. The scarab is a symbol of mesmerizing diversity and the ability to survive. There are about 30,000 *Scarabadaiae* variations within the beetle family.

249. The *bo'sun*, first mate, is the second in command from the ship's captain. S/he is a sailing master.

250. The infamous secret the fox utters to *Le Petit Prince* (*On ne voit bien qu'avec le cœur. L'essentiel est invisible pour les yeux*/ One sees clearly only with the heart. What is essential is invisible to the eyes) has traditionally been translated through the lens of love (en.wikipedia.org/wiki/The_Little_Prince). We would like to stretch the possibilities of this interpretation of love to include a commitment to embracing multiple perspectives, multiple truths, even multiple universes—a multiverse— the possibility that our Milky Way galaxy is one among many. *Kutub al-a'ja'ib* translates from Arabic as 'books of wonder,' "not only what one sees and hears on one's travels, but also what one could not have possibly seen because it did not then nor did it ever exist. …Fusing the world of the impossible with the world of the merely strange-but-true…" (Bejarano Escanilla and Werner 36-39, 36). Our story suggests that love is thoroughly enriched by finding connections with the unfamiliar.

251. Paralleling Adichie's recognition of empathy, Karen Barad provokes us: "The only possibility we have of catching a glimpse of ourselves is through the eyes of another" (11).

252. The word 'grain' has been derived from old Fr. *grein* and from Latin *granum*, which means seed. We can think of sand giving birth to water—sand as a seed for water. In his *Sand: The Never-Ending Story*, Michael Welland tells us: "There are beetles in the Namib that seem to use sand to solve the water problem. The same cold offshore current that dries out the coastal Namib also creates fogs that roll in over the dunes. Button beetles excavate furrows in the sand at right angles to the fog-carrying wind; the

furrows disrupt the airflow, causing eddies from which moisture condenses and the beetles can drink. There is often dew in the driest desert…" (174). And then there is the fog beetle, also from the Namib Desert, one of the most arid places on earth. *Stenocara gracilipes*, also known as the *Fogstand Beetle*, like the button beetle, collects minute quantities of moisture from the morning fog and dew. Learning from nature, such biomimicry could offer one alternative to our escalating water crisis. If we were to shift the scale, using both button and fog beetles as models for water collection in the desert by extracting moisture from the air, perhaps we will not be left high and dry once desertification engulfs our planet.

An example of this productive creativity is taking place in one of the driest deserts in the world: Chungungo, Chile. Camanchaga is a climatic phenomenon, a very heavy fog, often accompanied by a cold wind. Mimicking the action of the leaves on the town's eucalyptus trees, the villagers have manufactured fog catchers or mist nets to remediate its chronic water shortage. Just as the leaves catch moisture and form droplets, the villagers construct huge mesh nets, simulating the leaves to harvest water droplets. They collect the water in gutters, then into a pipeline that drains into tanks, and finally into the taps of homes and businesses throughout the village. Most significantly, the water is cleaner than the former system of trucks delivering water—often contaminated with disease from the transport tanks. The Camanchaga water system has improved the health of the entire local community—providing enough water for domestic consumption and approximately 10 acres of community vegetable gardens (Swanson 42-3). Once again, we must be extremely careful when we take something that works perfectly well in a *small scale* and attempt to exponentially amplify it. Maintaining this ethics of scale is critical so a company like Nestlé would not gain control of such low-tech practices.

In T*he Women In The Dunes*, Kobo Abé's brilliantly depicts the transformation of sand into water. The main male character believes, as most of us do, that sand is fundamentally dry. Yet he learns that sand actually has hydrodynamic properties: the capillary action of sand is a kind of pump—surface evaporation draws up subsurface water (233). The silicic acid in sand does not retain heat, but releases the warmth it has absorbed—a thick milk-white mist (Ibid., 164). The enormous quantity of mist across the dunes every evening and dawn is because capillary attraction never matches the speed of evaporation; water in sand is constantly replenished. The entire sand dunes are essentially an immense suction pump. Moisture clings to the pillars and walls; it rots wood, it rots everything (Ibid., 233-34). Perhaps Abé's character's sand-moisture revelation can be linked to the era of the Green Sahara or African Humid Period (see endnote 29).

253. To insulate itself from the cold, the grouse (in the same family as the endangered prairie chicken) fly-dives head first into a snow bank—one version of an igloo.

254. Sand rejects any stationary state; rather, it is "a world where existence was a series of states" (Abé 182). Sand is neither solid nor liquid, although it tends to behave like a liquid or gas, and can chemically transform into a solid and a liquid. Both sand and salt are dry liquids—again we see contradiction in action! "Dry sand itself behaves eerily like a liquid, but wet sand behaves more like a solid—as long as it's not too wet" (Welland 51). Sand is magic—it is contradiction in action! Competition arises because one tries to cling to a fixed position: "If one were to give up a fixed position and abandon oneself to the movement of the sands, competition would soon stop. Actually, in the deserts flowers bloomed and insects and other animals lived their lives. These creatures were able to escape competition through their great ability to adjust—for example the man's *beetle* family" (my italics) (Abé 15).

255. "For look! Within my hollow hand, / While round the earth careens, / I hold a single grain of sand / And wonder what it means/ Ah! If I had the eyes to see, / And brain to understand, / I think Life's mystery might be / Solved in this grain of sand" (Robert W. Service's poem cited in Welland 2). Because every grain of sand has a story to tell of past and present (Ibid., xiii), we must listen. Gottfried Willhelm Leibniz (1646–1716), a philosophical alchemist (as well as a mathematician and a logician), thought that the entire universe could be found within a grain of sand (Ibid., 29). The first line of William Blake's poem "To see a World," "To see a World in a Grain of Sand," echoes Leibniz, Spinoza, and Carson's micro-macro perception.

Dr. Barad coaxes us, "Can we trust our eyes?" (377). Her answer is rooted in how the brainless, eyeless brittlestar, a cousin of the sea slug, embodies multiple perspectives: empathic existence beyond optical site. Its fluid negotiations exemplify non-hierarchical, *convivial* "knowing, being, and doing" (Ibid., 380). Ralph Nader affirms: "When strangers start acting like neighbors... communities are reinvigorated."

256. Spinoza remarked: "We feel and we know that we are eternal. For the mind feels those things that it conceives by understanding no less than those things that it remembers. For the eyes of the mind, whereby it sees and observes things, are none other than proofs" (Benedictus de Spinoza, *Improvement of the Understanding / The Ethics / Correspondence,* Mineola, NY: Dover Publications, 1955).

257. Functionally, although by no means aesthetically or architecturally, reminiscent of the 'stepwells of India,' the 'singing wells' come from groups of men and boys in Ethiopia who form bucket brigades inside deep wells and chant as they pass the pails of water from person to

person. Singing helps them keep a rhythm to work quickly. Apparently, their process is more efficient than a machine would be. The Little Prince tells us: *Ce qui embellit le désert, dit le petit prince, c'est qu'il cache un puits quelque part…*/ "What makes the desert beautiful," said the little prince, "is that somewhere it hides a well" (Chapter XXIV).

258. Poop, like bacteria, is magic: the epitomy of *both/and*—deadly waste or abundant life-giver. When properly prepared (dried), feces can be transformed from harbinger of disease to generator of entire economies of extraordinarily valuable medicines (as mentioned earlier, dried dung has antiseptic properties that stave off fungi and bacterial infections), all-weather construction material, electrical usage, fertilizer, and insect repellant. Planet earth offers astounding models of unexpected juxtapositions—a balance of opposites. For instance, in the coldest, deepest parts of the ocean, hot water boils out of vents in the ocean floor.

259. This is a direct quote from the documentary "Dirt!" James Jiler is the director of The Greenhouse Program at Riker's Island Prison in New York City, one of the biggest prison complexes in the world. Jiler emphasizes: "What we give to the soil, what we give back to the soil, how we recycle our waste back into the soil, that is how we will survive" ("Dirt!"). Similarly, the two primary concepts of *The Humanure Handbook* are: "1) one organism's excretions are another organism's food, 2) there is no waste in nature" (J. Jenkins 223). Our country, on the other hand, operates from a *'toilet assumption:'* Philip Slater's concept of toilet assumption identifies US democracy as that which functions through institutional concealment—the collusive concept that "unwanted matter, unwanted difficulties, unwanted complexities and obstacles will disappear if they're removed from our immediate field of vision" (*The Pursuit of Loneliness*. Boston: Beacon Press, 1970: 19). See also: Alhadeff's *Viscous Expectations: Justice, Vulnerability, The Obscene* in which I explore multiple versions of this *ob-scene*, the off-stage. Joseph Jenkins' call to action is to incite awareness through our plumbing: "A household drain [or toilet] is not a waste disposal site. Consider the drain as a conduit to the natural world" (J. Jenkins 225). The key is how we choose to understand this process and take collective action. Our choices must be informed by the fact that 95% of urban, mostly untreated sewage ends up in the ocean; the world's rivers have become open sewers. More than 10 million people die every year from waterborne disease caused from sewage pollution and incinerators—that burn all types of household waste, including sewage. According to Greenpeace, incinerators actually encourage the production of waste. They need to be fed constantly, and *incinerator companies fine local governments if they don't deliver enough rubbish*! (my italics) (Toscani 107). See also: Jonah Winter's *Here Comes the Garbage Barge!* about the infamous trash displacement fiasco in 1987 in which the town of Islip, NY repeatedly failed in its attempts to dump its garbage elsewhere.

In company with the sewage and trash industries, toilet paper is big-business—an annual $3 billion market. Most toilet paper "contains traces of dioxin—a toxic by-product of the bleaching process that is the most potent cancer-causing agent in laboratory animals" (Toscani 42)—let alone in humans. When forming coalitions for integrative social change, we must recognize the perverse irony of wiping away potential helpful matter using extraordinarily harmful matter. Also, like giving birth lying down rather than squatting, for example, Western toilets are engineered counter to efficient fecal evacuation. In her *The Chair: Rethinking Body, Culture, and Design*, Galen Crantz argues that one of the downfalls of Western civilization is our status-obsession marked by the chair. See also analyses of the chair as a disciplinary tool in Ivan Illich's *Deschooling Society* and Michel Foucault's *Discipline and Punish: Birth of a Prison*. In addition, toilet seats can harbor parasites like ringworm and tapeworm. See Toscani p. 57 for unpleasant details.

260. Because of the vast contradictions among the politics/applications/history of salt, I am riffing on Michel Foucault's analytics of power—a game of power: (Michel Foucault, *Psychiatric Power: Lectures at the Collège de France 1973-1974.* translated by Graham Burchell, New York: Palgrave Macmillan, 2006: 16).

Relational history unfolds. Grotesquely ironic, in 1901, an abundance of oil was accidentally discovered in the quest for salt: "Anthony Lucas who, ignoring the advice of geologists, drilled an east Texas salt dome in 1901 and discovered an oil reserve so large it gave birth to the age of petroleum" (Alley's PSU lecture; See also: Mark Kurlansky and S.D. Schindler, *The Story of Salt*. New York: G.P. Putnam's Sons, 2006 (children version), Kurlansky's *Salt: A World History*, Toronto: Vintage Canada, 2002 (adult version)).

Until 100 or so years ago, humans and animals could not live without salt. Technology has made our need for salt both less necessary (we now have refrigeration and canning) *and* more urgent (we need therapeutic, construction, and transportation alternatives). Historically, salt has shaped multiple civilizations and their eating habits. Currently, salt is used in the manufacture of PVC, plastics, paper pulp, and a plethora of other inorganic and organic compounds. Prior to canning and refrigeration, salt was used as a preservative. In addition to tanning hides and the construction material for beautiful buildings (as we have seen in Iran), salt can be used to make roads—on its own, like some Caribbean islands where roads are made from salt, or mixed with sand like in Japan: "When salty sand is full of fog, it gets hard like starch…tanks can drive over it…" (Abé 36).

If corporations continue to pillage our planet for fossil

fuels, sea levels will continue to rise. For years there has been incontrovertible evidence that if this trend continues at its current rate, every coastal city across the globe will be wiped out. On one hand, melting glaciers will exponentially increase fresh water. For instance, the icecap covering Antarctica is about 1.3 miles thick, containing 60-70% of all Earth's fresh water. This staggering quantity of melt-off (non-potable in great quantities due to its lack of minerals) will radically undermine its surrounding saltwater ecosystems. On the other hand, ocean storms will (and are) more frequent and ferocious than ever before as sand increases due to desertification. What will we do with all that salt? With impending global blackout due to global warming, we may have to return to salt to preserve our food, build our homes, and heal our bodies. Since salt is one element we undoubtedly will have in abundance, perhaps we need to focus on its benefits. Otherwise, the water wars of "Mad Max," terraforming of "Dune," and moisture farms of "Star Wars" may colonize our future economies.

261. Mellâh (ملح or mallâh) in Arabic and מלח in Hebrew means salt—both are pronounced *melach*. The mellah in Fez was built on a salt marsh. *Mellah* also refers to a time when Muslim soldiers would return from battle with enemies' severed heads, salted in order to preserve the soldiers' booty. Jews were sometimes also seen as salting (contaminating) the soil they walked on. An ancient war-time practice was to 'salt the earth,' scattering salt throughout a defeated city in order to prevent anything from growing, thereby forcing starvation on the city's inhabitants.

262. This line from "The Rime of the Ancient Mariner" underlies the treacherous fact that only 2.5% of the water on Earth does not contain salt. Of this small percentage, only a fraction is acceptable for drinking and bathing.

263. "Singing and sound rituals were dedicated to cleanse the water, and so this ancient relationship of co-evolution between human and water has been going on [in Chile among the Incas] for more than 3,000 years" (Vicuña).

According to Corporate Accountability International's (CAI) Public Water Works campaign, "providing the needed funding for public water infrastructure over the next five years would create close to 1.9 million jobs and generate an additional $265.6 billion in economic activity" (The Story of Stuff e-newsletter, 2015). Additionally strategic taxes could provide critical resource: Chicago's tax on bottled water generates millions of dollars in revenue for public water projects. A penny per bottle on the estimated $13 billion in annual U.S. bottled water sales could support enormous infrastructural improvement.

264. Rob Nixon writes about 'slow violence' to describe how the threats wrought by climate change, toxic drift, deforestation, oil spills, and the environmental aftermath of war insidiously work their way into our daily lives (see Nixon's 2013 book, *Slow Violence and Environmentalism of the Poor*).

265. In Robert Kenner's "Merchants of Doubt," the 2014 documentary film on climate change disinformation, former South Carolina Republican Congressman, Bob Inglis (2015 recipient of the John F. Kennedy Profile in Courage Award for his stance on Climate Change), reminds viewers that climate change denial is hyper-functional because US citizens/ consumers "*want* to believe that the science is not real." The house in the suburbs represents this panic-denial: "You mean the way I am living is wrong?!"

266. July 2016 was the hottest month on the planet in recorded history (beginning in 1880). The earth's natural air conditioner can no longer function because the Arctic is rapidly melting. In July 2014, 40,000 square miles of Arctic ice melted *per day* (Gretel Ehrlich, "Rotten Ice: Traveling by dogsled in the melting Arctic," *Harper's Magazine*. April 2015: 41-51, 42).

267. Global warming leads to mass desertification in some regions and extreme flooding in others.

268. The compound salt is a combination of sodium (Na+) and chlorine (Cl-). When combined the two elements stabilize one another. Individually, they are potentially deadly: sodium is an extremely unstable, easily combustible metal, while chlorine is a poisonous, lethal gas.

A somewhat ridiculous extension of this quite literal metaphor is SALT, the Strategic Arms Limitation Talks. Organized in 1968, SALT's attempt at one form of conviviality consisted of a series of negotiations between the U.S. and the Soviet Union intended to limit or reduce nuclear armaments. SALT produced the Strategic Arms Limitation Treaty and was eventually superseded by the START (Strategic Arms Reductions Talks) negotiations in 1983, followed by Strategic Arms Reduction Treaty in 1991. Among all of these Talks and Treaties, the author of *Zazu Dreams* think Joha the Trickster must have been up to something!

269. The Salt Restaurant of Shiraz in Iran is reminiscent of Antonio Gaudi's outrageously whimsical architecture in Barcelona. The following are examples of salt buildings: an underground mosque in Punjab, Pakistan, cathedrals in Krakow and Bochina, Poland, and Palacio de Sal, a hotel made from one million blocks of salt on Salar de Uynni, the largest salt flat in the world, located in Bolivia (also where lithium for electric car batteries is harvested—see footnote 271).

270. Salt harvesting ranges from very low-fi, small-scale family operations to high-tech commercialized techniques, massive-industrial productions. As we have learned from history, the moment we identify a 'resource,' large-scale production takes off and frequently havoc ensues. This includes ongoing road construction (and all the destruction that road building entails), recreational

development, corporate monocultures, agribusiness, urbanization, dangerous mines, excessive logging, smuggling, abusive working conditions for both the laborers and the earth, and air/water pollution. Vandana Shiva explores the concept of 'resource' rampant in proclamations from both the Left and the Right: "Resource implied an ancient idea about the relationship between humans and nature—that the earth bestows gifts on humans who, in turn, are well advised to show diligence in order not to suffocate her generosity. In early modern times, 'resource' therefore suggested reciprocity along with regeneration. With the advent of industrialism and colonialism, however, a conceptual break occurred. 'Natural resources' became those parts of nature which were required as inputs for industrial production and colonial trade" ("Resources," ed. Wolfgang Sachs, *The Development Dictionary: A Guide to Knowledge and Power.* London: Zed, 1991: 206-218, 206). Historically, we see the curse of countries having an abundance of natural 'resources' (including silver, gold, tin, oil, cacao, and now salt). They tend to be at the whim of the international aid organizations, particularly the World Bank and International Monetary Fund (IMF). For instance, control, extraction, and exportation of natural 'resources' positions members of the Organization of the Petroleum Exporting Countries (OPEC) (Iran, Iraq, Libya, Nigeria, Angola, Saudi Arabia, and Venezuela) as frequent victims of their own treasures. In 1976, Pablo Perez Alfonzo, the Venezuelan founder of OPEP (*Organizacion de Paises Exportadores de Petroleo*), decried fossil fuels as the "*el excremento del diablo.*"

271. When commodified, even abundant materials can become symbolic ammunition in market-driven economies. Two examples include salt mines that can be dangerous and have an accompanying history of violence and smuggling, and the new demand for lithium. Lithium is derived from salt found beneath a salt flat's thick crust layer of milky brine. Bolivia's four thousand square miles (10,000 square km) salt flat, Salar de Uynni, under which is buried half the world's salt 'resource' is being called 'the Saudi Arabia of lithium.' Lithium, 'gray gold,' may compete with petroleum for future fuel needs. Poorly positioned to exploit this twenty-first-century fuel, Bolivia's pre-industrialized infrastructure is economically and ecologically precarious—unprepared to meet global energy supply demands. Cell phones and computers use small lightweight lithium batteries and the burgeoning market for electric cars depends on lithium for its batteries.

272. In the 14th century, the Arab explorer ibn Batuta found the saltworks at the oasis of Taghaza; Herodotus in the 5th century BCE also knew of this city made of rock salt with camel skin rooves.

273. Salt can be found in dry salt beds, underground springs, rocks beneath the soil, and the ocean. Desalinization, solar evaporation during which ocean water is turned into salt, has been explored throughout history. The Chinese began evaporating salt water in 1800 BCE. In 4th century BCE, Aristotle wrote: "Saltwater, when it turns into vapor, becomes sweet...and the vapor does not form saltwater again when it condenses." 250 years later, Julius Cesar's legions experimented with solar distillation, successfully converting seawater on a small scale for drinking. By the mid-nineteenth century, the British and American navies were using desalination devices onboard ships. Propelled by the need for fresh water, yet complicated by rapid population growth and poor water management, Middle Eastern peoples have been developing salt-removal processes for over 50 years (large.stanford.edu/courses/2013/ph240/rajavi2/). Currently, desalinization plants are extremely costly and have vastly damaging environmental impacts. Differing in their energy consumption and financial costs, there are three most common desalination technologies used in the Middle East: multistage flash (MSF), reverse osmosis (RO) and multi-effect distillation (MED). Desalinization could be a phenomenally beneficial 'solution' if it weren't so expensive and didn't involve an enormous energy demand—leaving a hefty carbon footprint. Additionally, the input process kills marine life in its larval stages, while the heavy brine extracted from the seawater is pumped back into the ocean, destabilizing a myriad of ecosystems. Yet, over $10 billion is currently being spent to develop desalinization plants all over the world.

Producing one-quarter of the 1% of humankind's daily fresh water needs (exponentially higher rates in the US than anywhere else in the world) as of 2013, there were approximately 17,000 desalinization plants throughout the world. Because of the high costs, 60% of these plants are in the Middle East; 70% of Saudi Arabia's potable water (essential for their agriculture) comes from distilled seawater.

Reverse osmosis in conjunction with solar power may be a viable alternative to the high financial and environmental costs of desalinization. Another 'space-age technology,' the patented irrigation product called DRiWATER, may be an additional sustainable option. Egypt has been investigating how to irrigate the Sinai and Sahara desert. Because industrial sized irrigation infrastructure is impractical, rather than engaging in a battle to control natural resources, scale-limitations have led to creative research. DRiWATER is a water-holding gel compound in the form of capsules used for irrigation that are 100% harmless to people and animals. Microbes eat the food-grade gel (zero polymers ingredients), allowing the water to slowly release into the ground—potentially transforming the terrain from barren desert to fruitful oasis. The process is chemical-free, completely biogradable, and wastes almost no water as it is delivered directly to plants roots (Swanson 136, 137). It can be shipped anywhere in the world in huge containers. DRiWATER is made to be mixed and packaged at a small scale, but still requires packaging infrastructure. Even with this knowledge, consumers still need to ask questions about DRiWATER's water transportation and distribution politics.

274. Biova is a German salt company that sells salt building materials in multiple colors.

275. We are suggesting the possibility of re-appropriating the derogatory usage of *mellah* in order to rewrite our future histories as symbiotic interrelationships. For example, we are researching what an ecologically conscious urban environment constructed using primarily salt would look like. The Emitaz Designing Group who designed and built the Salt Restaurant in Shiraz is a potential collaborator on this project.

276. The *Tripartite Mahzor,* a three-animal-headed being with human figures (whose three parts are kept in Budapest, London, and Oxford), merges "together with faces covered in other ways as well as with normal human faces, which is the most complicated category to understand" (Zsofia Buda, "Zoocephalic Figures in the Tripartite Mahzor," *Jewish Museum of Berlin Journal*. Nr. 12, 2015: 51). The apparitions in the climax of our story emerge from this Judaic history. Embracing contradiction and ambiguity, we should also mention that the biblical figure Lilith is seen as a conflation of three demonic women: Lilītu, Ardat Lilī, and Lamashtū.

277. In describing Gershom Scholem's perspective on the apparition of the Double, Borges tells us, "A tradition included in the Talmud tells the story of a man, searching for God, who met himself" (Jorge Borges, *Manual de zoología fantástica (The Book of Imaginary Beings)*. Buenos Aires: Breviarios, 1957; New York: Penguin: 1969: 62).

278. We would like to encourage the reader to consider the gift of the polymath, (Spinoza, Maimonides, Tagore, Ibn Sina, Marie Curie, Queen Margrethe of Denmark, Hypatia, Hildegarde de Bingen, Olympe de Gouges, to name of a few pre-20th and 21st century polymaths), and suggest we take up the possible implications of what an interdependent, transdisciplinary world could look like.

279. Moses de Leon was a Spanish mystic deeply influenced by Maimonides. His appeal was widespread because of his uncanny ability to access the mysteries of divinity through exegesis, narrative, and meditative practice. He offered a strategy for living *mitzvot*, embodying the mysteries of God. Again, we recognize the connections between Judaism and Hinduism.

280. Daniel Matt distinguishes between mystics (those who take the essence and hide in the mountain) and *Jewish* mystics (those who specifically *apply* the essence and live it out in community). As a weaver of stories and a journeyer, Zazu, like many deeply committed activists and artists, becomes a 'Jewish mystic.' Again, we return to *Abracadabra*, I create with words. Creativity enables community.

281. The Zohar tells us: "The term 'the world of separation' is used to describe the fragmented condition of this world. This term implies a dialectical relation between fragmentation and integration, by way of absence and yearning" (Zorenberg 400, nt. 47).

282. "Al' Garnati tells the story of the Sole, a flat fish that looks like it is sliced down the middle from tip to tail and often called the 'sole of Moses' after the Biblical story that in the parting of the Red Sea, the fish too was parted and thus became two live halves" (Bejarano Escanilla and Werner 37).

283. We are including Carson and Hawking in our story because, although neither were/are Jewish, nor from North Africa, India, or the Middle East, Carson's life-work focused on the web of terrestrial life while Hawking's life-work focuses on the web of cosmology and the 'theory of everything.' (On a side note, Hawking's first wife was a scholar of ancient Iberian poetry).

As a point אברה of reflection and discussion, we would like to offer the idea of paralleling quantum physics/mechanics and *tikkun olam*—a physics of the Kaballah. *Tikkun olam* is in constant process—like quantum physics, a continual non-arrival. Similarly, Charles and Ray Eames's "Powers of Ten," in which the microcosmos mirrors the macrocosmos, we are suggesting readers consider the relationships among individual bodies, social bodies, and celestial bodies. Albert Einstein stated, "I believe in Spinoza's God who reveals himself in the orderly harmony of what exists, not in a God who concerns himself with the fates and actions of human beings."

284. In letters to her editor, Carson wrote about her plan to "achieve…a synthesis of widely scattered facts, that have not heretofore been considered in relation to each other. It is now possible to build up, step by step, a really damning case against the use of these chemicals as they are now inflicted on us" (Linda Lear, *Rachel Carson: Witness for Nature*. New York: Henry Holt and Company, 1997: 340). Her commitment to evolving a comprehensive understanding reflects Judaic tenets.

285. Iranian-born American architect, writer, and humanitarian Nader Khalili's later work focused on housing structures for refugees, disaster victims, and the colonized poor. He taught them how to use the earth beneath their feet. The Israeli-born Canadian architect, urban designer, educator, theorist, and Syrian-Jewish author Moshe Safdie and Egyptian architect Hassan Fathy, the Middle East's Father of Sustainable Architecture using appropriate technology, also pioneered architecture for the poor.

286. Noor Inayat Khan was a freedom fighter in WWII. Khan was an East Indian-American Muslim who became a spy for Britain's covert unit, the Special Operations Executive (SOE) who supported an underground resistance network, in Nazi-occupied Paris. "Khan took her assignment knowing the average survival time for an underground wireless operator in occupied France was six weeks. She lasted 16. …Betrayed by a double agent, she was kept prisoner for almost a year until she was executed at Dachau concentration camp" (Omar Sacirbey, "The Quiet Muslim Heroes of World War II," *Saudi Aramco World*. Sept./ Oct. 2014). See the docudrama, "Enemy of the Reich: The Noor Inayat Khan Story."

287. Harriet Tubman was a freedom fighter leading up to and during the US Civil War. An African-American abolitionist who escaped slavery and near death as a young girl, Tubman led hundreds of runaway slaves to freedom along the Underground Railroad—a secret network from the Southern states to the North through which 60,000 to 100,000 fugitives escaped to freedom. People hid in carts, rode on horseback, and traveled by foot for hundreds of miles across forests, swamps, rivers, and ice. Slave-owners tried to capture Tubman by offering a $40,000 reward. Not only was Tubman never caught, she worked as a spy for the Northern Army during the Civil War. And after slavery was abolished, Tubman was an out-spoken activist for women's rights, black children, and poor black families.

288. In *The Woman Who Defied Kings*, Andrée Aelion Brookes chronicles the amazing journey of converso banker, Doña Gracia Nasi (Gracia Mendes Nasi 1510-1569). Doña Gracia fled the Inquisition in Portugal and wandered throughout Europe. In Antwerp where she found sanctuary, she eventually became a financially powerful banker. Doña Gracia lived the end of her life in Turkey where she was seen as the uncrowned Queen of Jewry in the Ottoman Empire.

We introduce Noor Inayat Khan, Harriet Tubman, Sol Hachuel, and Doña Gracia Nasi as a unified being who worked politically in alliance with other freedom fighters or who sacrificed their lives for their undying commitment to empathy and the common context of struggle. The liberation of Jews, of blacks, of women, of our natural world is fundamentally linked to socio-economic, political, and cultural liberation of all people. As stated in footnote 21: *We believe that only by understanding how all forms of oppression are interconnected can we understand that all forms of emancipation are equally interconnected*. Similarly, the Old Testament belief, "We are all flesh" (Isaiah 40:6), echoes the values of millions of small-scale farmers.

289. Mario Chiodo's "Remember Them: Champions of Humanity," located in downtown Oakland, California, consists of 25 humanitarians. The monument also includes an education curriculum that is taught in middle schools. Some schools divide these phenomenal people into categories to better understand how various issues are connected.

- Women's Rights: Shirin Ebadi, Susan B. Anthony, Coretta Scott King, Maya Angelou, Mahatma Gandhi, Helen Keller
- Freedom Struggles: Mahatma Gandhi, Martin Luther King, Jr., Nelson Mandela, Malcolm X, Tiananmen Square Protestor, Chief Joseph, Frederick Douglass, Abraham Lincoln, Oskar Schindler, Elie Wiesel, Ralph Abernathy, Rosa Parks, Coretta Scott King
- War against Nazism: Winston Churchill, Franklin Delano Roosevelt, Elie Wiesel, Oskar Schindler
- Advocates of Underserved Peoples/ Communities: Thich Nhat Hanh, Rigoberta Menchu, Cesar Chavez, Harvey Milk, Chief Joseph, Helen Keller, Martin Luther King, Jr., Mother Teresa
  Anti-Slavery: Abraham Lincoln, Frederick Douglass, Susan B. Anthony
- American Civil Rights: Martin Luther King, Jr., Malcolm X, Coretta Scott King, Rosa Parks, Maya Angelou, Ralph Abernathy, Ruby Bridges, Cesar Chavez
- Economic Justice: Helen Keller, Mahatma Gandhi, Martin Luther King, Jr., Coretta Scott King, Malcolm X, Cesar Chavez, Nelson Mandela, Maya Angelou, Rigoberta Menchu, Susan B. Anthony
- Focused on Class Issues: Rigoberta Menchu, Winston Churchill, Abraham Lincoln, Mahatma Gandhi, Malcolm X, Frederick Douglass, Martin Luther King, Jr., Cesar Chavez, Helen Keller.
- Time Spent in Jail/ Civil Disobedience: Mahatma Gandhi, Nelson Mandela, Martin Luther King, Jr., Rosa Parks, Susan B. Anthony, Ralph Abernathy, Malcolm X, Oskar Schindler, Frederick Douglass.
- Anti Colonialism: Mahatma Gandhi, Chief Joseph, Martin Luther King, Jr., Coretta Scott King, Susan B. Anthony, Abraham Lincoln, Frederick Douglass, Rigoberta Menchu, Malcolm X, Nelson Mandela.

290. Our ancestors include Sephardi, Ashkenazi, Mizrahi, Jewish people called Romaniotes from Greece, and Jews indigenously from China, India, Ghana, and Ethiopia.

291. The 'spy hop' is one of the unique behaviors of humpback whales in which they orient their bodies vertically so that they can 'spy' across the surface of the sea—keeping an eye out for potential food. They generally can be seen 'spy hopping" during the winter months in Hawaii.

292. *Megaptera* means 'big winged.' Their flippers (*Megaptera novaengliae*) are a third of their body length, longer than any other whale's. Unlike a fish's soft fin, these flippers are made up of bones like a hand or a wing.

293. Approximately only 20% of the Middle East is arable, usable agricultural land. During the 'Green Revolution' of the 1930s-1960s, hybrid strains were incorporated into mass production. The spread of new technologies led to a radical increase in crop production. These modernized management techniques included: expanding irrigation infrastructure, distributing hybridized seeds, developing high-yield grain varieties, and using artificial fertilizers and pesticides (in contrast with, for example, cow urine that has recently been discovered to not only be an extraordinarily effective fertilizer, but an equally effective pesticide). During the 'Green Revolution' corn yields increased by 70%, durum wheats and new 'adaptable' strains of rice were introduced, and ancient millet and sorghum varieties were revived.

This mass productivity acceleration resulted in proto-fascist agribusiness. One of its legacies is Monsanto, the monstrous FDA-patsy GMO giant. In March 2012, the "FDA deleted 1 million signatures on the 'Just Label It' Campaign calling for GMO labeling." More than one million Americans have demanded that the FDA label GMOs, yet in the biggest campaign history for the labeling of genetically modified foods, the FDA 'consolidated' the signatures to 394 (Mike Barrett, www.naturalsociety.com/corporate-giant-nestle-contradicts-gmo-stance/#ixzz3zEOWWO8t). GMOs inflict some of the most lethal impacts on the environment and human bodies. The interwoven worlds of food, agriculture, nutrition, and the environment are inseparable from the ways in which we raise our children and from those who drive daily decision-making (such as the EPA, CDC, FDA, and WHO). The insidiousness of standardization-for-profit, first developed and implemented during the Green Revolution, is now integral to our political structure. One perspective is that "abolishing the Senate [i]s a first step toward reducing the hegemony of monoculture" (Mark Bitton, *The New York Times*. Sunday, Sept. 13, 2015).

Infinite incidents demonstrate back-door monoculturization of minds, bodies, and environments. In 1991, while working with the Quijos-Quechua in Ecuador on an ethno-botany program, I witnessed multiple culturally inappropriate projects that were implemented by 'aid' organizations. Two examples of this corporate-imposed dependency include when a major seed distributor planted soybeans along the sides of the most traveled roads. Villagers picked and used the soybeans, but couldn't produce the plant on their own and ended up having to buy it from the transnational agribusiness who had originally planted the soybeans. Another example of insidious colonial control in the same community is the sickening absurdity of replacing thatched roofs with aluminum. Since the women cook on open fire in their homes, the roofs no longer absorbed the smoke. The rates of lung cancer, asthma, etc. soared. They then had to seek medical assistance from urban areas (often involving pharmaceutical dependency), travel expenses, etc.

294. *Al-haram al-sharif* ('the noble sanctuary') in Old Jerusalem is home to Judaism, Islam, and Christianity.

295. Arbil, the capital of Iraqi Kurdistan, is made up of layers upon layers of ruins that date back before 5000 BCE.

296. In 1934, King of Saudi Arabia 'Abd al-'Aziz Al Sa'ud granted permission for oil exploration to the United States.

297. Using the hypersensitive heat-sensors on its body that detect infrared radiation, the fire beetle (*Melanophila*) can locate a fire from more than 20 miles (32 kilometers) away. Following the direction of the signals (like a bloodhound), these beetles fly to a fire to mate while the trees are still burning and lay their eggs in the charred wood that no longer has predators. They have evolved to breed in dead trees because a live tree cell growth would crush their pupating larva bodies, or they would drown in the tree's sticky resin that is a natural pesticide. (Botanical resin is an evolutionary adaptation of plants and trees to protect themselves against insects). Engineers are applying the beetle's evolutionary strategies in designs for military infrared radiation detectors.

298. In many cultures throughout the world, The Milky Way was interpreted as variations of 'The Great Sky River.' For example, in Hindu mythology the name for The Milky Way is *Akasaganga*, meaning 'The Ganges River of the Sky.' In Judaic traditions, The Milky Way is called 'the River of Fire,' (*nehar ha-esh* in Hebrew and *nehar di-nur* in Aramaic—found in chapter 10, verse 7 of the book of Daniel).

299. Like ancient seafarers, dung beetles of the species *Scarabaeus zambesianus* navigate using the starry glow from the Milky Way—they are the only known non-human animal who use the Milky Way to navigate and orient themselves. While many animals (including humpbacks, honeybees, butterflies, birds, and seals) use the stars and sunlight's polarization pattern to navigate, the *Scarabaeus zambesianus* dung beetle is the first animal discovered to use the million-times dimmer polarization of moonlight and gradient of light provided by Milky Way to guide its travels. Moonlight polarization occurs when partial light from the moon mingles with atmospheric particles. Beetles climb on top of their dung balls and dance in circles as they examine the night sky to get their bearings. When a beetle looks up, it's registering the sun, moon and shifting patterns of ambient polarized light. Biologist Marie Dacke from Lunde University in Sweden states, "The dorsal (upper) parts of the dung beetles' eyes are specialized to be able to analyze the direction of light polarization—the direction that light vibrates in. …These celestial cues help the beetle avoid accidentally circling back to the poo pile, where other beetles may try to steal its food" (Marie

Dacke, Emily Baird, Marcus Byrne, Clarke H. Scholtz, Eric J. Warrant, "Dung Beetles Use the Milky Way for Orientation," Current Biology. 2013; DOI: 10.1016/j.cub.2012.12.034). Using various filters to alter the pattern of the polarized moonlight, researchers have determined that dung beetles are looking to roll their poop-prize away from their competition the fastest way possible—in a straight line: "Scientists noticed that when the moon was visible, these dung beetles did just that; they traveled in straight paths. But when it was a cloudy night, the beetles' paths became shaky and erratic. …To be sure, the beetles were indeed using the moon's polarization and not the moon itself, the researchers used a filter that changed the pattern of the polarized moonlight by 90 degrees. The beetles responded by changing their course by 90 degrees" (www.indianapublicmedia.org/amomentofscience/the-eye-of-the-dung-beetle/; news.nationalgeographic.com/news/2003/07/0702_030702_dungbeetle_2.html).

300. Once coprolites are soaked and re-softened, the poop smell returns, and its bacteria can live indefinitely.

301. "American babies are born with the highest levels of flame-retardant chemicals of any place in the world." And, the scientist whose studies were used by the Tobacco Industry to promote the necessity of such chemicals, "fireproofing the world around the cigarette," explicitly states that his research was 'distorted'—in fact, it has been repeatedly proven that these flame-retardants protect no one (*Chicago Tribune*, Patricia Callahan, cited in "Merchants of Doubt").

302. Unlike many unintended victims (including both people and wildlife), beetles are an example of how the assumed target may actually be completely off-target. In the case of beetles, their phenomenal capacity to adapt has proven that they cannot be the target of successful chemical extinction. Beetles out-survived pesticides intended to eradicate them and instead passed genetically based immunity onto its next generation. In response, these chemical controls have been replaced with attempts to sterilize pests by radiation, genetic engineering (GMOs), and the accession of predators, parasites, and pathogens. Because plants, animals, and humans are impacted by all of these pest-eradication methods, a domino-effect of ecological crises is now the norm. Rachel Carson's *Silent Spring* opened the door to public awareness, but industry, advertising, and convenience-culture has distorted the facts. One of too many examples, DDT and BHC, both proven carcinogen-inducing chemical pesticides now banned in the US, are shipped to other countries (predictably to the global South); the US then imports those products and the cycle of cultural and corporeal sickness continues. Arundhati Roy reminds us: "Colonialism, apartheid, slavery, ethnic cleansing, germ warfare, chemical weapons—[Western 'civilization'] virtually invented all of it" (112). She decries the relentless waste exported to the "Third World:" including dams, old weapons, superannuated aircraft carriers, and banned pesticides (Ibid., 15). Since Roy's *The Cost of Living* was published, we must now add high-tech trash to the litany of hazardous waste shipments sent to non-industrialized countries. This environmental colonialism includes computers, TVs, cell phones, audio components, baby monitors, e-waste, e-scrap—containing mercury, arsenic, cadmium, beryllium, and other toxins that may leak into the soil and ground water (Chris Carroll, *High Tech Trash*, ed. Elizabeth Kolbert, *The Best American Science and Nature Writing*. New York: Houghton, Mifflin, Harcourt, 2009: 33).

The politics of disposal go hand-in-hand with the politics of production—equally devastating manifestations of consumer colonialism. For Samsung's new smash hit cell phone, cobalt-powered handset Galaxy S7, children labourers in the Congo (as young as seven) are 'employed' to extract cobalt, a mineral used in rechargeable cell phone batteries. In the process, they inhale toxic dust—potentially leading to fatal lung disease. While Samsung boasts "the longest battery life ever," their child-labor-cobalt-supply chain is responsible for uncounted illnesses and death (secure.avaaz.org/en/dark_side_of_galaxy_cs/?bmVMybb&v=73055&cl=9582518532).

Proponents of overcoming 'The Digital Divide' (non-industrialized countries gaining 'access' to modern technologies —mobile devices, laptops, etc.), many of whom originate from countries who suffer the most from the production and disposal of such consumption, too often fail to recognize the wrenching irony of such imperialist practices.

303. "At death, human bodies often contain enough toxins and heavy metals to be classified as hazardous waste" (David W. Orr, *Earth in Mind: On Education, Environment, and the Human Prospect*. Washington D.C., Island Press, 1994: 1). Orr wrote this in 1994; now, just over 20 years later, given vaccines and their adjuvants administered through the CDC *required* schedule, the measurable toxins and heavy metals in human cadavers have exponentially increased.

Our bodies are toxic waste dumps even before we are born. Exposed to a myriad of toxic substances, about 45 chemical contaminants circulate throughout the average American pregnant woman's body. Some examples of aggressive heavy metal circulation include: vaccine ingredients and adjuvants directly injected into infants' and children's bodies, antibiotics in our food supply, and lead paint in poor neighborhoods as a manifestation of environmental racism and institutionalized classism.

The public water system crisis in the US is a blaring example of these consciously implemented injustices. Investment in public water infrastructure has decreased significantly over the past couple of decades in the United States; the results are found in the increasingly sick children's bodies from our poorest sectors. In 2016, Governor Rick Snyder of Flint, Michigan was responsible for redirecting known contaminated water into his district's poorest communities. All 10,000 of Flint's children under six years old are being tracked for lead poisoning. Such exposure can lead to extreme developmental disabilities, numerous physical and emotional side-effects, and in some cases death. In addition, ten Flint residents recently died from Legionnaire's disease originating from the bacteria in the water.

Many US cities are on the brink of reenacting the Flint water tragedy. Los Angeles has switched to chloramine, the disinfectant believed to have compounded Flint's water crisis. Los Angeles residents are taking a stand to hold their utilities accountable to this transition. When it comes into contact with dirty water, chloramine disinfection by-products (DBPs) are created. DPBs are 10,000 times more toxic than chlorine by-products and are completely unregulated. The World Health Organization states that in terms of killing many diseases (E. Coli, rotaviruses, and polio), chloramine is 2,000 to 100,000 times less effective than chlorine. Chloramine strips lead and copper piping and releases these heavy metals directly into our water supply. At current levels in Los Angeles, drinking water is deadly to fish.

Unfortunately, not a solution for bathing, but citizens can remove harmful chlorine by putting their filled glass water receptacles in sunshine.

304. We must learn from our natural environments (including sea slugs who clean the ocean and dung beetles who clean the earth). We must learn from those who consume waste matter. Carbon-bacteria-human co-existence offers a model within our own bodies in which gazillions of microbes in our gut (in addition to the gazillion of microbes in our skin and mouths) work symbiotically (Eric Roston, *The Carbon Age: How Life's Core Element Has Become Civilization's Greatest Threat*. New York: Walker and Company, 2009). Some parasites and worms strengthen our immune system from our insides, protecting us from multiple *auto-immune* diseases. Asthma and allergies have increased as our surroundings have become less dirty. "If we all moved into a completely sterile (germ-free) environment, we would die" (Dr. Joel Weinstock, Tufts University).

Simultaneously, our culture's sanitary ideologies' (Virilio) obsessive germ-frenzy that requires antibacterial hand-sanitizers distributed throughout our public space is creating an unprecedented chemical overload on women's and children's bodies. The high-volume chemical compounds triclosan and triclocarban (found in hand-sanitizers mouthwashes, toothpastes, deodorants, bedding, washcloths, towels, kitchen utensils, and toys) are known carcinogens. These pesticides disrupt hormone levels and tragically, are commonly found in breast milk. In daycares throughout the US, children are required to 'clean' their hands before snack time—essentially eating triclosan. Like flame retardants and polychlorinated biphenyls (PCBs), its effects include mpaired skeletal growth and muscle function that has led to cardiac arrest, lung damage, and an increased risk of allergies and immune-system-dysfunction in children. In 2013, the FDA announced: "There appears to be little or no evidence that antibacterial soaps and household products help prevent us from being exposed to germs, and they may even pose significant health risks" (Melanie Haiken, "Anti-bacterial Soaps May Pose Health Risks, FDA Says; Should They Be Banned?" *Forbes*, Dec. 16, 2013). Although the American Medical Association stated that this chemical is creating superbugs and is responsible for mutating viruses, it is still used in hospitals, which in turn sparks the consumer market. In 2012, Kline & Company antibacterial soaps comprised almost half of the $900 million liquid-soap market. Big Pharma has capitalized on germ-phobia—conveniently selling products that disable our natural immunity. The reality is "[m]odern research has discovered that only a very small number of microorganisms are pathogenic...able to make us sick. The vast majority of bacteria are beneficial... we cannot live without them" (Sally Fallon Morell and Thomas S. Cowan, *The Nourishing Traditions Book of Baby and Child Care*. Washington DC: The New Trends Publishing Co., 2013: 242). We must shift our focus from bacteria-phobia to environmental toxicities. Another layer to the irony of our modern poop predicament is that although most 'civilized' people see themselves as 'appropriately' fecophobic, we are obsessively addicted to Jurassic poop, dinosaur poop, fossil fuels.

305. "Similarly toxic are the bodies of whales and dolphins washed up on the banks of the St. Lawrence River and the Atlantic shore" (Orr 1).

306. This third poop is compost. J.I. Rodale, aka 'Mr. Organic,' and founder of the Rodale Institute in 1947, stated: "Compost is more than a fertilizer or a healing agent for the soil's wounds. It is a symbol of continuing life" (cited in Jenkins 48). Joe Jenkins' *The Humanure Handbook* includes a list of the benefits of compost:

ENRICHES SOIL
- Adds organic material
- Improves fertility and productivity
- Suppresses plant diseases
- Discourages insects
- Increases water retention
- Inoculates soil with beneficial microorganisms
- Reduces or eliminates fertilizer needs
- Moderates soil temperature

PREVENTS POLLUTION

- Reduces methane production in landfills
- Reduces or eliminates organic garbage
- Reduces or eliminates sewage

FIGHTS EXISTING POLLUTION
- Bind heavy metals
- Degrades toxic chemicals
- Cleans contaminated air
- Cleans stormwater runoff

RESTORES LAND
- Aids in reforestation
- Helps restore wildlife habitats
- Helps restore mined lands
- Helps restore damaged wetlands
- Helps restore erosion on flood plains

DESTROYS PATHOGENS
- Can destroy human disease pathogens
- Can destroy plant pathogens
- Can destroy livestock pathogens

SAVES MONEY
- Can be used to produce food
- Can eliminate waste disposal costs
- Reduces the need for water, fertilizers, and pesticides
- Can be sold at a profit
- Extends landfill life by diverting materials
- Is less costly bioremediation technique

(US EPA (October 1997). Compost-New Applications for an Age-Old Technology. EPA530-F-97-047; Jenkins 48).

One example of the remarkable benefits of compost is its bioremediation potential. Following clouds of radioactive fallout from the Chernobyl reactor meltdown that drifted over the Ukraine and northern Europe in 1986, there were multiple reports of gaps in the fallout map where biodynamic farms were located. From a bird's eye view lush, fertile regions were clearly designated—areas where biodynamic farms had radically reduced land plant contamination. The compost included cow manure mixed with yarrow and nettle stuffed into empty spiral horns. In addition to Rudolf Steiner's Agriculture Course and lectures on The Spiritual Foundations for the Prosperity of Agriculture that he gave in 1924 in which he discussed transmutation of atomic elements, "Maria Thun's barrel compost (BC) formulation [was] born out of concern for atmospheric fallout from above-ground nuclear weapons testing in the 1950s" (Lia and Linder 35).

307. "Under the Dome" is a film and presentation by Chai Jing. She made this for her daughter, who, because of the relentless smog infiltrating Bejing, has never seen clouds floating in a blue sky.

308. The burning forests in both Indonesia and Brazil can be seen from outer space.

309. Blindingly white, Bolivia's Salar de Uyuni looks like a frozen sea and can be seen from outer space. When Neil Armstrong saw it from the moon, he mistook the Salar for a giant glacier.

310. This legend comes from local Quechua or Aymara Indians of Bolivia. Beneath the glistening pale-blue salt crust of Salar de Uyuni lies the bountiful milky brine of the future—if we are careful and alter our consumption habits while committing to small-scale productions.

311. Humpbacks make one of the longest migrations of any land or sea mammal. Paralleling dung beetles that exclusively use the polarization of moonlight to navigate in straight lines, humpbacks also use the earth's solar system to guide themselves through their migration cycle and eventually back home, also in straight lines. "Humpback Whales May Be Migratory Astronomers" explores the research of how and why these whales can travel "uncannily straight paths for weeks at a time…using a combination of the sun's position, Earth's magnetism and even star maps to guide their 10,000-mile journeys" (www.wired.com/2011/04/humpback-whale-migration/).

Activist biologists work to convince governments to shift the routes of tankers out of the path of whale migrations. But, tankers and large and small boats are only part of steamrolling whale migration safety. It is hypothesized that migrating animals such as whales, eels, locusts, terns, caribou, monarch butterflies use electromagnetic frequencies (EMFs) to find their way (www.hbelc.org/about/about-emr-emfs). Magnetite is a metalloid substance in humpback brains that help them navigate using the earth's magnetic field to orient themselves. Because it severely disrupts electromagnetic fields, electro-pollution is creating havoc on animals' capacities to follow their migration routes. This sea of man-made electromagnetic radiation (EMR) (electromagnetic pollution or electropollution) disrupts their ability to navigate because of electrical impulses in the water and air.

We have little idea of how high the stakes really are. "Human beings are bioelectrical systems. Our hearts and brains are regulated by internal bioelectrical signals. Environmental exposures to artificial EMFs can interact with fundamental biological processes in the human body" (www.bioinitiative.org). (See also: *An Electric Silent Spring: Facing the edangers and Creating Safe Limits*. Katie Singer MA, Porter Books, An Imprint of Steiner Books, Anthroposophic Press).

Like DNA strands communicating with each other at same frequency, the earth's electromagnetic frequency has the exact resonance as alpha waves generated by a human brain (vimeo.com/54189727). This frequency is known as Schumann Resonance 7.83H2. (Patient Zero Productions "Resonance: Beings of Frequency" Directed by James Russell and J. Webster). Schuman Resonances, the airspace between the earth's surface the ionosphere (80 km or so above the ground), "functions like a giant spherical flute for electromagnetic waves." We are constantly immersed in these seven resonances—all part of the electromagnetic spectrum. The lowest of these resonance parallels human alpha brainwave activity (*Sonifications created for the Rhythms of the Universe,* collaboration among Mickey Hart, George Smoot and Mark Ballora, Pennsylvania State University 2105). The human brain has evolved in concordance with the earth.

Given the onslaught of wireless transmissions, radio transmissions, and cell phones, birds are frequently unable to navigate and bee colony collapse syndrome is accelerating. Cell phone technology propagates some of the most insidious impacts on both our environment and people. Cognitive deterioration in young people dependent on digital crutches resembles that of head injury victims. 'Digital dementia' is a modern physical condition arising from our ever-encroaching electric toxic soup (vimeo.com/17251471: How to protect yourself from EMF's, Elizabeth Kelley, director of Electromagnetic Safety Alliance). In 2011, the World Health Organization issued a public statememnt that mobile phone radiation is a possible carcinogen. They claimed that nobody should carry a cell phone in their pocket (Dr. Devra Davis, "The Truth about Mobile Phone and Wireless Radiation," University of Melbourne, Nov. 30, 2015: www.youtube.com/watch?v=BwyDCHf5iCY; See www.ehtrust.org for further details). Cell phone waves are actually very short—only about a foot long. Again, our refusal to shift basic behavior, like keeping the phone next to our head, will cause irreparable damage. Electromagnetic hypersensitivity (EHS) is another recent diagnostic emerging from our sci-fi age of microwave technology: EMFs and RFs from cell phones and towers, Wi-Fi, utility companies' AMI smart meters, smart phones, routers, monitors, etc. and other electronics that can send and receive visual and auditory data (www.activistpost.com/2016/01/environmental-refugees-electromagnetic-hypersensitivity-ehs-sufferers.html).

We have no choice but to be technology specimens—sacrificial guinea pigs. A few months ago, when the electrical company was removing my broken electrical meter, I specifically requested an analog replacement and explained why I did not want a smart-meter outside my son's bedroom. Obviously, they denied my request. Public Utility Commissions maintain their federal funding by denying the scientific validity of citizen's choices to defend their bodies and those of our children. Again, freedom of health is curtailed.

The PUC is also ignoring the World Health Organization's statement: "EHS is characterized by a variety of non-specific symptoms that differ from individual to individual. The symptoms are certainly real and can vary widely in their severity. Whatever the cause, EHS can be a disabling problem for the affected individual" (Yael Stein, MD, Slide 67 of 83 / UNESCO 10th Word Conference on Bioethics, Medical Ethics and Health Law). Those suffering from EMF Sensitivity have a legal disability, yet disability laws are consistently ignored. These potentially disabling electrical bombardments begin in the womb with ultrasound technology, continue as infants in the crib with 49 megahertz frequency baby monitors, and persist throughout our lives through electric blankets, microwave ovens, fluorescent lights, utility wires (power lines), cell phone towers, smart technology, and computers.

Melatonin is an anti-oxidant that regulates the immune system, and is thoroughly disrupted by digital technologies. Yet again, the medical establishment has a built-in captive audience. The more our bodies are required to adapt, the sicker we become—increasingly requiring 'professional' medical care and health insurance. Although many 'scientists' claim the Radition-EMF argument is a faulty one, NASA is simultaneously conducting research on the EMFs of spider feet in relation to space walking. How can they justify this irony?

Those who are taking these issues seriously include the UNESCO 10th World Conference on Bioethics, Medical Ethics and Health Law held January, 2015 in Jerusalem, the EHS Refuge Zone Open in France, WEEP-Canada (Wireless Electric Electromagnetic Pollution), ElectroSensitivity UK, the Swedish Association for the ElectroHyperSensitive, the BioInitiative Report working group (a public advocate in our Plasticene Age), and those exploring the German field of *Baubiologie* (See The Institute of Building Biology + Sustainability (IBN) in which thousands of architects, civil engineers, tradespeople, medical doctors, naturopaths and other individuals have the opportunity to stay informed about the latest developments in building biology: www.baubiologie.de/international/institute/).

312. As in the beginning of our story (the beginning of all of our stories), clouds of gas and dust are the origin of life, the origin of home.

313. While living in Spain, Maimonides learned of ibn Sina's (and other Persian and Arab polymaths') Aristotelian philosophies.

314. The Milky Way is the light created from about 100 billion distant stars that belong to the same family as our Sun. Its spiral arms are made up of giant clouds of stars, dust, and gas called nebulas. Galileo Galilei was the first astronomer to use a telescope to observe the movements of the night sky. In 1610, because he refused to succumb to the Catholic Church's lies, Galileo was imprisoned by the Inquisition—accused of heresy because of his defense of the Copernican system and Johannes Kepler's laws addressing elliptical planetary motion. They disproved

geocentric theories that planets circle around the earth, and proved that the earth and planets travel in elliptical paths (stretched out circles) around the sun. As with the theories of evolution and the mesochinyd, this process of proving and disproving demonstrates the dynamism of history. Like the universe, history is in constant flux.

We highlight these scientists in the context of our theme: *L'essentiel est invisible pour les yeux* (What is essential is invisible to the eyes). Kepler explained how telescopes work, describing the physics of magnification and the properties of reflection. He also determined that two eyes facilitate depth perception in the visual process—he created near and farsightedness eyeglasses. As a lens-grinder for telescope construction, we are (playfully) suggesting that Spinoza followed Kepler's lead. In contrast to grinding down glass, current nanotechnology development (such as scientists conducting research with Bell Labs) is building up calcite layers—exploring the brittlestar's microlens optical systems. Again, we revisit Dr. Barad: "Brittlestars don't *have* eyes; they *are* eyes" (375).

315. Like the Bolivian Aymara story about the breast milk and tears of a goddess creating their legendary salt flats, the Milky Way is said to come from breast milk. According to Greek myth, when Hera awoke, realized that Zeus had put his mortal mistress's baby Hercules to suckle at *her* breast, and quickly unlatched him, Hera's breast milk sprayed across the night sky. It was thought that each star was formed from a drop of breast milk.

316. Navajo mythology describes the creation of the Milky Way as a result of Coyote speeding up the process of the Holy People as they placed the stars in the sky.

317. The Milky Way is just one among a hundred billion other galaxies, none of which have a single center; it is the same, yet different. Dark matter holds the Milky Way together. It keeps its spiral shape because dark matter's gravity pulls on stars from all directions. Dark matter, like sand, is an intermediate substance.

318. By experimenting with auditory space, Kepler "mapped the universe and sought its inner harmony and structure" (Welland 54). We would like to think that Kepler's orchestral cosmos, his "celestial music," may have influenced Spinoza's process as an instrument maker. "Sounds are internal vibrations that reveal themselves as a subtle, rhythmic brightening and dimming of a star, a celestial symphony—turbulent rise and fall of hot gases on the star's surface, the vibrations penetrate deep into the stellar interior and become resonating tones that reveal the star's size, composition and mass" (www.goodsearch.com/search-web?utf8=%E2%9C%93&keywords=Kepler%E2%80%99s+Planet+Sounds&button=).

319. Baleen whales' skulls have acoustic properties that capture sounds as they vibrate along the whale's tympanoperiotic complex (TPC), an "interlocking bony puzzle" of ear bones that is solidly attached to the skull. In a process called bone conduction, the energy of low frequencies (which include their own vocalizations along with human-made noises) is directed to their TPC (ear bones). Many people hope this new discovery will influence legislators' decisions to limit oceanic human-made noise. Also, "This research has driven home one beautiful principle: Anatomic structure is no accident. It is functional, and often beautifully designed in unanticipated ways" (Ted W. Cranford, Petr Krysl. Fin Whale Sound Reception Mechanisms: Skull Vibration Enables Low-Frequency Hearing. *PLOS ONE*. 2015; 10 (1): e0116222 DOI: 10.1371/journal.pone.0116222 / San Diego State University. "Baleen whales hear through their bones," *Science Daily*. Jan. 29, 2015; www.sciencedaily.com/releases/2015/01/150129143032.htm).

320. In 1977, Voyager Golden Records sent recorded sounds of humpback whales to outer space on Voyager 1 and Voyager 2—sounds and images selected to present the diversity of life and culture on Earth. In addition to the humpback songs, the recordings included the beating of a human heart, birds and crickets chirping, and greetings in 55 different languages. They were intended for any one who might find them: intelligent extraterrestrial life forms or for future humans.

321. Whales used to live past 100 years old. Now due to marine ecology demolition their lifespan has radically decreased—ranging between 30 to 60 years.

322. A 50,000 year-old Neanderthal coprolite (fossil feces, frozen, dried, or lithified—the gradual process of a plant or animal turning to stone) was discovered in Gibraltar Cave, Spain (Jacob Berkowitz and Steve Mack, *Jurassic Poop: What Dinosaurs (and Others) Left Behind*. Toronto: Kids Can Press, 2006: 28). Bacteria cannot breathe when there is no oxygen. For example, in a compressed poop pile, bacteria cannot decompose the dung; this is the perfect environment for coprolites (poop fossils) to form.

323. The Dalai Lama has deemed Boulder, Colorado as one of the most spiritual communities in the world. Paleoecologist Karen Chin studies the relationships between ancient animals, plants, and the environment at the University of Colorado in Boulder. Dr. Chin is the only scientist in the world whose full-time focus is fossilized poop. She found the earliest case of dung beetles eating poop—75 million year old dinosaur poop (Ibid., 27).

324. When examining our culture's food politics (GMOs, monoculture industrial agriculture, crimes of the agrichemical lobby and of Nestlé food giant, environmental and corporeal effects of pesticides, fast food, obesity, and diabetes—the leading cause of death in the US), poop is a powerful magnifying glass. The individual body and social body cannot be separated. What a society accepts

and encourages as appropriate food for its citizens reflects the health of society. "The evidence is in the trash" (See Zal Batmangliji's 2013 film, "The East"). The recent popularity of 'fecal transfer' (transferring healthy fecal matter into a diseased colon to help heal the ill digestive tract) demonstrates a deep-seated need to re-align our bodies with our own more basic human functions.

325.   Dr. Chin's research is leading to a coprolite family tree that will help uncover relationships between ancient animals (including dinosaurs) and how their poop influenced the cycle of life. "Plants convert sunlight into food, animals digest the plants into feces, then insects and bacteria eat the poop and release nutrients that feed plants. It's the great cycle of life, and poop helps hold it all together…The soil we grow our food in is largely made from the poo of worms and other small animals" (Ibid., 7). By understanding this cycle, we can determine what food was grown where and how people prepared their meals. We can also learn about methane and artificial fertilizer. "In the 1840s, farmers in England didn't have enough animal manure to fertilize their crops. The solution? Dinosaur coprolites [dinosaur poop]. Hundreds of people in southeastern England were hired to dig up coprolites, which are rich in calcium phosphate, the main ingredient in fertilizer. Ground up coprolites mixed with sulfuric acid, the coprolites became the world's first artificial fertilizer" (Ibid., 21). A revolution in the way we grow food took place. Poop family trees also tell us stories about evolution by examining the excrement of the first multi-celled animals called metazoans, and stories about the history of pollination. Microscopic ancient beetle poop has been found full of pollen grains—proving that pollination relationships have been at play for 84 million years (Ibid., 36).

Farmer's have always understood the remarkable value of manure. "They know that animal manures are digested crops, and that the crops are soil, water, air, and sunshine converted into food, and the best way to use that manure is to put it back inot the fields from where it originated. …But what about *human* manure?" (J. Jenkins 42). Humanure, like 'night soil,' is NEVER supposed to be used fresh on crops (as it breeds potential pathogens—disease-causing microorganisms); rather, when it goes through the necessary process of bacterial digestion (composting), human feces becomes an ideal fertilizer—hygienically safe soil-building material. This information may help us understand how to more effectively use our bodies' waste products to our environment's benefit. Whether human ejecta or an apple core, "[o]rganic refuse is stored solar energy" (Ibid., 50).

326.   *Mazalot* are heavenly constellations that live among us. The Zohar and Midrash tell us, "There is no blade of grass that does not have a 'constellation'—*Mazal*—over it, telling it to grow" (www.chabad.org/library/article_cdo/aid/361901/jewish/Angels-and-Mazalot.html). At the center of the mosaic floor of the synagogue in Sepphoris is a circular representation of the Hebrew Zodiac, the twelve months with their corresponding animals revolve around the sun.

God tells us stories through the stars and planets. Stephen Hawking and his daughter, Lucy, declare we are all children of the stars. Some sources describe the stars as having intelligence; they were commonly thought to be angelic beings; each angel star a word, while constellations communicated full ideas. Because the Talmud continues to expand with infinite interpretations, it looks like a constellation (Simon Schama, *The Story of the Jews*, PBS, 2014).

327.   In a 1980s interview with Philip Roth, Milan Kundera reminded us, "The novelist teaches the reader to comprehend the world as a question. …There is wisdom and tolerance in that attitude. …It seems to me that all over the world people nowadays prefer to judge rather than to understand, to answer rather than ask, so that the voice of the novel can hardly be heard over the noisy foolishness of human certainties." In her *Harper's Magazine* article, "The Mother of All Questions," Rebecca Solnit shares, "On of my goals in life is to become truly rabbinical, to be able to answer closed questions with open questions…" (Oct. 2015).

328.   We all come into the world as a whole vessel (capacity to hold things that are nourishing, such as water or olive oil). Over the course of our lives, we are all shattered by the world; our work during our lifetime (Zazu's journey) is to put the pieces back together—even more beautifully than our original vessel (as in mosaics throughout the Middle East). When we recreate our selves/ recreate the vessel, it is stronger in the broken places—able to contain/ nourish with a restored sense of beauty and wholeness of our own creation. This is home.

329.   The myth of *tikkun olam* is known as "The Shattering of the Vessels" (*shevirat ha-kelim*). In the 12th century, Maimonides expanded the original meaning of *tikkun olam* to include a re-alignment of the world.

Additional Resources for Further Reading/Discussion

In addition to the sources (books, journals, articles, films, websites, blogs, poems, and interviews) cited in the "arcades:"

One Plastic Bag: Isatou Ceesay and the Recycling Women of the Gambia, Miranda Paul and Elizabeth Zunon

The Boy Who Harnessed the Wind, William Kamkwamba and Bryan Mealer

Beatrice's Goat, Page McBrier

One Hen: How One Small Loan Made a Big Difference, Katie Smith Millway

Mama Miti: Wangari Maathai and the Trees of Kenya, Donna Jo Napoli

The Ecology of Commerce, Paul Hawkens

Taboo Memories, Diasporic Voices, Ella Shohat

Israeli Cinema: East/West and the Politics of Representation, Ella Shohat

Between the Middle East and the Americas: The Cultural Politics of Diaspora, Ella Habiba Shohat and Evelyn Azeeza Alsultany

A People's History of the United States, Howard Zinn

The Book of Questions, Edmond Jabes

Tribe of Dina: A Jewish Women's Anthology, Melanie Kaye-Kantrowitz and Irena Klepfisz

The Essential Kabbalah, God and the Big Bang, and translator of *Zohar: The Book of Enlightenment,* Daniel C. Matt

Two Sephardic Giants of the Modern Age: Elijah Benamozegh, Sabato Morais, and Vichian Religious Humanism, Joel Kraemer

I Remember Rhodes, Rebecca Amato Levy

Refranes de los Judíos Sefardíes, from the Biblioteca Nueva Sefarad Volumen V

Sephardic Folk Dictionary, IV Edition Albert Morris Passy

Poesia Tradicional de las Judios Españoles, Manuel Alvar

The Rabbi's Cat, Joann Sfar

Folktales of Joha: Jewish Trickster, Matilda Koen-Sarano

Betraying Spinoza: The Renegade Jew Who Gave Us Modernity, Rebecca Goldstein

An Apprenticeship in Philosophy: Gilles Deleuze, Michael Hardt

The Night Moses de Leon Died, Daniel Y. Harris

500 Years In The Jewish Caribbean, Harry Ezratty

The Mezuzah in the Madonna's Foot, Trudi Alexi

Wedding Song: Memoirs of an Iranian Jewish Woman, Farideh Dayanim Goldin

Stephen Hawking: Breaking the Boundaries of Time and Space, John Bankston

The House of Nasi: Doña Gracia, Cecil Roth

Nurture Shock: New Thinking About Children, Po Bronson and Ashley Merryman

Emmanuel's Dream: The True Story of Emmanuel Ofosu Yeboah, Laurie Thompson

Ubiquitous: Celebrating Nature's Survivors, Joyce Sidman and Beckie Prange

The Particulars of Rapture: Reflections on Exodus, Avivah Gottlieb Zornberg

The Beginning of Desire: Reflections on Genesis, Avivah Gottlieb Zornberg

I Wonder Why the Sahara is Cold at Night, Kingfish Publishers

Here Come the Humpbacks, April Pulley Sayre, Illustrations by Jamie Hogan

The Hand: A Philosophical Inquiry into Human Being, Raymond Tallis

The Golem and the Jinni, Helene Wecker, Illustrations by Joseph Daniel Fiedler

The Blessing of a Skinned Knee, Wendy Mogel

A Book of Beetles, Josef R. Winkler, Illustrations by Vladimir Boháč

"Blow-Ups in the Borderzones: Third World Israeli Authors' Gropings for Home," in *New Formations: Hybridity,* Smadar Lavie

The Gazelle, Medieval Hebrew Poems on God, Israel and the Soul, Raymond P. Scheindlin

The Story of Emma Lazarus: Liberty's Voice. Erica Silverman, illustrated by Stacey Schuett

Rachel Carson and Her Book That Changed the World. Laurie Lawlor, illustrated by Laura Beingessner.

Beyond Courage: The Untold Story of Jewish Resistance During the Holocaust. Doreen Rappaport

The Man in the White Sharkskin Suit: My Family's Exodus from Old Cairo the New World, Lucette Lagnado

The Last Jews in Baghdad, Nissim Rejwan

The Road to Fez, Ruth Knafo Setton

The One Facing Us, Ronit Matalon

To Live with the Palestinians, Eliyahu Eliachar

After Jews and Arabs: Remaking Levantine Culture, Ammiel Alcalay

Keys to the Garden, Edited by Ammiel Alcalay

Sephardic Jews in America, Aviva Ben-Ur

Remnant Stone: The Jewish Cemeteries of Suriname, Aviva Ben-Ur

Sephardi Lives: A Documentary History, 1700-1950, Julia Cohen and Sarah Stein

The Physician, Noah Gordon

My Father's Paradise, Ariel Sabar

Iraq's Last Jews, Tamar Morad, Dennis and Robert Shasha

Flowers in the Blood, Gay Courter

India's Jewish Heritage: Ritual, Art & Life-Cycle, Shalva Weil

Across the Sabbath River: In Search of a Lost Tribe of Israel, Hillel Halkin

Book of Rachel, Esther David

Let Jasmine Rain Down: Song and Remembrance Among Syrian Jews, Kay Kaufman Shelemay

The Jews of Spain and Portugal, E.H. Lindo

Hispanic Culture and Character of the Sephardic Jews, Mair Jose Benardete

Profit Over People, Noam Chomsky

A History of the Marranos, Cecil Roth

Dona Gracia of the House of Nasi, Cecil Roth

Salonica, City of Ghosts: Christians, Muslims, and Jews, Mark Mazower

The Tyranny of Oil, Antonia Juhasz

Black Tide, Antonia Juhasz

The End of Nature, Bill McKibben

Children's Literature: A Reader's History, from Aesop to Harry Potter, Seth Lerer

The Brightening Glance: Imagination and Childhood, Ellen Handler Spitz

Irony, Claire Colebrook

Dangerous Emotions, Alphonso Lingis

The Haraway Reader, Donna Haraway

The Sixth Extinction: An Unnatural History, Elizabeth Kolbert

Zombie Politics and Culture in the Age of Casino Capitalism, Henry Giroux

The Nervous System, Michael Taussig

Unstoppable: The Emerging Left-Right Alliance to Dismantle the Corporate State, Ralph Nader

Who's That Stepping on Plymouth Rock? Jean Fritz

Alvin Fernald, Superweasel, Clifford B. Hicks

Beatrix Potter, The Complete Tales, Beatrix Potter

My Book of Best Stories from History, Hazel Phillips Hanshew

Ecology and the Jewish Spirit: Where Nature and the Sacred Meet, Ellen Bernstein, Editor

Acknowledgments

We thank Zazu's preschool at Jewish Community Center and children's librarians at Schlow Library in State College, PA. *Saudi Aramco World*, the bi-monthly magazine on the Arabic and Muslim world, has been a tremendous creative and intellectual component of our collaborative process. We are also grateful for Dr. Devin E. Naar, Dr. Alan Benjamin, and Aron Hasson's enthusiastic support. My infinite gratitude goes out to Nicole Sumner whose sense of play continues to demand the most delightful creative risks. And a special note of appreciation to Penny Eifrig, thank you for being such a vital part of our team!

About the Author and Artist

Dr. Cara Judea Alhadeff engages embodied feminist theory, publishing essays in philosophy, art, gender, ethnic, and cultural studies' journals and anthologies. Alhadeff has exhibited her photographs and performance videos internationally, and her work is in numerous public and private collections including MoMA Salzburg and SFMoMA. She is the subject of several documentaries for international public television. Her transdisciplinary book *Viscous Expectations: Justice, Vulnerability, The Ob-scene* (Pennsylvania State University Press, 2014) explores the intersections of eroticism, global corporatocracy, petroleum-parenting, and the pharma-addictive health industry. She is professor of Critical Philosophy at The Global Center for Advanced Studies (GCAS), and lives with her son, Zazu, in Ecovillage, Ithaca, New York.(www.carajudea.com)

Micaela Amateau Amato is a a multi-disciplinary artist and curator who has exhibited her work across the globe. She is included in the collections of Albert and Vera List, Rockefeller Collection of the Chase Manhattan Bank, Museum of Art & Design, Denver Art Museum, Bard Museum Collection, Rose Art Museum Brandeis, and the Museum of Contemporary Photography. She is the recipient of several National Endowment for the Arts and Pollock Krasner Awards. Amato is curator and editor of *Couples Discourse* and *Uncanny Congruencies*, and Professor Emerita of Art and Women's, Gender, and Sexuality Studies at Pennsylvania State University. She lives in Boalsburg, Pennsylvania. (www.micaelaamato.com)

As mother/ daughter collaboration team, Alhadeff and Amateau Amato have exhibited their visual work together across the US and Europe in multiple two-person shows, and have co-presented their research on "petro-pharma-culture" and "petroleum-parenting" (see description below) at international conferences since the early 1990s.

Afterword

The story of *Zazu Dreams* began long before my (Alhadeff 's) search for kids' books that represent Arab Jews and Jews of Color and their crises of assimilation. It began when I was eight years old after seeing a photograph of a logger, chainsaw in hand, arrogantly posing next to a giant redwood tree with the caption: "It took 20,000 years for this tree to grow, and 20 minutes to cut it down." Arundhati Roy reminds us: "This world of ours is four thousand, six hundred million years old. It could end in an afternoon." As individuals and as a team, and as minorities within a minority, we (author and artist) consider imminent disaster along with another warning: Rob Nixon's description of "slow violence"—how the threats wrought by climate change, toxic drift, deforestation, oil spills, and the environmental aftermath of war insidiously work their way into our daily lives. In order to educate a new generation of young people prepared to realize paradigm shifts, we must convey not only the urgency, but the potential for collective agency within our human ecology. Thus, our fable shares disturbing facts *and* expands the scale of time and space in which people and animals individually and in community connect with one another—a social ecology of empathy. "The bacteria are *evolving*. We should, too."*

We believe that a critical element of our evolution is the parent-child relationship. As a single mother raising my five year-old son in the US, I have intimately experienced the intra-cultural impacts of the institutional segregation of children from adult terrain. It is this intergenerational chasm that I hope *Zazu Dreams* bridges. Spinoza, "the philosopher of joy," claimed that *scientia intuitiva* is simultaneously an emotional and cognitive state. This third kind of knowledge, knowledge as the intuitive unconscious, spawns a deterritorialization of the child-adult binary. Storytelling as a pedagogical strategy can elicit Spinoza's *scientia intuitiva* and its concomitant uncanny alliances. Our story is committed to rupturing our culturally arrogant illusion that adult capacity to be educated/entertained is more complex than children's innate intelligences.

How we raise our children is critical to our agenda for radical social justice. Particularly in our Anthropocene Era, sustainable, collective ethics must challenge how we think about parenting. My concept of "petroleum-parenting" explores the choices that parents make that substantially contribute to both environmental destruction and body-phobic institutional practices, and is at the core of *Zazu Dreams* as an eco-literacy project. Embodying my ethics as a parent includes my commitment to live communally and barter 98% of services and goods—acquiring *everything* through swaps (I have never purchased anything new or used for my son; and for myself, no new or used clothing or accessories for over twenty-five years). Despite my "advanced" age of 40, I chose no prenatal medical interventions (ultra-sounds, cervical examines, blood-tests) and no vaccinations-*ever*. We practiced *elimination communication* (diaper-free as much as possible), never used disposable-diapers (or menstruation products for myself), never used a pacifier or stroller, but wore Zazu on my body. I choose to sleep and bathe together, never own a credit card or a car (bike/walk everywhere). I do not own a smart-phone. As I weaned Zazu at four years old, I taught him, and continue now to teach him how to creatively use "resources." We playfully disentangle *le propre*, propriety, and property (ownership, entitlement, individualism). We explore the implications of our Plasticene Age and Roland Barthes' prescient essays (*Plastics* and *Toys*) that illustrate the treacherous collision/collusion between property and impotency: "[T]he child cannot constitute himself as anything but an owner, a user, never as a creator; he does not invent the world, he utilizes it."** I am not suggesting an idealist reaction devoid of realistic responsibilities and relationships. Rather, I encourage parents as citizen-activists to learn *how to be* informed decision-makers. Like the metabolism of the human body and the earth's tendency towards homeostasis, the metabolism of our culture must be scrutinized as a relational organism—one that parents and children can help shape. Together, Zazu, his grandmother (Amateau Amato), and I learn how to shift the myth of individualism to an integrated recognition of interdependency.

Zazu Dreams is the first in a series of books. "Zazu Dreams: The Musical!" is an upcoming collaboration with Adam McKinney (of Jewish-Ghanaian descent), a former Alvin Ailey dancer and cofounder of *DNA-WORKS: Dialogue and Healing through the Arts.*. Also, in progress is an animated film of *Zazu Dreams* with Steven Vargas (of Portuguese descent), a SONY Pictures' lead animator.

*Stephen Harrod Buhner. *Natural Treatments for Lyme Coinfections*. Rochester: Healing Arts Press, 2015: 33.

**Roland Barthes. Trans, Annette Lavers. *Mythologies*. New York: Hill and Wang, 1972: 60.

The keystone species Mauritia palm was considered the "tree of life'... the perfect symbol of nature as a living organism" (Wulf 74).